GLOBAL
IMPERATIVE

GLOBAL IMPERATIVE

Harmonizing Culture and Nature

CHRIS MASER

STILLPOINT

STILLPOINT PUBLISHING
Building a society that honors The Earth,
Humanity, and The Sacred in All Life.

For a free catalog or ordering information, write
Stillpoint Publishing, Box 640, Walpole, NH 03608, USA
or call
1-800-847-4014 TOLL-FREE (Continental US, except NH)
1-603-756-9281 (Foreign and NH)

This book is manufactured in the United States of America.
Text design by Karen Savary

Published by Stillpoint Publishing, Box 640
Meetinghouse Road, Walpole, NH 03608

Library of Congress Catalog Card Number: 92-60988

Maser, Chris
Global Imperative: Harmonizing Culture and Nature

ISBN 0-913299-90-1

1 3 5 7 9 8 6 4 2

**This book is printed on acid-free recycled paper to save trees and preserve
Earth's ecology.**

To all who went before us.
To all who will come after us.

*How do all the energies of the universe
originate? Through struggle, contest, conflict!
Supposing all the particles of matter were
continuously in equilibrium; would there then
be any creative process at all?*

—VIVEKANANDA

CONTENTS

FOREWORD

Chris Maser is a personal friend of mine and a respected colleague. I consider him one of the best role models for professionals and scientists who choose the treacherous path of citizen advocacy. But Maser has gone beyond just advocacy for better science. He's been able to communicate and advocate the need for internal personal change as a precursor to changing the external physical landscape.

His thoughtful and informative book provides an abundance of facts and ideas about the war our culture is waging against nature. Unlike most books that sound the alarm about environmental catastrophe, however, Maser's insights equip us to save our environment—and our culture—from the road to extinction.

The author knows that our society traditionally views nature as a source of endless material wealth. Yet, we are at the same time capable of feeling a deep spiritual love for the beauty of nature. We revere our "spacious skies," then pour pollutants into them. We praise our "shining seas," then fish them to near-extinction. We love our "purple mountains' majesty, above the fruited plain," then plow the plains and clear-cut the forests, destroying the habitat of our fellow creatures.

Trained as a scientist, Maser refuses to confine his thinking to one narrow discipline. He calls upon economics and psychology to show how we view a forest—either as a landscape we value for its beauty alone or predominantly as a "resource" for the price of its timber. Using history as a backdrop, Maser provides evidence of past civilizations that failed mostly because of the exploitive way their cultures viewed nature.

While groups of human beings can be very adaptable, living almost anywhere from deserts to ice caps, culture is far more vulnerable to extinction. Maser warns that a culture that clashes with its environment cannot repair the damage through technological "management." It is thus highly vulnerable to extinction.

We can, however, "manage ourselves," Maser writes with hope. His message is simple: to restore the despoiled landscape, we must first work on our "internal landscape" before the clear-cutting, the toxic waste dumping, and the hunger and poverty can be halted.

Second, we must realize that change starts at home. Although our area of concern is global, we must determine how we can use our individual power to create effective change where we feel the deepest commitment. Whether we are teachers, carpenters, sales clerks, or foresters, each of us can wield considerable influence locally and use it to create the changes needed to bring us to a sustainable society globally. Using our influence means talking with and informing our immediate families and friends, electing political leaders and commissioners who hold a reverence for the land, and revising the way our companies do business.

Change will come from motivated individuals, as Maser reminds us, when we human beings honor the inextricable spiritual bond we have with the natural world and all living things.

> Jeff DeBonis
> Executive Director
> Association of Forest Service
>   Employees for Environmental
>   Ethics

ACKNOWLEDGMENTS

William Moir, a research ecologist with the United States Forest Service, and Jean Holt, science editor for the National Park Service, both graciously accepted my request to review the entire manuscript of *Global Imperative*. They helped me organize the text when organization eluded me, and they helped me smooth many of the rough places.

When I sent the manuscript to Stillpoint Publishing, I thought it was clear and concise. Then Meredith Young-Sowers, the publisher, took over. She recommended many improvements in the organization of the text, and with patience and humor she answered my queries when at first I didn't understand her point of view. With Meredith's help the reorganization took shape and felt good.

I still harbored a mild notion, after twenty some years of struggling to learn how to write, that I knew something about writing. I learned with Dorothy Seymour's editing, however, that if I know anything about writing it's only that I love to write. Dorothy worked magic with the manuscript. Under her tutelage, cloudiness became clarity, and convoluted sentences became simple and direct. As for grammar, it's with the greatest humility that I admit to knowing virtually nothing about the English language. Consequently, my empathy has reached profound proportions for any non-English speaking person trying to master the nuances of this language.

Finally, it's with a great deal of gratitude that I acknowledge Zane, my wife, who accepted the many months of my working on this book, months when my attention was stolen from her. I can only imagine what it was like for her to be replaced by an idea called *Global Imperative* and a Macintosh computer, at times with no end in sight.

To each of you: thank you for your patience, your help, and your faith in the outcome.

PREFACE

Global Imperative sums up knowledge gleaned from more than twenty years as a research scientist, knowledge I found out of balance with my spiritual knowing, which lies beyond such knowledge. In *Global Imperative*, I recognize that the problems of a society teetering on the brink of spiritual bankruptcy cannot be mended with scientific Band Aids and technological quick fixes. Nevertheless, out of the current growing social chaos can come a society with a better balance between the materialistic and the spiritual, the masculine and the feminine, the intellectual and the intuitive, the unconscious and the conscious, and the present and the future. But to achieve that better balance, we must view the world and society differently.

Humanity has taken for granted the world as designed by Nature and has exploited it in such a way and to such an extent that human society cannot long endure in our present course. People within a society compete with one another for the goods and services of Nature, and each society competes with every other society for the same goods and services. In that competition, each society has become so needy and so specialized in the materialistic sense that today we live in a global community, which stands like a house of cards. If one major society falls, the ripples of collapse are felt with stunning rapidity throughout the world.

The day must arrive, however; when the citizens of this planet come to understand that, if human societies are to survive, we must set aside our historic exploitive environmental competition and begin instead to cooperate and to coordinate with one another. Only then will we be able to bring our various cultures in harmony with Nature so that there will be room for all planetary citizens, both human and nonhuman. Only then will Planet Earth be adaptable to change by the ecological hand of humanity.

To this end, Part 1 of *Global Imperative* examines a few aspects of the world of Nature as evolutionary harmony to set the stage for the introduction of human society. Part 2, in turn, presents some of the cultural constructs with which society has justified the greedy exploitation of Nature in the name of material progress. And Part 3 is a view beyond exploitation to the conscious artistry with which culture can meet Nature if we choose to make it so. Cultural harmony with Nature is a global imperative if each form of life is to contribute its singular gift to our home planet by fulfilling the naturalness and the excellence of its ecological fit in Nature's dynamic dance of evolution.

I

NATURE AS CREATIVE HARMONY

*Scholars in our century have forgotten that theory
owes its existence to practice and that Nature
existed before there were rules.*

—ECKARTSHAUSEN

1

A GLOBAL IMPERATIVE

What sets us apart from our fellow creatures is not some higher sense of spirituality or some nobler sense of purpose but our deeming ourselves wise in our own eyes. Therein lies the fallacy. We are no better than or worse than other kinds of animals; we are simply a different kind of animal—one among the many. We are thus an inseparable part of Nature, not a special case apart from Her.

As a part of Nature, what we do is natural even though it often is destructive. This is not to say our actions are wise, or ethical, or moral, or desirable, or even socially acceptable and within the bounds of Nature's laws. As a part of Nature, we will of necessity change what we call the "natural world," and it is natural for us to do this, since people are an integral part of the total system we call the Universe. The degree to which we change the world, and the motives behind and the ways in which we make these changes, however, are what we may justifiably question. And it is the motive behind the

creation—God's spirituality versus humanity's materialism—that is knocking at the door of our consciousness.

Today, many of us are trying somehow to reach back
into human history to find our mythological roots and to
recapture some primordial sense of spiritual harmony with
Nature. Our search is urgent, because at some deep level we
know we are an inseparable part of Her. We have an intuitive
feeling that we humans as a whole have lost something we
must find—the lessons of the Holy Grail, one of which is that
humanity and Nature are one.

Our European forebears, having long forgotten their
tribal roots, misplaced the lesson of the Holy Grail when
they began to prize material wealth above the sacredness of
Nature's cycles. As the sacred became the profane, our forebears perceived themselves increasingly as both separate
from and above Nature, until what they saw as natural and
native was something to be subjugated and exploited for
personal gain.

Coming from culturalized, pastoral landscapes of Europe, our ancestors first arrived in and began to settle the
islands of the Caribbean in the New World in 1492 and La
Florida, now the state of Florida, in 1513. They considered
both the forests and the people who inhabited them as both
natural and native, but in what sense?

They had already lost their spiritual connection with
Nature and had become almost totally materialistic. They
therefore saw not a land and a people with which to connect
spiritually but only the apparently-free products of the
land—including the "native peoples"—to be exploited in
order to grow economically wealthy. To reap such wealth,
however, they had to dispose of the native peoples—which
they did, and which we in many ways are still doing culturally.

As our ancestors became more and more materialisti-
cally removed from the land through the process of urbanization, they lost their spiritual connection with the creation
of Nature and with the nature of Creation. Their relationship

with Nature changed almost completely from one of spirituality and reverence to one of materialism and exploitation.

Today we also see ourselves as separate from Nature, but in two different ways. Some people still envision humanity's role in life as the master species whose duty it is to harness Nature strictly for the benefit of human society. Others perceive themselves as unnatural, non-native intrusions into the world of Nature where their very presence defiles Her. Here the connotation of natural and native is of something apart from human society, a purity without contamination by human activity or artifact.

Neither view, however, is accurate. What we perceive as natural and native is not an either/or proposition but rather a degree of naturalness and a degree of nativeness based on our personal feelings of the sacredness with which we participate with Nature. The way we as a society participate with Nature is currently one of our most pressing struggles— to balance spirituality and materialism.

Unfortunately, this struggle often takes place in the courts of the land rather than in our hearts and souls, where such a battle belongs. In our struggle to find a sustainable place within Nature and to participate with Her in a sacred manner, we must recognize and accept that for thousands of years human society has been converting Nature's landscape to a human-designed cultural landscape. And we shall continue to do so in perpetuity. It's all we can do, simply because we exist and because we as a global society occupy and use the whole world, leaving nothing untouched from the blue arc of the heavens to the depths of the deepest sea.

Even Native North Americans, who were in spiritual harmony with Nature when the Europeans arrived, were in fact altering the landscapes in which they lived. But they did not change them in the same way as did the Europeans who colonized the New World and superimposed their materialistic demands forcefully on the spiritual customs of the natives.

Most of us who are European-Americans from North,

Central, or South America still feel and act as though we are alienated from Nature. We still don't have a clear sense of naturalness and nativeness as concepts joining us with Nature. We still see our concepts of naturalness and nativeness as somehow excluding us as participants in the creative process of designing the landscapes in which we live and work.

But we are a natural part of the landscape in which we live, even if we don't understand it, and what we do in the way of converting Nature's landscape to our cultural landscape is natural. The "naturalness" of a landscape is thus not an absolute value but rather a relative value, which ranges from no alteration by humans at the most pristine end of the ecological scale to any kind of artificial alteration at its most humanized end. By the same token, "nativeness" ranges from the most ancient, continuous habitation of an area to the most recent immigration into an area.

Our living in and altering the landscape are natural aspects of Creation, and by the very fact that we exist we are active participants in redrafting Nature's design. Therefore, as Co-Creators made in the image of God, we not only belong here and have a right to be here in the sense of our "nativeness" but also have a duty to consciously participate in the creation of our landscape in the sense of our "naturalness." So the question is: How do we consciously participate in the sacred care of the Earth while we help sculpt and texture Her landscapes with our cultural designs?

Conscious participation in the sacred care of the Earth leads to the moral question: do those living today owe anything to the future? If our answer is "No," then we are surely on course, because we are consuming resources and polluting the Earth as if there were no tomorrow. If on the other hand the answer is "Yes, we have an obligation to the future," then we must soon determine what and how much we owe, because our present irresponsible course is rapidly destroying the environmental options for generations to come. Meeting this obligation will require a renewed sense of morality—to be "other-centered" in doing unto those to come as we wish those before us had done unto us.

To change anything, we must reach beyond where we are, beyond where we feel safe. We must dare to move ahead, even if we don't understand fully where we're going, because we'll never have perfect knowledge. We must ask innovative, future-oriented questions in order to make necessary changes for the better.

True progress toward an ecologically-sound environment and an equitable world society will be expensive in both money and effort. The longer we wait, however, the more disastrous becomes the environmental condition and the more expensive and difficult become the necessary social changes. No biological short-cuts, technological quick fixes, or political hype can mend what is broken. Dramatic, fundamental change, both frightening and painful, is necessary if we're really concerned with bettering the quality of future life. It's not really a question of "can we change?" or "can't we change?" It's one of human morality: "will we change?" or "won't we change?" It's a sad fact that from world leaders down, we have, with few exceptions, so far chosen "WON'T."

2
THE UNIVERSE IS BORN

Before time, the Universe was naught, and, according to the Bible, "the earth was without form, and void; and darkness was upon the face of the deep."[1] Then, says current scientific thought, arose a great cataclysm, the "big bang," which created a supremely harmonious and logical process as a foundation of the evolution of matter, and the Universe was born. So began the process of evolution, which proceeds from the simple to the complex, from the general to the specific, and from the strongly bound to the more weakly bound.

To understand that evolution, consider an extended family. The strongest bond is between a husband and wife, then between the parents and their children. But as the family grows, the bonds between the children and the various aunts and uncles and their first, second, and third cousins become progressively weaker as relationships become more distant with the increasing size of the family.

To understand the creation of the Universe, it's necessary

to examine its basic building blocks and the way they evolved into organized systems. The big bang created particles of an extremely high state of concentration bound together by almost unimaginably strong forces. From these original micro-units, quarks and electrons were formed. (Scientists propose quarks as the fundamental units of matter.) Quarks combined to form protons and neutrons; protons and neutrons formed atomic nuclei, which were complemented by shells of electrons. Atoms of various weights and complexities could, in some parts of the Universe, combine into chains of molecules and, on suitable planetary surfaces, give birth to life. On Earth, for example, living organisms became ecological systems and human societies with the remarkable features of language, consciousness, free choice, and culture.

In this giant process of evolution, relationships among things are changing continually as complex systems rise from subatomic and atomic particles. In each higher level of complexity and organization we find an increase in the size of the system and a corresponding decrease in the energies holding it together. So as evolution proceeds, the forces that hold together the evolving systems, from a molecule to a human society, weaken as the size of the systems increases.

Earth has been exposed for billions of years to a constant flow of energy streaming from the sun and radiating back into space. On Earth, the flow of energy produces the vast variety of living systems from the simple, such as an individual cell, to the complex, such as a human society. Each system uses the sun's energy to fuel its own internal processes, and each in turn provides fuel to others.

During its evolution, every system must develop the ability to constantly balance the energy it uses to function with the energies available in its environment. Ecosystems and social systems, like organisms, constantly bring in, break down, and use energy not only for repair but also for regeneration and to adapt to changing environmental conditions.

Keep in mind that we live in a world where everything seems to have its exact opposite, such as love/hate, black/

white, life/death. So the relationship of cause/effect seems also to be one of opposites. Consider that the first relationship between two things, whatever gave birth to cause, also gave birth to effect. But rather than being discrete opposites, cause and effect are part of a process of both creation and extinction.

Creation was the initial cause of extinction when the world was formed, and since that instant, extinction has been the continual cause of creation. Thus, in effect, the act of creation also becomes the act of extinction, and the act of extinction becomes the act of creation, as Marcus Aurelius intimated when he wrote: "Time is a . . . river of passing events, and strong is its current. No sooner is a thing brought to sight then it is swept by and another takes its place, and this too will be swept away." This river of passing events, of cause and effect, of creation and extinction, is the continual, fluid motion of change, which gives rise to the diversity.

So change, which includes both creation and extinction, is the basis of the world around us. As such, change is the catalyst of diversity.

3

DIVERSITY, THE QUALITY
OF BEING DIFFERENT

Diversity is not only the quality of being different but also is the richness of the world and our experience of it. Diversity means variety, as shown in Figure 1. Diversity comes in many forms, each of which is a relationship that fits precisely into every other relationship in the Universe and is constantly changing.

Nature crafted the world inherited by human beings through the principle of cause and effect, which gave rise to the diversity of nonliving matter. When the first living cell came into being, diversity not only became limitless but also gave rise to the possibility of the extinction of life.

We are losing the diversity of life (biodiversity) world-wide. So we need to have some notion of diversity itself, because biodiversity is in many ways the cumulative effect of diversity in all its various dimensions. How can we understand and describe diversity?

11

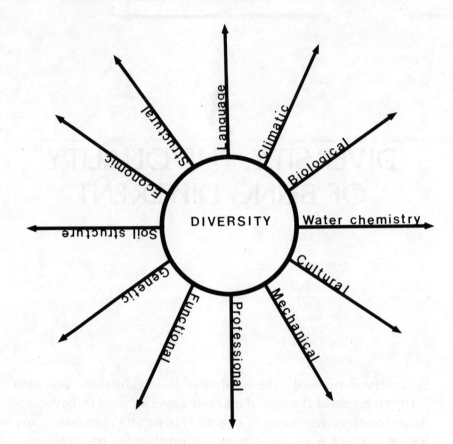

Figure 1. *Diversity:* A few of the faces of diversity are indicated here.

Diversity as a Matter of Dimension

Diversity is partly a matter of dimension. Dimension is in a general sense a measure of spatial extent, such as height, width, or length. It also is a physical property—often mass, length, time, or some combination of those characteristics. Speed, for example, has the dimensions of length divided by time, so speed is both spatial and physical.

Scale, from the Microscope to Infinity

We also see diversity in scale, from the infinitesimal through the electron microscope to the infinity of space. The dimension of scale is important, because it adds greatly not only to our perception of diversity in the landscape but also to our perception of the way one part of the landscape relates to another. And both perceptions are necessary for us to make the wisest possible decisions concerning the best use of such things as our backyard gardens and our national forests.

Scale is a progressive classification in size, amount, importance, rank, or even a relative level or degree. When dealing with diversity, however, we often overlook space or distance as a dimension of diversity.

Space and distance as a scale of diversity is right in our own backyard—and always has been. If, for example, you took a high-powered microscope and studied a pinch of soil, you would see things that you never imagined to be living in your backyard, but you cannot see the roses or even your house so long as you focus your attention into the microscope.

Now, if you were to use a ten-power hand lens to look at the same pinch of soil, you could not see what you saw through the microscope, but you would see more of the way the particles of soil and some of the larger soil organisms relate one to another. But so long as you're looking through the hand lens, you still couldn't see the roses or your house.

On the other hand, if you put the pinch of soil back where you got it and stand up straight and look down, you have still a different scale of diversity. Now you see a wider patch of soil, but without the detail. If you climb onto the roof of your house and look down on the patch of soil, you now see even less detail of the soil, but you see the roses growing out of the soil, and you see your house. Imagine, therefore, what you would see if you hovered in a helicopter a hundred feet, a thousand feet, or ten thousand feet above the patch of soil in your backyard; what would you see? What would you see from a satellite in outer space?

Let's look for a moment at the scale of distance and space in still another way. What would you see in your backyard if you were a microorganism peeking out of the soil from under a grain of sand? What would you see in your backyard if you were an ant (Photo 1), a mouse (Photo 2), a cat, or a dog? Then again, what would you see if you were a sparrow, first feeding on the ground and then suddenly flying into the tree and then just as suddenly flying to the other end of the neighborhood?

Scale, as we perceive it, is an aspect of diversity in distance and space. Diversity includes every conceivable scale, such as time, viewed from every conceivable place in distance and space simultaneously, from the viewpoint of the ant to the viewpoint of the sparrow and beyond.

Photo 1. *Ant's-eye view:* The view of a lawn through an insect's eye—the same sort of blurred-edge vision we have when we focus on something small.

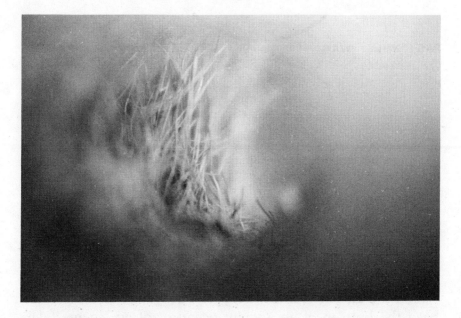

Photo 2. *Tunnel Vision:* A mouse's-eye view of its own tunnel, through tall grasses in the corner of the garden by the back fence.

Diversity in Time

Time is our invisible creation. We created time and are now stuck in our creation. Our society is run by the clock, so we try to manage our landscapes by that measure. In dealing with our renewable natural resources, for example, we try to rush Nature's processes, because to us time is money. To Nature, however, both time and money are non-existent. We must therefore learn that Nature will never bow to society's clock.

In our culture, we often think of time as a nonspatial continuum in which events occur in an apparently irreversible sequence from the past through the present into the future (Fig. 2). Time also is thought of as an interval separating two points on this continuum, points we select centering on a regularly-recurring event, such as the sunrise,

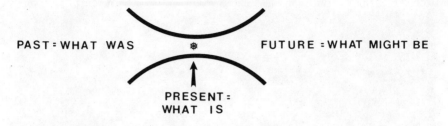

PAST = WHAT WAS   FUTURE = WHAT MIGHT BE

PRESENT =
WHAT IS

Figure 2. *Our Concept of Time:* Time is seen as past, present, and future. This is our normal concept of time as a nonspatial continuum.

and counting the number of its occurrences during the interval. And time is represented as numbers, such as seconds, minutes, days, weeks, months, years, centuries, millennia, or geological epochs.

In the dimension of time, your backyard may once have been the bottom of an ancient ocean or of an ice-age lake. Or it could have been a mountain top, a tropical forest, a tundra, or a desert. And it could have been all of these things. What you perceive your backyard to be today is only an instant in an ever-expanding explosion of diversity, one aspect of which is time.

Consider a simple example, the backyard of my home when I lived in a small town in northeastern Oregon. Behind my house I had a vegetable garden, which I used to Rototill every spring. And just as soon as I was finished Rototilling the soil I began picking up squarish nails and clinkers from coal that someone had burned in a forge to heat and shape mule shoes and horse shoes. Why? Because a hundred years earlier, where I set up my garden had stood a blacksmith shop.

The acre of ground I used for a garden in 1978 was the same physical acre a hundred years earlier, but the diversity of materials in the soil of that acre was very different from that of my neighbors on either side, both of whom had gardens but neither of whom found any of the artifacts that I did. And today, for all I know, that acre of ground could have a garage built on it. So if we add the dimension of time to all the other forms of diversity, we learn that diversity is really an infinity. It's something we cannot define. We can only crudely and imperfectly characterize it.

Life, the Wonder of It All

The most wonderful diversity of all lies in life itself. Just imagine: since that first living cell, nothing has ever again been alone on Earth, because since that first living cell, the diversity of life has literally filled the planet. And the experiment continues.

How exactly that part of Creation called life began is a question as old as the first human being to wonder about it. Nevertheless, the first animated cell opened up not only the possibility of life and living diversity but also a whole dimension of diversity beyond our present comprehension—infinite diversity, created out of nonliving substances and living tissue as well as a combination of the living with the nonliving. As an example, think of the vast array of marine snails, each of which makes its own peculiar shell out of nonliving materials, and yet without the living snail the shell could not exist.

The wonder of biological diversity is the wonder of its having begun with a single living cell, or maybe even a handful of cells scattered throughout the seas of the world. From that cell, or perhaps those cells, arose the longest-known living experiment on Earth—the genetic experiment of life. You could argue that combinations of genetic materials are really no different from the original combinations of chemicals that gave rise to chemical compounds. If you omit the spark of life from this equation, you'd be right. But that undefinable spark of life is there, and that changes everything.

Today, therefore, as I meet each living thing that shares the world with me, I see the pinnacle—the culmination—of billions upon billions upon billions of genetic experiments, all of which have taken place over millions of years, all embodied in each butterfly, each rose, each tree, each bird, and each human being. Every individual living thing on Earth is the apex of Creation, because every living thing is the result of an unbroken chain of genetic experiments—each individual that ever lived being part of a single experiment—that began with the original, living cell that filled the lifeless sea with life.

How Diversity Compounds Itself

Diversity as a dimension of itself may seem like an odd idea. But just think: all the various dimensions of diversity ultimately come together to create diversity in the form of a seascape, a landscape, the Earth, a moonscape, the moon, or even the Universe as a whole. So when we alter one thing, we alter everything. That cumulative alteration is the ongoing Principle of Creation. To see how this principle works, how diversity continually creates itself, we'll examine the history of a landscape in the southern Appalachian Mountains at a place where the states of Tennessee, North Carolina, and Georgia meet.

It's been 260 million years since the Appalachian Mountain chain was last affected by significant upward thrusting of the Earth's crust. At mid- and high elevations, during the last period in which the glaciers of the Pleistocene Epoch reached their maximum development, about 20,000 years ago, the ground surrounding the glaciers was permanently frozen. In addition, the potential area of alpine tundra extended from an elevation of about 5,000 feet to the summits of the highest mountain peaks. (Tundra is a treeless area that has a permanently frozen subsoil and supports such low-growing vegetation as lichens, mosses, and stunted shrubs. Tundra occurring above the tree line on high mountains is termed "alpine tundra" as opposed to "arctic tundra.")

During this time, sediments in all sizes, ranging from boulders to silt and clay, surrounding the glaciers were frozen in place. With the warming of the climate about sixteen thousand years ago, both the frequency and the intensity of the cycles of freezing and thawing increased. Finally, the climate warmed sufficiently so that the once-frozen materials began to move downslope with the pull of gravity.

With the onset of recent times, about 8,000 years ago, the climate warmed again. This change resulted in the sediments, such as boulders, pebbles, or clay, washing downslope through the force of water, as opposed to moving downslope by the pull of gravity as in colder times.

From the time when the last glacial period was at its height to the present, the major factor in forcing the landscape to change was shifts in climate. Freezing and other ice-related phenomena were the main causes of disturbance in the biological system. The combination of cold temperatures and cycles of freezing and thawing, which churned the soil, resulted in a landscape mosaic of permanent snowfields and alpine tundra above 5,000 feet elevation, while below 1,600 feet there was a species-rich boreal forest. (Boreal forest means "northern forest," which today is characterized by the vast, short forest of small trees that occurs across central and northern Canada and throughout interior Alaska.)

As the climate warmed, herbaceous species of plants that formerly grew in alpine tundra either died out or were restricted to high-elevation sites kept open by disturbances like fire, falling rocks, and landslides. In addition, the boreal forest has spread upslope to the summits of the highest mountain peaks, and a deciduous forest has replaced it at mid- and low elevations. The forest communities as we know them today have evolved only recently, some within the lifetimes of the oldest living trees.

So the diverse elements of diversity itself, such as the scales of time, space, and temperature, the processes that shape the Earth, and the Earth's living organisms have molded and remolded the landscape into an ever-changing kaleidoscope of mosaics.

Perception, What I See that You Don't

When Margaret Shannon, a professor of natural resource policy and sociology at State University of New York, said, "the world does not define itself for us; rather we choose to see some parts of the world and not others," she opened the door of a whole new way to think about diversity: that of our individual and collective perceptions. Her statement "puts us on notice" that we do not "see" diversity but rather that we have some perception of diversity—which in itself creates diversity, because my perception is more or less different from yours.

Shannon's observation points out that I'm right from my point of view, you're right from your point of view, and Jill is right from her point of view. Thus we can, if we choose, view the world and one another from the position of right, right, and different—as opposed to "I'm right" and "you're wrong." With this view, negotiating a new relationship with one another and with our home planet would be much easier than constantly fighting the emotional gridlock we all too often find ourselves in.

Our perceptions can even be thought of in a manner similar to that of an insect's compound eye, because it is through perception that we "see" one another and everything else. The cornea of an insect's compound eye is divided into a number of separate facets, which, depending on the insect, may vary from a few hundred to a few thousand. Each compound eye is formed from a group of separate visual elements, each of which corresponds to a single facet of the cornea. Each facet has what amounts to a single nerve fiber, which sends optical messages to the brain. Seeing with an insect's compound eye would be like seeing with many different eyes at once.

Each human perception is like a facet in the compound eye of an insect, with its independent nerve fiber connecting it to our local, national, and global society (the brain). Thus each perception, which at the same time represents both an individual's own cultural foundation and moral limitations, has its unique construct, which determines the possibilities of the individual's understanding. A person who tends to be negative or pessimistic, for example, sees a glass of water as half empty while a person who tends to be positive or optimistic sees the same glass of water as half full. Regardless of the way it's perceived, the level of water is the same— which illustrates, as Shannon says, that we see what we choose to see. And what we see may have little to do with reality.

So it seems reasonable that the freer we are as individuals to change our perceptions without social resistance in the form of ridicule or shame, the freer is society—the collective of the individual perceptions—to adapt to change in a healthy, evolutionary way. On the other hand, the more rigidly monitored and controlled "acceptable" perceptions are, the more prone a society is to the cracking of its moral foundation and to the crumbling of its infrastructure, because nothing can be held long in abeyance, least of all social evolution.

For this reason, I suggest that the perception of an individual human being both adds to and compounds diversity, because an individual's perceptions change with age and with life's experiences. They also change with the individual's degree of focus, centeredness, personal identity, and formal education, both secular and religious. And finally, they change with changing social and peer pressures and with the ever-changing relationships of human beings to one another, each of which has different perceptions, which also are constantly changing.

In this sense, each human being is the sum total of all his or her perceptions of everything in life, and it is the cumulative integration of these perceptions that makes not only each individual unique but also the collective of individuals into a unique society. If, therefore, we could add diversity to diversity, we would find in the end that it is human perception that at once creates, integrates, and re-

creates diversity in an ever-widening sphere of consciousness. This being the case, we create what we think, and what
we think we create. The richness or the poverty of our individual and collective life's experience is our choice.

Diversity as a Matter of Relationship

There are, beyond dimensions, three other relationships of
diversity. When these are added to the various dimensions—
scale, time, life, diversity itself, and perception—diversity
becomes an infinite novelty of Creation.

Oh, What Chemistry!

Diversity in chemistry is another aspect of diversity in
our Universe. Chemical diversity is the diversity of physical
things, which are individual elements, such as nitrogen, and
the compounds produced by combining elements in relationship with one another. If it is true that the first two
physical things were chemicals, then the initial relationship
between these two chemicals produced the initial chemical
reaction, which in turn produced something else. This means
that a third thing—a chemical compound—arose out of the
initial chemical reaction. That chemical compound simultaneously created the possibility of new relationships and a
new definition of relationship. So the result of the interaction
between the two chemicals—the compound—becomes an
integral part of the definition of each parent chemical. At
some point, in the classic concept of cause and effect, the
growth of possible physical-chemical relationships becomes
exponential.

When a Chair is Not a Chair

Things are not what they seem. We perceive objects by
means of their obvious structures or functions. Structure is

the configuration of elements, parts, or constituents of a thing, be it simple or complex. The structure can be thought of as the organization, arrangement, or make-up of a thing. Function, on the other hand, is what a particular structure either can do or allows to be done to it or with it.

Let's consider a common object—say, a chair. A chair is a chair because of its structure, which gives it a particular shape. A chair can be characterized as a piece of furniture consisting of a seat, legs, and back, and often arms, an object designed to accommodate a sitting person. Because of the seat, we can sit in a chair, and it's the act of sitting that makes a chair a chair.

But now I'll remove the seat so that the supporting structure on which we sit no longer exists, and now to sit, we must sit on the ground between the legs of the "chair." By definition, when I remove a chair's seat, I no longer have a chair, because I have altered the structure and therefore also altered its function. So the structure of an object defines its function, and the function of an object defines its necessary structure, and both add to the ever-widening ripples of diversity.

Context Affects Relationship

Besides structure and function, our Universe contains the characteristic of context—the way an object relates to its environment. The context of any object affects the relationship of that feature with its surroundings.

Because this notion of context affecting relationship is so important to an understanding of extinction, I'm going to give three examples of the way this dynamic works. The first example deals with an old-growth forest and human alteration of that forest.

Suppose you had access to a 5,000-acre tract of undisturbed, old-growth forest. Now, I'm going to put an imaginary boundary around the central hundred acres. That section becomes the feature, and I'm going to start clearcutting the surrounding rest of the land, beginning along the outer edge of the 5,000-acre tract. How will clearcutting affect the relationship of the central hundred acres with the surrounding 4,900 acres?

First, noise from road-building and logging equipment will begin to pollute Nature's silence, Her birdsong, and the whispering of the wind in the tops of the trees. With the noise comes a sense of intrusion—a violation—of the millennial, symphonic harmony of Nature's forest. As the clearcutting draws nearer and nearer, the noise of the large machinery becomes louder and is now punctuated with the scream of chain saws. Finally, the sense of violation becomes unbearable as the death knell of ancient trees is added to the roar of machinery and the wailing of chain saws, each time a forest giant crashes to earth, its life severed by a speeding steel chain of opposing teeth ripping through its fibers.

In the beginning, clearcutting seems remote from the hundred acres, but on the heels of the mechanical noise comes the first sense that the central portion of the 5,000 acres is becoming an island as the noise comes from here and from there and from over there. Next, the crashing of the falling trees brings a real sense of the forest's being cut down, forever altering Nature's evolutionary experiment that is the forest. And suddenly the clearcutting is close enough that the trees are seen falling. Now there exists a hundred-acre patch of old-growth trees in the middle of a sea of stumps and the mangled bodies of plants.

The hundred-acre patch of old-growth trees is no longer a forest but an unprotected island, which is too small to support many of the species of vertebrate wildlife that require or find their preferred habitat in the old-growth forest. These species will become extinct within the hundred acres because the context of the landscape (unbroken forest as opposed to a vast clearcut) has changed the relationship of the hundred acres with its surroundings.

The hundred acres, once protected by the surrounding forest from the drying winds of summer and the freezing winds of winter, is now unprotected and exposed to the whim of the winds. In addition, one hundred acres is too small an area for old-growth species, such as the marten and the pileated woodpecker, to live in, breed, and survive, and there may be no place else for them to go. So the demise of the marten and the pileated woodpecker further changes the hundred acres' relationship to its surroundings.

Our second example of context is a farmer's field in the flatlands of Nebraska. The field is not far from a farming community that is rapidly pumping the stored water out of a millennia-old underground lake for use in peoples' homes and for irrigating the surrounding farm crops. Over a period of years, far more water has been pumped out of the ground than can possibly be replaced, and the farmer under whose field the lake lies begins to notice that his field, instead of being flat, is sinking in the middle.

He notices a bare spot gradually developing in his crop, because cold air drains into the sunken middle of the field and freezes the wheat. Draining the underground lake altered its structure, and that alteration caused the sinking of the field, which in turn changed the air-flow patterns of the landscape—which created a different relationship between the field and its above-ground surroundings.

In this case human society has created the feature, the farmer's field, and it also created the alteration—the massive pumping of underground water—that changed the field's underground surroundings, thus causing it to sink. Depletion of the water in turn changed the field's above-ground surroundings, causing the air-flow patterns to shift in relationship to the field and freeze the wheat in the bottom of the sunken area.

The third and final example of context is the Bonneville Salt Flats in Utah. This desolate white plain, one of Nature's more bizarre geological inventions, is so flat that the curvature of the Earth is visible from the level of the ground.

Geologically speaking, the salt flats are a relatively recent phenomenon. During the Pleistocene Epoch, which began about a million and a half years ago, Lake Bonneville covered a third of Utah as well as parts of Nevada and Idaho, to a depth of nearly a thousand feet. But with the end of the Pleistocene Epoch about ten thousand years ago, Lake Bonneville was already drying up, depositing its dissolved salts and other minerals in the lowest part of the Great Salt Lake Basin, the area now known as the "salt flats."

Long a magnet for tourists, filmmakers, and daredevils who thunder across the salty, concrete-smooth surface in the world's fastest automobiles, the salt flats are disappearing more than seven thousand years after they formed from the dried-up remnants of Lake Bonneville. Since 1926, when surveyors first mapped the area, the salt flats have shrunk from 96,000 acres to about 25,000 acres. So the salt is vanishing at a rate of about one percent a year—which means that the salt flats could be gone within decades.

Although proof is inconclusive, one of the reasons for the loss of salt is thought to be a nearby mine, which pumps salt-laden groundwater to produce potash, an ingredient in fertilizers. As we lower the water table by pumping and removing the ground water, the water, which is replaced by rains, percolates downward through the flats, dissolving the salts and carrying them into the lowering water table from which they are continually removed.

In addition, construction of an interstate highway may also have modified the hidden movement of water in the shallow aquifers that underlie the plain. By creating yet another "conduit" for the drainage of salt-laden water, the building of the highway has lowered the water table in many directions around the salt flats.

Regardless of the cause or causes, measurements taken since 1960 show that the salt crust of the Bonneville Flats has thinned from seven feet to five feet at its thickest point and to mere inches in some spots. This thinning of the salt crust constitutes an estimated loss of a million and a half tons of salt per year.

Few places on the surface of the Earth are so well-suited

to the pursuit of speed as the Bonneville Flats, and it was here in 1970 that the world's land-speed record was set, 622 mph, in a jet-powered automobile. This speed was attainable because the flats, covered with water throughout the winter and spring, are dry as a bone, hard as concrete, and about as smooth by late summer. In recent years, however, cracks, holes, and pressure ridges have begun to appear around the edges of the thinning, weakening flats, which soon may be more mud than salt—a change that will forever alter the context of the salt flats with their surrounds as they dissolve into extinction. As the context of the Bonneville Salt Flats changes through human-caused alterations to its structure and function, so the diversity of the entire area changes through the loss of this unique feature.

4
CREATION AND EXTINCTION

Creation means something has come into being that heretofore did not exist physically. Where did it come from?

Creation is generally thought of in terms of theology or of biological evolution. But think about the destruction or extinction of a habitat; after the change, doesn't it become another, very different habitat? A swamp, for example, may be drained to create an agricultural pasture. In draining the water, the swamp-dwelling organisms become extinct, but the resultant pasture becomes inhabited by pasture-dwelling organisms. This doesn't mean that the draining of the swamp is either desirable or undesirable. It means only that in some cases we can easily see the creative side of extinction.

Extinction means that something no longer exists in its living form; its spark of life has died out like embers of a dying fire. Extinction is generally thought of only in terms of the disappearance of a living entity. But the concept of extinction goes far beyond living things. The disappearance, the irreparable alteration of the nonliving components of the environment, such as a lake, is linked inseparably to the extinction of living things.

This link is important to appreciate, because by the time a species is documented as extinct, the alterations wrought by humans have caused one or more physical/chemical/structural/functional extinctions in the habitat. It's these "hidden extinctions," the ones we are unaware of, the ones we pay no heed to, that cause habitats to change.

As habitats change, they in effect become extinct not only in a particular place but also to the species living in them. In turn, the species that are adapted to that specific habitat become extinct in the area where their required habitat no longer exists—such species as the passenger pigeon and the Carolina parakeet.

Creation and extinction can hardly be discussed today without including the influence of humanity as a species. Human social activity is, for example, changing the chemistry of the water in Colorado's high-mountain lakes through the spread of air pollutants. Each winter the pollutants are scrubbed from the air by falling snow and stored in the snowpack until released with the spring thaw to alter the lakes in a way that kills their living organisms. Human social activity is also deforesting most of Canada, the Pacific Northwest of the United States, and the tropical rainforests of the world. This deforestation is eliminating habitats and altering the global climate.

What we are doing to Earth is natural, even though it may be viewed as destructive, because we are one species of animal among the many populating our home planet. But the changes we create are faster, more radical, more thoroughly systematic, and simultaneously more widespread than any changes caused by any single species at any other time in the history of Earth. Humanity, especially through society, is constantly altering the Earth. To illustrate, I'm going to present a few examples of creation and extinction, all but the first one achieved by the influence of humans.

Such alterations create something "new" at the expense of something already in existence.

Can Rocks Change, Too?

A volcano is a vent or opening in the earth's crust through which gases and melted rock, called molten lava, are ejected. A volcano that is ejecting gases and molten lava is said to be active; it is in creation. On the other hand, a volcano that has "run its course" of activity is said to be extinct because the "life" has gone out of it.

A volcano is built from within by fire and is eroded from without by wind and rain and ice. A volcano defies gravity in its growing and falls to gravity in its dying. A volcano is born and dies and is reborn as something else. This means that volcanos, which form mountains, are not eternal, but, as with all mountains, they come and go, are born and die, in concert with all living things.

Consider that children, flowers, and grasses are living entities, which grow almost fast enough to actually watch them increase in size. Trees grow more slowly. And some rock-dwelling lichens (a lichen is a combination of a fungus and an alga) grow just a fraction of an inch in a century— so slowly that historians use their growth to date events.

And, yes, rocks also grow, but more slowly yet. At a rock's pace of growth the history of the Egyptian pyramids is a wink of time and the Rocky Mountains a yawn.

Rocks even have a life cycle of birth and death and birth again. Some geologists estimate that since the Earth was born four and a half billion years ago, its rocks have been through only ten generations.

As mountains are born and die, as pieces of continents come and go like ships at dock, the rock formed on the floor of the sea is raised to the tops of mountains only to be eroded and returned to the floor of the sea where it once again begins its journey through the Earth. And in approximately 450 million years, the rock may reappear on the surface of the continent to begin a new life. So even rock participates in the ever-changing, ever-flowing cycle of fire and ice, of creation and extinction.

On Species

If rocks are born and die, so are entire species. A species is thought of as the basic building block of biological diversity and the epitome of creation. In fact, the concept of a species is so fantastic in evolutionary terms and so important ecologically that the United States Congress passed a public law—the Rare and Endangered Species Act—specifically to protect species and subspecies from extinction by an act of human society.

What Is a Species?

The word "species" has one significance to a student of taxonomy and another to the student of evolution. To the student of taxonomy, the concept of a species is a practical device designed to reduce the almost endless variety of living things to a comprehensible system of classification. To the student of evolution, a species is a passing stage in the stream of evolution. And here the concept of extinction is simple: it is what happens when whatever we call a species disappears.

Before 1935, scientists based most definitions of species on the degree to which they were distinct in form and structure. They paid little attention to evolutionary relationships. In 1937, scientists revisited the definition and began to emphasize the dynamic aspects of species—their potential for change. Today, species are thought of as groups of natural populations that can or do interbreed and are isolated from other such groups in a reproductive sense. To be reproductively isolated means that even if the two species were put together they could not produce fertile offspring.

An example of such populations are the Oregon and the California red tree voles, which are reddish "mice" that live primarily in Douglas fir trees of western Oregon and northwestern California. These two species meet occasionally in the vicinity of the Smith River just south of the Oregon-California border. Although voles of the two species may interbreed now and then, hybrid males, those produced by such a union, are sterile, and hybrid females, although fertile, can breed only with a male of one species or the other. Because the habitat is not well suited to the tree voles of either species there are not enough voles to populate the area. So the scarcity of voles, plus the fact that hybrid males are sterile, maintains the integrity of the two species.

Where Do Species Come From? Where Do They Go?

To find out where species come from, we need to think about two theories of evolution, beginning with Darwin himself, who was of the opinion that evolution was both continuous and gradual. His theory says that evolution proceeds by mutation and natural selection. Mutations, which are simply random "typing mistakes" in the repetition of the genetic code passed from parent to offspring, are produced by all species at a more or less constant rate. Most individuals with mutations are eliminated through time, because they are "faulty" in some respect and unable to reproduce or to adapt as well as "normal" individuals.

But occasionally a mutation arises with a genetic make-up that renders the individual more, rather than less, fit to survive and reproduce. When this happens, the individual is given a chance to pass its mutant genes on to its own offspring, which in turn passes them to its own offspring, and so on until the mutant trait becomes both dominant and "normal" in the population.

So through the combination of random mutations and natural selection, evolution continually adapts species to their environments by weeding out the less fit in favor of the more fit. Here the notion is that species continue to evolve until they at last occupy all available habitat niches in the biosphere, which keeps changing, so that the species must continue adapting.

Darwin probably adopted the two basic but unnecessary assumptions—that evolution is both gradual and continuous—more out of innate conservatism than out of weighty scientific evidence. Darwin thought that Nature made no "great leaps." Sudden leaps in Nature resembled for Darwin the uncomfortable, sudden changes, such as revolutions, that transform human society. The dominant personalities of Darwin's time abhorred the revolutionary process of wholesale transformations. They clung instead to the idea of tiny, continual changes, which gradually adjusted one thing to another. Then, a hundred and twenty years after Darwin's *Origin of the Species* was first published, Jay Gould and Niles Eldredge, two American paleobiologists, wrote a seminal paper introducing the theory of evolutionary leaps. In their theory, these leaps, although dramatic, occur relatively infrequently.

Evolutionary stability or plateaus, it appears, are the normal course of events in the persistence of species over long periods of time. Paleontologists have long dismissed this "lack of evolution" as faulty judgments based on "apparent" gaps in the fossil record. The Darwinists believed that such gaps could be explained by the imperfection of the record, which had nothing to do with a lack of ongoing evolution. The fossil record, although perhaps imperfect, does not prove that evolution is a continual process.

In fact, evolution, as it now appears, proceeds through leaps of "speciation" (the sudden dominance of new species) rather than through a slow, gradual, continuous perfecting of existing species to fit changing conditions. These periodic leaps of speciation are like major earthquakes, which suddenly relieve the gradually-building pressures of the Earth's mantle.

In this new theory of periodic leaps of speciation, evolutionary change, rather than affecting individuals as survivors and reproducers, affects the entire system, which is composed of living organisms as they interact within their environments. Evolution occurs when a dominant species is destabilized within its habitat, when its cycle of dominance is broken by a new species, which may have emerged "haphazardly" at the edge of the cycle of dominance. Thus the dynamic equilibrium is broken as the old species is suddenly replaced by the emerging new species in a leap of evolution.

So, according to this most recent theory, new species are selected in sudden bursts of evolution during periods of critical instability within the cycles of dominant species. This sort of change is like what happens to an established singer who has long held an uncontested place in the spotlight. Suddenly, from somewhere backstage, emerges seemingly "out of nowhere" a new, hot star who commands the audience's attention and thereby takes over the spotlight and permanently displaces the old star.

Where do old species go when they become extinct? To find out, we need to visit the coelacanth ("SEAL-a-canth"), a rare fish that has survived deep in the Earth's seas almost unchanged for 380 million years. Humans are threatening this fish through greed, curiosity, superstition, and the pollution of its deep-sea habitat with toxins.

A team of scientists at the Virginia Institute of Marine Science in Gloucester has found high levels of DDT and PCBs in the tissues of frozen coelacanth specimens taken from deep water off the southeast coast of Africa. This situation alarms the scientists.

"It's a very scary situation," said John A. Musick, who headed the study at the institute. "It's even more alarming because if we lose the coelacanths, we're not losing a species, or a genus, or a family. We're losing a superorder—the last member of a species that dominated the world's ecology for millions of years."[2] The loss of a superorder is, to scientists, the loss of a gigantic branch in the tree of life.

Some ancient species, such as opossums, are unlikely to

become extinct because they meet Nature's criteria for persistence. In addition, they live in environments that vary so much from day to day, month to month, and year to year that they are unlikely to meet anything in the future they have not already survived in the past. Another category of organisms, however, called living fossils, is in much more severe danger of extinction.

Organisms like the coelacanth are called "living fossils" because they are the only surviving species of a taxonomic group that was once considerably richer. As the last living species in that group, they have not changed in millions of years. This notion of the living fossil has an air of doom about it, as though the coelacanth were living on borrowed time, a holdover from a more aristocratic era. Some "living fossils" are indeed living on borrowed time because they are adapted only to specific habitats threatened with drastic modification, or the species themselves are simply disappearing into extinction.

In the game of survival, the coelacanth has three strikes against it: it is the only surviving species of a taxonomic group that was once considerably richer; it has not changed in millions of years; and it is adapted to a specific habitat that is now threatened by human-caused pollution and exploited by human intrusion.

The continued survival of the coelacanth, after 380 million years of history in the deep sea off the coast of southeast Africa, is suddenly threatened by major changes in its environment. These changes have been created by an upstart species that has been around for only about five to eight million years. If we, the human species, critically destabilize the coelacanth's habitat and its patterns of self-maintenance to the point that it becomes extinct, what does this mean?

In the case of the coelacanth, it means that a whole, major line of evolution will suddenly disappear—forever. It means that all living individuals in the species, each one of which is the culmination of 380 million years of an unbroken chain of genetic experiments, will cease to be. And the loss of these individual genetic experiments amounts to the cumulative loss of the collective individuals that comprise the species.

The loss of the coelacanth after 380 million years because of human-caused disturbance to its habitat shows us something else: that the effects of our materialistic form of society are now reaching into the furthermost recesses of the planetary ecosystem. So the impending extinction of the coelacanth is a warning that the effects we are having on the environments of our home planet are deleterious to the survival of human society. The coelacanth is perhaps the most ancient living form of the "miner's canary." Yet the greater meaning of our having caused the coelacanth's extinction rests privately in our hearts.

But what about you and me? Each of us is also the culmination of an unbroken chain of genetic experiments reaching back millions of years into antiquity. When you and I depart this Earth, we too, in the Earthly sense, are individually extinct, although if we have living children, our genes are passed on. But we have disappeared, vanished from the scene, and the play of human speciation goes on without us. The millennial genetic experiment of an individual life is suddenly terminated with a finality that only the bereaved can understand.

Extinction carries two meanings: one local and one global. A local extinction refers to a particular population, such as the red squirrel on Mount Graham, a mountain-top island in the desert of Arizona. A global extinction, on the other hand, refers to an entire species (all the squirrels, in this example).

Local populations may—and often do—disappear, either temporarily or permanently, without implying extinction or even the near extinction of the species. A species, on the other hand, is composed of the sum of its populations, both plants and animals, so the loss of populations will affect the species as a whole and may imply danger to its survival.

Global extinction happens at the exact moment when either one of the last breeding pair dies.

The minimum size of a population is critical to its continued survival in the face of change; the smaller a population is, the more susceptible it is to extinction from any of various causes. This scenario is exemplified by the recent extinction of nine populations of the northern leopard frog in the mountainous Red Feather Lakes region of Larimer County, Colorado.

Between 1973 and 1982, the nine populations of frogs failed to reproduce, so they became extinct. Although one area that had formerly supported a population was recolonized in 1980, nobody saw any frogs at any of the sites in 1981 or in 1982. Six of the populations became extinct because the ponds in which they bred dried up. The remaining three populations were so small that they were susceptible to other events, the nature of which remains unknown.

Even though nine populations of the northern leopard frog have become extinct, the significance of such extinctions to a species with a network of populations is vastly different than it would be to a species with few populations. A species subdivided into a large number of semi-autonomous populations that cover a vast geographical area is less susceptible to extinction than a species of only one or two populations.

The salmon is an excellent intermediate example of the way such a dynamic might work. Salmon have discrete populations of adults, often called "strains" or "runs," which breed in particular streams—those in which they originally hatched. Once the young reach a certain size, they swim downstream and mingle in the ocean with individuals of all the other populations. With maturity, however, members of each population leave the ocean and swim up the particular river they originally descended on their way to the ocean, once again seeking the exact stream in which they hatched and in which they will lay their eggs.

Someone interested in managing a population of salmon in a particular river must pay close attention to the dynamics of that population, which only become apparent when the salmon are actually in the river. On the other hand, when salmon from all of the rivers are massed in the ocean in a "superpopulation," the management of the marine salmon fishery is a vastly different affair.

Today the Pacific Northwest region of the United States has a number of discrete populations or "runs" of breeding salmon in particular rivers, such as the Columbia and the Snake, that face extinction because of hydroelectric dams. The dams not only trap many of the young fish upstream, preventing them from reaching the ocean, they also kill other fish passing through the hydroelectric turbines in their efforts to reach the sea. Still others die when the impounded waters behind the series of dams are drawn down to accommodate large irrigation projects. Bear in mind that people constructed both the dams and the irrigation projects without regard to the habitat requirements of the salmon.

Losing a given run of salmon will affect the superpopulation in the ocean through the loss of genetic diversity, a sort of "secret extinction" hidden in the totality of the superpopulation. Such a loss is hardly noticed because the superpopulation is a collective of immature salmon growing to reproductive maturity.

But if you are responsible for the health of a particular population of breeding adults once it leaves the ocean and arrives in the river, the secret extinction in the superpopulation is no longer a secret. It's a permanent disaster. The impact of that extinction on the river, which may never again see a salmon, differs significantly from its impact on the ocean, which still sees millions of the same species of salmon, though none from that particular run.

Secret extinction or not, where do species come from? Where do they go? Species arise out of the Creative process of evolutionary change, and when their time is over, they disappear back into that process, making way for yet another species, much as the rocks of the Earth have cycled through creation, destruction, and re-creation as something entirely different.

After all, you and I are but refabrications composed of the atoms borrowed by the earliest invertebrates of the Cambrian Period, about 600 million years ago, then passed on to the dinosaurs of the Cretaceous Period, about 130 million years ago, then on to the woolly mammoths, dire-wolves, saber-tooth tigers, and cave bears of the Pleistocene Epoch, about a million years ago, until now, finally, it's our turn to borrow them. When we die, when we become extinct as individuals in this world, where will the atoms go? That is the Eternal Mystery!

How Species Enrich the World

Why do we need such a variety of species anyway? Would the coelacanth really be so great a loss? What effect does a variety of species have on the world ecosystem?

One marvelous effect they have is increasing the stability of ecosystems by means of feedback loops. Feedback loops are the means by which processes reinforce themselves.

Strong, self-reinforcing, feedback loops characterize many interactions in Nature and have long been thought to account for the stability of complex systems. Ecosystems with such strong interactions among components that feedback loops contribute can be complex, productive, stable, and resilient under the conditions to which they are adapted. When these critical loops are disrupted, such as in the extinction of species, these same systems become fragile and easily affected by slight changes.

It's the variety of species that create the feedback loops. That's what makes each individual species so valuable: each species by its very existence has a shape and therefore a structure that in turn allows certain functions to take place, functions that interact with those of other species. All of this is governed ultimately by the genetic code, which by replicating species' character traits builds a certain amount of redundancy into each ecosystem.

Redundancy means that more than one species can perform similar functions. It's a type of ecological insurance policy, which strengthens the ability of the system to retain the integrity of its basic relationships. The insurance of redundancy means that the loss of a species or two is not likely to result in such severe functional disruptions of the ecosystem so as to cause its collapse because other species can make up for the functional loss. But there comes a point, a threshhold, when the loss of one or two more species may in fact tip the balance and cause the system to begin an irreversible change. That change may signal a decline in quality or productivity.

Although an ecosystem may be stable and able to respond "positively" to the disturbances in its own environment to which it is adapted, this same system may be exceedingly vulnerable to the introduction of foreign disturbances to which it is not adapted. We can avoid disrupting ecosystems supported by feedback loops only if we understand and protect the critical interactions that bind the parts of an ecosystem into one.

Diversity of plants and animals therefore plays a seminal role in buffering an ecosystem against disturbances from which it cannot recover. As we lose species, we lose not only their diversity of structure and function but also their genetic diversity, which sooner or later results in complex ecosystems becoming so simplified they will be unable to sustain us as a society. So any societal strategy aimed at protecting diversity and its evolution is a critically important step toward ensuring an ecosystem's ability to adapt to change. Diversity counts. We need to protect it at any cost.

For Want of a Squirrel, a Forest is Lost If diversity of species is essential, how do they act in concert as a whole? "For want of a squirrel, a seed was lost; for want of a seed, a tree was lost; for want of a tree, a forest was lost; for want of a forest . . . . " But what exactly does this all mean? It means that we could lose the tremendous biodiversity of the tropical rain forests without cutting a single tree! How?

Let's consider the rain forest in Gabon, Africa, where to biologist Louise Emmons its fascination lies in "its stunning complexity." In this forest, says Emmons, "You can stand anywhere and be surrounded by hundreds of organisms that are all 'doing something,' going about their living in countless interactions—ants carrying leaves, birds dancing, bats singing, giant blue wasps wrestling with giant tarantulas, caterpillars pretending they are bird droppings, and so on."[3]

In Gabon, Emmons found that nine species of squirrels all live together in one forest. Each is a different size; three species have specialized diets or habits, which leaves six that feed on nuts, fruits, and insects and could therefore be potential competitors for food. But a closer look reveals that three of the six species—a large, a medium, and a small— live exclusively in the canopy of the forest, with the largest one, a "giant" squirrel, feeding primarily on very large, hard nuts while the smaller ones eat proportionally smaller fruits and nuts. The other three species—again a large, a medium, and a small—live exclusively on the ground, where they eat the same species of fruits and nuts as do their neighbors in the canopy, except they eat the fruits and nuts after they fall to the ground.

The forest in Gabon is evergreen, and fruit can be found on the trees throughout the year, but any one species of tree produces fruit for only a short period each year. To support three species of squirrels, eight species of monkeys, and eight species of fruit-eating bats (and so on) in the canopy, the Gabon forest must have a wide variety of species of trees and lianas (high-climbing, usually woody vines), each producing fruits and nuts in its own rhythm. The varying sizes of the fruits and nuts can support different sizes of squirrels with different tastes, whereas these same fruits and nuts when they fall to the ground can feed a whole analogous array of species, those that feed on the ground.

But just how rich in species is a tropical rain forest? Al Gentry of the Missouri Botanical Garden has for many years been counting the species of trees and lianas in tropical rain forests. The richest site he has found thus far is a plot two and a half acres in extent near Iquitos, Peru, where he counted an incredible 283 species of trees over four inches in diameter. There were 580 trees of this size in the two-and-a-half-acre plot, which means there was an average of only two individual trees per species, and there were an astounding 58 species among the first 65 individual trees that Al counted.

Worldwide, tropical rain forests seem to have from about 90 to 283 species of large trees within every two and a half acres, and this is not counting the other plants and the animals. Even the "poorest" of tropical rain forests have an average of about five individual trees per species every two and a half acres.

In contrast, a dry tropical forest, such as occurs in northern India, has about half as many species of trees as does a wet tropical forest. And the richest forests of the United States have about twenty species of trees over four inches in diameter, with an average of about thirty individuals per species, in each two and a half acres of ground. But most temperate forests are much poorer than this.

So it seems clear that tropical rain forests are amazingly rich in species of trees. But not just any trees: especially those trees whose fruits are eaten and dispersed by birds and mammals. Not surprisingly, therefore, tropical rain forests also are rich in species of mammals and birds. But not just any mammals and birds: especially those that eat fruits and disperse their seeds. There are, for example, 126 species of mammals within a single area of forest in Gabon and 550 species of birds within a single lowland site in the Amazon basin of Peru. Further, the life cycle of each species is interdependent on the life cycles of the other species. The enormous number of vertebrate animals appears to be supported by the large number of species of plants acting as sources of food the year round.

If all this biodiversity is to be maintained, each individual tree must succeed in leaving offspring. Seeds and tender young seedlings are amongst the richest foods available to forest animals, and their succulence greatly increases their chance of being eaten by the large numbers of hungry animals searching for food around the bases of fruit- and nut-bearing trees. Likewise, such organisms as fungi, worms, and insects soon accumulate where the seeds and seedlings are concentrated, and they spread from one seed or seedling to another.

Under such circumstances, seeds carried away from such concentrations of hungry organisms are more likely to succeed in germinating. Another major benefit of seeds being carried away from the parent tree is the availability of a wide variety of places with different conditions into which a seed is likely to fall. A new condition might offer a pocket of better soil on a mound created by termites, or in a spot where a dead tree has created a hole in the canopy, a hole that admits sunlight.

It is certainly no accident that about eighty to ninety-five percent of the species of trees in tropical rain forests produce fruits that are dispersed by birds and mammals. By dispersing those seeds, the birds and mammals also are maintaining the rich diversity of species of trees, which not only formed their habitat in the first place but also perpetuate it. This is an ideal example of a self-reinforcing feedback loop.

Many species of trees in the tropical rain forests, especially those germinating in the dark understory, have large seeds that carry enough stored energy to put out leaves and roots without much help from the sun. Such fruits and seeds are often so large that only proportionately-sized birds and mammals can swallow or carry them. In Gabon, for example, monkeys dispersed sixty-seven percent of the fruits eaten by animals in Emmons's area of study.

Seed-dispersing animals like large birds and large monkeys are the most important animals for replacing the large trees and lianas of the forest canopy and thus helping them survive. Those animals are, however, the first species to disappear when humans hunt them for food. These species, along with elephants, have already been hunted so heavily that they have either been drastically reduced in numbers or eliminated completely over vast areas of African forest, and the situation in the tropical rain forests of Central and South America is much the same.

Foresters for the most part have overlooked the whole subject of the way the interdependency of plants and animals affect biodiversity of a plant community. Elephants of the Ivory Coast, for example, disperse the seeds of 37 species of trees. Of those, only seven species had alternate ways of being dispersed—by birds and monkeys. In one study area, out of 201 individual trees, 83 species were dispersed by elephants.

In one forest where humans had eliminated elephants a century earlier, few juvenile trees of the elephant-dispersed species were left, and the two major species had no offspring at all. One of these two species just happens to be the single most important species for the two largest squirrels that Louise Emmons studied in Gabon—the one that eats the large, hard nuts in the canopy and the other that eats the same nuts once they've fallen to the ground.

Once the large species of birds and mammals are gone, the stunningly rich tropical rain forests will change and gradually lose species of trees, lianas, and other plants. Smaller seeds dispersed by wind will replace large seeds dispersed by large animals. Those species of plants whose seeds grow in the shaded understory will not survive, and the land will gradually be forested by fewer, more common species.

As the forests become poorer in species of plants, the number of species of birds, mammals, and other creatures will decline accordingly. All the complex, interconnected, interdependent feedback loops among plants and animals will gradually simplify. The species of which the feedback loops are composed will be lost forever—and the feedback loops with them. This is how the evolutionary process works. Ecologically, it is neither good nor bad, right nor wrong, but those changes may make the forest less attractive, less usable by species, such as humans, that used to rely on it for their livelihoods and for products. So if we want to think about the survival of humans, we have to think about all interrelationships of animals with plants.

The same types of self-reinforcing feedback loops that take place in tropical rain forests occur also in the temperate coniferous forests of the world, and they represent the same four basic elements of diversity: genetic, species, structural, and functional. Genetic diversity is the way species adapt to change; it is the hidden diversity that is so often subjected to the "secret extinctions" mentioned earlier. The most important aspect of genetic diversity is that it can act as a buffer against the variability of environmental conditions, particularly in the long term. So healthy environments can act as "shock absorbers" in the face of catastrophic disturbance.

Here looms a critical concept: the past function of an ecosystem determines its present structure, and its present structure determines its future function. This means that structure is defined by function and function is defined by structure! So as we alter the composition of species in an area, so we at the same moment alter its function in time. Over time, this new arrangement of species will respond to conditions differently than the original arrangement of species would have.

Genetic Steppingstones Species come and go, enriching the world with their presence. Having considered those points, it's time to contemplate the genetics of place—that is, local populations adapted to specific habitats. Their importance lies in the understanding that as we fragment the landscape in which we live, we're putting our fellow planetary travelers at risk often without even realizing it.

As we fragment landscapes, both plants and animals

become vulnerable to "secret extinctions"—the loss of lo-cally-adapted populations, such as people or trees that have evolved over centuries to millennia. Such a loss can be more or less permanent and may inexorably alter the habitat. That's because other populations of the same species might prove unable to reoccupy the habitat or might not even be able to reach it, because of major environmental shifts. We produce these shifts by pumping unprecedented amounts of energy into and through the ecosystems of our home planet.

To help you understand what I mean, I'll present two instances of the genetics of place. One deals with the Temuan culture of Malaysia. The other deals with sugar maple trees in the eastern United States and Canada.

First, the Temuan. The Temuan natives living along the fringe of the Malay jungle may be much the same as they were thousands of years ago. This tribal group has stayed remarkably separate through the centuries, with little blend-ing into other nationalities, such as the Chinese, the Indians, or the British who most recently ruled the area.

The Temuan natives display some interesting genetic traits that they probably maintained by isolating themselves culturally. Among the most significant traits is a special con-dition of red blood cells, an "elliptocytosis," found only in Southeast Asia; it offers some protection against malaria. *Elliptocytosis* means elliptical cells.

Malaria, which has been around for thousands of years, has devastated populations of humans. To the Temuan, re-sistance to malaria not only has survival value in evolution-ary terms but also offers a window into their past. To understand ourselves as a species, therefore, we must learn more about our cultural diversity and about the specifics of our genetic development, because the way we are genetically today reflects our environment of the past.

Although many scientists tend to study only the people of wealthier nations and their characteristics, some other groups of humans around the world represent unique gene pools. In some cases, as history has proven again and again, a disease as simple as the common cold could decimate a particular people who, through isolation, lack immunity to it. And we would rue the day such peoples become extinct, because our global society would lose an irretrievable part of itself. This potential loss reveals the need for a new concept in protecting our environment: the conservation of unique communities of humans. It's an idea worth considering.

The second example of the genetics of place deals with sugar maple trees, which in New England range from sea level up to about 2,500 feet in elevation. Populations of sugar maples differ in a number of physiological characteristics depending on the elevation of their habitat. Sugar maples from high elevations, for example, can photosynthesize much faster than those populations at middle elevations. Not only that, but the structure of their leaves is quite different.

Leaves of sugar maples growing at high elevations are thin. That is, for the same area of a leaf, the weight of the leaf is lowest at the high elevations and highest at the middle elevations—something suggesting that sugar maples at high elevations produce cheap, throw-away leaves.

Trees can produce large, thin leaves at far less cost in energy than they can thick leaves. Despite this low investment in leaf tissue, the trees' rates of photosynthesis are very high. It stands to reason, therefore, that such characteristics of low-energy, throw-away leaves coupled with high rates of photosynthesis are best adapted to the short growing seasons of high elevations. Indeed, one can expect leaf-out to occur ten days later at high elevations than at middle elevations and leaf-drop to be ten days earlier—a difference of nearly three weeks in the growing season.

Because sugar maples shed their leaves each autumn and produce new ones each spring, the length of the growing season is critical to the type of leaves they produce. The high-elevation sugar maples are right on the border of conditions to which the maples are suited, and the short growing season must exert a tremendous pressure in selecting for individual trees that can photosynthesize quickly and produce cheap, rapidly-deployed, throw-away leaves.

Suppose a population of sugar maples was removed from the top 325 feet of its elevational range. Could it be replaced by sugar maples from middle elevations? You could physically transplant them, but they wouldn't survive, because they lack the local genetics of place. Without the local adaptations necessary to survive at the top of the species' elevational range, sugar maples simply would not be part of the plant community. If the high-elevation population becomes extinct, the high-elevation environment is less diverse by at least one species of tree.

So what, you say? One species of tree is missing from the top of some mountain. Big deal! Well, let's consider another, more drastic, example. This time, however, the example is hypothetical, because it hasn't happened yet but could theoretically.

Let's assume that sugar maples range geographically from Georgia to just north of the Canadian border. Now, if the climate were to warm up rapidly by an average of three degrees, with correspondingly higher extremes in summer temperatures occurring more frequently, the sugar maples would become stressed throughout their range. In order to survive, the species would have to compensate for the increase in temperature by migrating northward in latitude and higher in altitude.

What happens when the temperature increases and the maples have to migrate northward in latitude? In the past, given Nature's continuous landscape and sufficient time to migrate and to adapt, such a change could have been handled, but now it could not. Why? First, the connectivity of Nature's landscape has been severely fragmented by our cultural tinkerings; this means there are large areas through which sugar maples can no longer migrate because there is simply no suitable habitat for them. Sugar maples cannot, for instance, march through cities or grow in concrete and asphalt. Nor can they grow in many other once-suitable habitats, ones that have been so drastically altered they need time apart from human activity to once again become habitable to sugar maples.

Second, too many of the locally-adapted populations of sugar maple within the network of populations no longer exist. They have succumbed to secret extinctions, which means those genetic steppingstones of place no longer exist as "a corridor of migration."

Forests, like people, migrate. In fact, forests migrate as entire systems—as interactive above-ground/below-ground communities of symbiotic plants and animals. Although individual species of trees may migrate singly by means of seeds dispersed by animals or by the wind, this is the migration of trees, not of forests. Even for one species of tree to migrate, however, the habitat requirements of the individual species of tree must be met.

Third, let's assume that global warming due to our human-induced greenhouse effect is unprecedented in speed and magnitude. So even if the first two conditions still favored the migration of sugar maples, the speed with which the climate would change would simply be too fast for the maple to accept. After all, the maple in Georgia would have to migrate at least to New England, and the trees in New England and southern Canada would have to occupy areas that now are boreal forest and treeline in northern Canada.

Even if we set aside this hypothetical case, we must still deal with secret extinctions. When locally-adapted, interactive, above-ground/below-ground communities of symbiotic plants and animals disappear, they cannot be replaced overnight—if ever. Nor can they be replaced through the myth of "management," a concept through which we give ourselves a false sense of power over Nature.

The adjustments in these plant and animal communities over thousands of years makes the genetics of place vulnerable to thoughtless human tinkering. Each secret extinction of a locally-adapted population weakens and impoverishes the genetic network of diversity, the sum of which constitutes not only the species as it survives today but also what the species must become if it is to survive tomorrow.

When Habitats Change

In addition to the genetics of local populations, there have been and again will be drastic changes in habitats, changes that affect whole groups of plants and animals. But then plants and animals help create a given habitat through their above-ground/below-ground symbiotic interactions, so in the sense that habitats change, habitats, too, can be thought of as part of the evolutionary process. After all, both plants and animals together help create new habitats as well as the extinction of old ones. To gain a sense of what I mean, consider conditions in eastern North America at the close of the Wisconsin glaciation, about 10,000 years ago.

The modern northern flora and fauna of eastern North America are composed largely of post-Wisconsin glacial-stage plants and animals that immigrated to ground previously stripped of life by glacial ice. Competition therefore favored species adapted to harsh northern environments, species that could disperse rapidly. Groups of animals composed of species from northern and temperate habitats lived on the southern edge of the glacier. Unadaptable temperate species continued to inhabit local areas of relatively unaltered climate while those that could adapt to some degree survived where the glaciers had not encroached.

As the climate changed, habitats around the glacier slowly changed. Those covered with ice were created and destroyed more rapidly than those along the edge of the ice. The gradual changes created a continuum of small habitats, which supported a richer collection of plants and animals than the flora and fauna in previously glaciated areas.

As the glaciers receded, most mammals followed habitats northward, migrated to higher latitudes, underwent physiological adjustments, or became extinct. The varied habitats available and the adaptability of other mammals allowed them to survive, too, and to move southward ahead of the advancing Wisconsin glaciation and northward again as the glacier melted. Only the less adaptable larger species were particularly prone to extinction.

On a smaller scale, changes in the Fort Rock Basin of southcentral Oregon, east of the High Cascade Mountain Range, which today is a shrubby, cold-desert steppe, caused species to become extinct in a particular area. During the Wisconsin Glacial Stage, the Fort Rock Basin was filled by a large lake (Photos 3 & 4). The Basin's habitat was a mixture of grassy plains, river-bank woodlands, and water. Two species of horses and three species of camels lived on the grassy areas of the lowland glades and upland prairies. The stream

Photo 3. *There Once Was a Lake:* Fort Rock, rising more than 300 feet, is the remnant of a tuff cone, rock formed of compacted volcanic ash. Much of the erosion was caused by wave action in a lake that covered the floor of the valley during the Pleistocene Epoch.

Photo 4. *Ancient Waves:* Close view of Fort Rock shows erosion at its base caused by centuries of waves in the Pleistocene lake.

valleys, with strips or clumps of woodland, were suited to the large ground sloth, woolly mammoth, two species of peccaries, and a bear, while the streams themselves held a giant beaver and muskrats.

These animals were hunted by wild dogs called direwolves and by people, who are thought to have moved into the basin about eleven thousand years ago. Three species of carp and two species of suckers as well as chinook salmon lived in the lake and streams. All these species, except the salmon, are extinct. Presence of the salmon reveals that there was an overflow through an outlet to the Pacific Ocean, which allowed the salmon to reach Fort Rock Lake. When the overflow ceased, the salmon became land-locked but persisted in the lake until the end of its existence about ten thousand years ago.

Not all species that became extinct in the Fort Rock

Basin, however, died out as a whole. Some species simply migrated with their habitats and live today in other areas. Before seven thousand years ago, for example, white-tailed jackrabbits lived in the lower elevations of the present Fort Rock Basin. The white-tailed jackrabbit is adapted to the colder climates of higher, more northerly regions and tends to occupy grassy habitats. Sage grouse, elk, and bison, each with similar habitat affinities, all lived in the Fort Rock Basin. In addition, the pika or rock rabbit lived in jumbles of broken rock.

Then the climate began to change. As the area warmed and dried the existing plant community became destabilized and shifted from one that was made up primarily of northerly grasses and herbs to one that was made up primarily of southerly shrubs. The shift in plant communities caused the local extinction of the white-tailed jackrabbit, sage grouse, pika, elk, and bison. None of the other species was affected, however.

The pika and the elk moved up in elevation, whereas the white-tailed jackrabbit, sage grouse, and bison followed the migration of their habitat eastward toward what today is the state of Idaho. The mountain cottontail and black-tailed jackrabbit (Photo 5) moved northward into the Fort Rock Basin as the habitat changed, because both are adapted to the warmer climates of lower, more southerly regions and tend to occupy shrubby habitats.

As we have seen, habitats change. Sometimes they evolve slowly and gradually and sometimes quickly and drastically, but regardless of the way they do it, all habitats change. When they do, there is a general reshuffling of plants and animals. More adaptable species may for a time survive a change in habitat, even a relatively drastic one, but in the end they too must change, migrate elsewhere, or become extinct.

Occasionally, however, a species like the coelacanth changes but little in habitat over vast periods of time. This

Photo 5. *Black-Tailed Jackrabbit.*

stability of habitat allows the species to exist for millions of years with little or no apparent need to adapt further—that is, until now, a time in which they have no place else to go.

We humans have changed and are changing the global ecosystem and all of its component habitats at an exponential rate. Today we have become the major cause of extinctions and of evolutionary leaps. Some ecosystems and their habitats may be able to mitigate the alterations to which we subject them. But alas, most alterations are damaging to the ecosystem as we know it and are prone to spread. Others evolve into ecosystems that we humans find less desirable, often because the new species, which quickly replace those lost, cannot live up to our human expectations. Consider, for instance, what human society is doing to the Amazon.

Deforestation in the Amazon—as well as in the Pacific Northwest and across Canada—shows that, as a culture, we have learned but little. Just imagine the forests from the crest of the Cascade Mountains in western Oregon and western

Washington to the Pacific Ocean, about a third of each state, all burning up within a year. That is roughly equivalent to the amount of land burned in only one year in the Brazilian Amazon. Each year, an area eighty percent the size of the State of Oregon burns in the Brazilian Amazon alone.

The major cause of deforestation by extensive burning is that people are converting the tropical forests to pastures for cattle. Simple harvesting of timber also causes problems, however, because once the canopy of the forest is opened, the understory environment changes drastically, and the forest can no longer sustain itself.

Never in the history of humanity have so many of the world's tropical forests been disturbed in such a foreign and catastrophic way on such a large scale as they have during the last thirty years. Think of the fact that tropical rain forests—one of the world's oldest ecosystems—occupy only seven percent of the Earth's surface and are home to more than fifty percent of all the Earth's species. What does this mean in terms of the Amazonian tropical forest?

An intact rain forest creates its own internal and external climate, in which about half of all the rainfall originates from moisture given off by the forest itself. When large areas of a rain forest are destroyed, local and regional climatic patterns change. Once the forest is gone, the result is usually drought, which increases the probability of fire and decreases the probability that the forest will ever return.

The environment in the deforested areas of the Amazon has been altered to such an extent that the ecological processes that once maintained the tropical forest are changing irreversibly. Once the forest has been even partly cleared or logged, environmental conditions change swiftly and dramatically.

Removal of the trees alters the forest's internal microclimate by exposing the heretofore protected, moist, shaded interior of the forest to the sun. It also leaves behind large accumulations of woody material exposed to the sun's drying heat. As a result, daily temperatures soar in the deforested areas by ten to fifteen degrees above that of the forested areas, causing the woody fuels to dry and become extremely easy to burn. It is therefore not a matter of *whether* the area will burn but of *when* it will burn. The ultimate result is a quick, dramatic change from a dense closed-canopy forest virtually immune to fire to a weedy, flammable pasture in which fires are common and often occur repeatedly. In those conditions, a new forest cannot grow.

Today as never before, the evolutionary script is in our hands. Through politics, we are writing, editing, and rewriting the next scene of the play, and the next, and the next. Through our motives and our behavior we have set in motion the direction the evolutionary tree will grow.

Today all habitats pass through the hands of time as well as through the hands of human society, if for no other reason than that we have polluted the atmosphere and, through the air, the soils and the waters of the world. And such pollution has reached even unto the coelacanth in the far, deep recesses of the sea!

In addition, the human-caused rate of change in the climate through the greenhouse effect is unprecedented. Scientists predict its speed at several orders of magnitude faster than any known previous climatic changes. In mountainous areas, for example, a predicted three-degree rise in temperature would mean that subalpine and alpine habitats, to compensate for the increased temperature, would have to migrate upward in elevation about 1,600 feet. That dramatic a migration would really affect the plants and animals of those habitats.

Such migration would lead to a reduction in both the total extent and the numbers of areas of subalpine and alpine habitats. As a result those animals that require large home ranges and these specific habitats may become extinct as their habitats shrink. Given this scenario, even a two-degree rise in temperature over the next fifty years could cause the extinction of from ten to fifty percent of the animals now living in the subalpine and alpine "habitat islands" on the tops of isolated mountains in the Great Basin of the American West.

Further, the major impact of such a fast rate of change will come not from average changes in the weather but rather from striking climate events like prolonged drought in the American Midwest or increased rainfall in the Indian subcontinent. Such climatic changes could lead to increased flooding in both India and Bangladesh. And speaking of rain, the total amount of the rainfall may not be critical for undisturbed habitats, such as forests, but changes in the timing of the patterns of rainfall would be catastrophic for many species that depend on the current weather patterns for part of their life cycles. In addition, increased temperature will cause polar ice caps to melt and sea levels to rise, with potentially-devastating effects on habitats in low-lying coastal areas.

What would happen, one might ask, to the biodiversity of tropical forests if no rain falls in the wet season, or if rain falls in the dry season? The patterns of flowering and/or fruiting of many species of plants would be disrupted, and that disruption would dramatically affect the vast array of species of animals whose reproductive cycles are finely tuned to the current patterns of renewal of these resources.

Changing the way these patterns of flowering and/or fruiting synchronize with the animals' cycles of breeding could lead to serious disruptions of these cycles. Those disruptions could lead to rates of extinction above and beyond those already being experienced. Taken one step further, the loss of those species of animals that act as pollinators and dispersers of seeds would lead ultimately to the loss of the dependent species of plants—in short, to the total alteration of today's tropical forests as habitats.

I hope it's clear that we human beings, as a young species, relative newcomers within the world, are redrafting the evolutionary play. We are choosing the characters that will survive to perform again, those that will meet their extinction in which act, and those relative unknowns who will come from backstage to command the spotlight of the future.

Today, in the United States alone, 592 species of plants and animals are threatened with extinction. And we in our arrogance and in our informed denial of the problem continue to direct our impromptu play—without a script or any idea of what we're staging!

II
CULTURE AS AN END IN ITSELF

[Americans'] one primary and predominant object is to cultivate and settle these prairies, forests, and vast waste lands. The striking and peculiar characteristic of American society is, that it is not so much a democracy as a huge commercial company for the discovery, cultivation, and capitalization of its enormous territory. . . . The United States is primarily a commercial society . . . and only secondarily a nation. . . .

—EMILE BOUTMY

5
EVOLUTION AND HUMANITY

For a society to function so that its human components can survive and reproduce, Nature must maintain its cycles in such a way as to provide enough energy for society to use. If some of the cycles that we humans tinker with and alter begin to deviate too much from the evolutionary track that Nature has established, then we tend to introduce "corrections": we seek new sources of energy, we nurture new varieties of plants, and we invent new modes of production.

When, however, enough human-altered cycles break down simultaneously, we must call into question the logic of our social system itself. Such scrutiny is wise, because what society thinks of as "corrections" are really self-reinforcing feedback loops, the outcome of which is not necessarily in keeping with our desires, regardless of what we try to do. Human societies therefore either transform in a truly corrective sense—realigning themselves with the Universal Laws—or they vanish.

Life and society are tenable so long as a particular human population remains within the carrying capacity of its habitat. Carrying capacity is the number of individuals that can live in an area without degrading the habitat that supports them. When, however, the limits of carrying capacity are exceeded, the social system must change and correct the way it overtaxes the environment's source of energy or disappear into its smaller, more strongly bound components, such as tribes, families, or even individuals.

To survive, all societies must evolve in response to environmental changes, those usually brought about by their own activities. So far, groups of humans have evolved through stages of gathering food, hunting, nomadic herding, agriculturalization, industrialization, and now post-industrialization. Each stage has had a successively greater impact on the environment, and each cultural shift has brought with it the need to transcend the socially-created, environmental problems it has caused.

Today as never before the environmental transgressions of a few powerful nations like the United States of America affect the whole world. Human society as we currently know it, in all its various stages of evolution, stands at the crossroads of extinction. Witness Eastern Europe.

If the industrialized nations insist on maintaining their present course of environmental destruction, human societies, including ours, will collapse worldwide. If, on the other hand, we humans are wise enough to transcend our destructive ways, we can, through conscious decisions, create the opportunity for our societies to evolve more harmoniously into the future than might otherwise be possible.

Language, the Key to Conscious Evolution

For us to continue our evolution, we need to protect one aspect of our culture that we normally neglect: language.

Perhaps one of the greatest feats of humanity is the evolution of language, especially written language, which made culture possible. Language, which we seem to take for granted, is not something we generally think of as becoming extinct. And yet languages are disappearing all over the world—especially those of indigenous people that are spoken languages only.

Of all the gifts of life, language is one of the most incredible. I can, in silence, understand what I think you wish me to know when you write to me. And I can perceive what I think your thoughts are and ask for clarification when you speak to me. You speak and you write and you allow me to share a small part of you.

Through language, we can create, examine, and test concepts, those intangible figments of human thought and imagination. Concepts can only be qualified, not quantified; only interpreted, not measured. And concepts can be requalified and reinterpreted hundreds or even thousands of years after they were first written.

Language is the storehouse of ideas. It allows each succeeding generation to benefit from the knowledge accrued by generations already past. It is a tool, a catalyst, a gift from adults to children. By means of language, each generation begins further up the ladder of knowledge than the preceding one began.

One of the greatest values of language is that it allows us to search for truth and to strive for those ideals that we, as a society, perceive to be right and just. In this sense, language has become an imperative for the survival of human society, because the tenets of society are founded on language. We simply must understand one another if our respective societies are to survive.

Every human language—the master tool representing its own culture—has its unique construct, which determines both its limitations and its possibilities of expressing myth, emotion, and logic. So long as we have the maximum diversity of languages, we can see ourselves—the collective human creature, the social animal—most clearly and from many points of view in a multitude of social mirrors. And who knows when an idiom of an obscure language, or a "primitive" cultural solution, or the serendipitous flash of recognition spurred by some ancient myth or modern metaphor, may be the precise view necessary to resolve some crisis in our "modern" global society.

A case in point is the mystery of the way Mayan farmers fed their huge population in the tropical forest of the Yucatán peninsula. Rather than cutting down the forest and practicing the destructive slash-and-burn agriculture of today, they managed the tropical rain forests with ecological acumen and cultural harmony long before the Spanish conquistadores set foot in the New World.

The Mayans practiced sustainable agriculture for centuries by constructing *pet kotoob* (plural of *pet kot*, Mayan for "round wall of stone"). These constructions are rock walls two to three feet high enclosing a small area about the size of a backyard garden. Within these *pet kotoob*, the Mayans grew many kinds of agricultural plants not native to the region.

The *pet kotoob* offers today's farmers in the Yucatán peninsula a form of sustainable tropical agriculture and forest management should they choose to create them, but only because the "tool"—*pet kotoob*—is still alive. What if the words *pet kotoob* had been lost to antiquity, and with the words the idea had become extinct?

How many potential answers, how much ancient wisdom, will be lost, because we are losing languages, especially obscure, "primitive" ones, to "progress"? As languages become extinct, we lose their cultural sources along with their perceptions and modes of expression. Because language is the fabric of culture, when a language dies the demise of the culture is imminent.

One such dying language is that of the coastal Tlingit Indians of southeastern Alaska,[4] so Richard and Nora Dauenhauer have raced time to collect the Tlingits' tales before the language dies with the few elders who still speak it. Nora remembers when speaking her native Tlingit tongue brought punishment at school and shame on the streets. Now it's too late for Tlingit to survive as an everyday language. To survive at all, it must be preserved as literature.

Since Nora began collecting Tlingit stories in the 1960s, only three of the twelve elders whose tales are printed are living. "We only know of two young men who can speak Tlingit, two under the age of 40. All of us who can speak it are now grandmothers," she says.

With the loss of each language, we also lose the evolution of its logic and its cultural myths and rituals—the metaphors of Creation that give the people a sense of place within the Universe. Each time we allow another human language to become extinct we are losing a facet of understanding, a facet of our collective selves. As a global society we are slowly making ourselves blind not only to ourselves and to one another but also to our relationship within the Universe.

Our growing blindness through the extinction of languages is exacerbated by the global spread of such languages as English, German, and French. They are replacing more obscure ones at a tremendous cost of lost cultural history, lost myths, and lost human dignity.

For a time now some have been pushing English as the "official language" in America.[5] Those who support the "English-only" movement claim that "bilingualism creates cultural divisions and hinders new immigrants' abilities to assimilate," but critics believe the English-only movement is a cover for racism. This may well be so, for as poet Allen Ginsberg said, "Whoever controls the language, the images, controls the race." But regardless of the motive, to lose one's cultural myth, which only one's own language can portray adequately, is to lose one's sense of place and identity in the Human Family and in the Universe.

And, if diversity at some point does equate to the stability of a dynamic society, we are simplifying and therefore destabilizing society not only through the loss of languages and their cultures but also through the proliferation of a few chosen languages. Both of these things are destroying the spiritual vitality of humanity's cultural myths and the rituals on which they are founded.

Our Cultural Choices

Language made culture possible, because it allowed a group of human beings to evolve a unique ever-increasingly complex social order that eventually became a society. A society is a group of human beings broadly distinguished from other groups by mutual interests, participation in characteristic relationships, a common culture, and shared institutions and agencies. Culture, in turn, is the totality of socially transmitted behavioral patterns, arts, beliefs, institutions, and all other products of human work and thought characteristic of a community or population.

As can be seen in Fig. 3, people think in one of two ways: (1) in a linear pattern that causes some to focus on the production and accumulation of material *products* as the primary purpose of life, or (2) in a cyclic pattern that causes others to focus on being an integral part of the *processes* that constitute the spiritual center of life's cycle. In turn, these patterns of thought determine the core of a society's culture.

Note that the linear pattern of human thought in Fig. 3 produces a culture like ours in which economics is the force that drives the society, determines its mode of institutions, and relegates religion to the bottom rung of the social ladder. On the other hand, the cyclic pattern of human thought in Fig. 3 produces a culture like that of the Native North Americans prior to the invasion by the Europeans, in which religion is the force that drives the society and determines the mode of its economics and institutions.

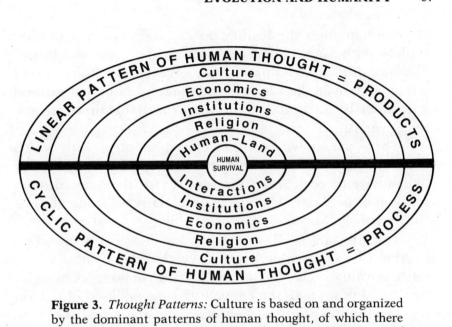

Figure 3. *Thought Patterns:* Culture is based on and organized by the dominant patterns of human thought, of which there are two dominant patterns. Through the cultural dynamics of human-land interactions, these patterns determine the care a given society takes of its land and the patterns it designs on the landscape.

Because a society's culture is the product of its dominant mode of thinking, given the same piece of land each culture would produce a different design on the landscape as a result of the pattern of its thinking, which is the template of individual values expressed in the collective mirror—the land. Because the land and the people are inseparably one, people unite with the land through their culture.

People and the Land Are One

As the social values determine the culture, so the culture is an expression of those values. The care taken of the land by the people is therefore the mirror image of the hidden forces in their social psyche. These secret thoughts guarded in the mind ultimately express themselves and determine whether or not a particular society survives or becomes a closed chapter in the history books. And history books are replete with such closed chapters as the great empires of Mesopotamia, Babylonia, Egypt, Greece, and Rome, all of which destroyed their forests and the fertility of their topsoil with their linear thinking and their insatiable drive for material wealth.

There are, however, other closed chapters with which most of us are not familiar, so we will travel back in history to examine three of them. First we'll visit the Anasazi; then we'll visit the Easter Islanders,[6] and finally we'll spend some time with the Mayans.[7]

The Anasazi (a Navajo word for "ancient strangers") lived in Chaco Canyon, Arizona, which today is mostly saltbush, nothing higher than one's knee, with no trees in sight. But 1,800 years ago, the canyon was a woodland of pinyon pine and juniper—that is, according to the remains of vegetation in the "fossilized" middens of the bushy-tailed woodrat.

In those middens, which range in age from 10,000 years ago to the present, researchers found 10,000-year-old remains of spruce and Douglas fir, along with a record of pinyon pine and juniper up to 1,200 years ago. Middens are missing, however, from the period of 1,200 years ago to 500 years ago, something that means during that period the Anasazi hunted the woodrats for food. When the middens reappeared, none showed traces of pinyon pine. What happened to change the landscape so dramatically? Mounting evidence strongly suggests the hand of the Anasazi culture itself.

More than a thousand years ago the Anasazi Indians moved into the area and established one of the most advanced civilizations that pre-industrial North America ever knew. The Anasazi built huge pueblos and developed sophisticated networks of politics and trading. Then, in the twelfth century, they mysteriously disappeared. Why? A question that has long been asked may now have an answer.

But first we must understand that the cliché about pri-

mitive peoples living in perfect harmony with the land may
not always have been the case. In fact, a number of ancient
cultures—such as the Anasazi—were nearly as adept at ecological destruction as we are today.

The peak of the Anasazi civilization occurred between
1075 and 1100 A.D., at which time the two Anasazi pueblos,
"Chetro Ketl" and "Pueblo Bonito," were the largest build-
ings north of what is now Mexico. They were five stories tall
and contained more than 500 rooms each. Their three-foot-
thick walls were made of flat, inch-high stones mortared with
the red mud of the canyon, and the roofs were supported
with massive timbers of spruce and fir, neither of which have
existed in the canyon since the Pleistocene Epoch, more than
10,000 years ago. This means that the Anasazi had to import
the huge timbers from distances of fifty miles or more.

Because the Anasazi brought the massive timbers for
their pueblos from that far away, they could also have imported firewood from similar distances. Heavy use of firewood meant deforestation. The decline of the culture must
have been caused by more than simple deforestation, however—perhaps by the concordant collapse of the elaborate
network of politics and trading, which in turn might have
been speeded up by a rapid increase in the region's population even as the region's resources decreased. Such an increase in population could have placed a tremendous strain
on the area's resources, from wood to water to arable land.
If the land could not support the population, the culture
would collapse with the collapse of the habitat on which the
culture was based.

Now let's look at Easter Island, a tiny, 43-square-mile
piece of land in the South Pacific 2,400 miles off the coast of
South America. The oldest pollen dates on the island go back
some 30,000 years, long before the first people, wandering
Polynesians, arrived. At that time, the island was forested.

The Polynesians settled on the island in about the year
400 A.D. They began gradually to clear the land for agriculture, and they cut trees to build canoes. The land was rela-

tively fertile, the sea teemed with fish, and the people flourished. Their population rose to about 15,000, and the culture grew sophisticated enough to carve the giant statues that have since become famous. So the people eventually also cut trees to provide logs for transporting and erecting those hundreds of eerie statues, or *moai*, some of which are about 32 feet high and weigh as much as 85 tons.

Unfortunately, when the trees were cut, they didn't grow back. Deforestation began about 1,200 years ago, a few hundred years after the people arrived, and was almost complete by 800 years ago. The people of Easter Island also exploited many of the island's other resources, such as its abundance of birds' eggs. The result was ecological disaster.

The people had cleared so much of the forest that they were without trees to build canoes for fishing. They probably also had exploited the eggs of the sooty tern to the point that the bird no longer nested on the island. And deforestation led to erosion of the soil and reduced yields of crops.

The downward spiral of culture on Easter Island had begun. Fewer fish, eggs, and crops led to a shortage of food. Hunger in turn brought warfare, even cannibalism, and the whole civilization was pushed to the brink of collapse. By the time European explorers arrived in the 1700s, only 4,000 people remained on the island, and the culture that produced the statues had completely disappeared.

Today, all we can do is marvel at the remains of the culture of Easter Island—statues that once stood erect on specially built platforms, others that lie abandoned between the volcanic quarries of their origin and their planned destinations, and still others that remain unfinished in the quarries. Easter Island is another example of the dependence of culture on the habitat on which it was based.

Finally, let's take a brief excursion to visit the Mayans of the Petén region of northern Guatemala, an area populated sparsely today but an enclave for the Mayans between 1,000 B.C. and 1,000 A.D. Over hundreds of years the population of the area had grown as much as tenfold, and the forest had been cut down for planting, building, and fuel. Since the tropical forest held most of its nutrients in the plants and little in the soil, much of the available nutrients was lost as the trees were cut. As the habitat disappeared, the animals, which provided a major source of protein, also vanished.

Here there is an interesting twist to the story. As the Mayan culture was collapsing, the forest was rejuvenating itself. What is sobering about this scenario is that the Maya were ingenious and knowledgeable conservationists. They knew a great deal about their own ecology, and all their systems of land management were sophisticated, as demonstrated by the Mayan farmers who fed their huge population in the tropical forest of the Yucatán peninsula. So rather than cutting down the forest to practice the destructive slash-and-burn agriculture of today, they managed the tropical rain forests with ecological acumen and cultural harmony. And they practiced sustainable agriculture by constructing *pet kotoob*, in which they grew not only native plants but also a variety of herbs, shrubs, and trees not native to the region.

The Maya didn't move in, raze the land, and move on. Yet it's as if the Mayan civilization choked itself on its own success. As the people caused the land to produce more, their population grew, and as their population grew, they coaxed more from the land. As more and more was demanded from the land, it began to change in subtle ways. These changes took place over a period of 2,000 years and were imperceptible to the people at any given time. Yet the hidden environmental damage caused by centuries of population growth increasingly taxing the land—what we today term "cumulative effects"—undoubtedly played a large role in the eventual collapse of the Mayan civilization.

How We Think

Although it is clear from the foregoing that both cyclic thinking and linear thinking can cause the destruction of the land, our Western, linear thinking is far more destructive in a far shorter time than is the cyclic thinking of most "primitive peoples." To understand why I say this, we need to examine both forms of thought. We'll start with cyclic thinking, because it is the older and because it arose at a' time when humanity had a better sense of its place within the Universe.

Cyclic Thinking Thinking in cycles ultimately causes us to see our life as a circular dance in which certain basic and necessary patterns of use and renewal, of life and death, are repeated endlessly. This is the ethical basis of Native American religious thought, as exemplified by Black Elk:

> Everything the Power of the World does is done in a
> circle. The sky is round, and . . . the earth is round like
> a ball, and so are all the stars. The wind, in its great-
> est power, whirls. Birds make their nests in circles,
> for theirs is the same religion as ours. The sun comes
> forth and goes down again in a circle. The moon does
> the same, and both are round. Even the seasons form
> a great circle in their changing, and always come
> back again to where they were. The life of a man is a
> circle from childhood to childhood, and so it is in
> everything where power moves.[8]

Those who think cyclicly humbly accept the mysteries of the Universe. They allow Nature to teach them, and Nature's reflective lessons of infinite Universal relationship are intrinsically valuable. To use something for its own sake and then to be the source of its renewal is to see it as a re-source. In the original sense of the word, "resource" was a reciprocal relationship between humanity and Earth, a circle of taking and giving and taking again. The very structure of the word— *re* and *source*—means reciprocal relationship, a cycle, to use something from the Earth and then to be the source of its renewal. "It is only in the processes of the natural world, and in analogous and related processes of human culture," says Wendell Berry, "that the new may grow usefully old, and the old be made new. . . . "

People who see life as a great circle see everything as interdependent, nothing as independent. There thus exists in Nature no such thing as an "independent variable." Everything in the Universe is patterned by its interdependence on everything else, and it's the pattern of interdependence and change that forms the only constant. This constant is the Principle both of Creation and of Infinite Becoming.

The cyclic *vision* is at once realistic and generous. Those who accept it recognize that in Creation lies the essential principle of return; what is here will leave and will come again; what I have, I must some day give up. They see death as an integral and indispensable part of life, for death is but another becoming, a view beyond a horizon.

Some cycles revolve frequently enough to be well known in a person's lifetime. Some are completed only in the memory of several generations—hence the notion of the invisible present, that which is ongoing but not seen now, and yet will manifest itself later. Still other cycles are so vast that their motion can only be assumed. Such is our galaxy and the Milky Way. But even they are not aloof from our humble, daily activities, for we are kept in touch with the Universe by just knowing they exist.

Linear Thinking In contrast to cyclic thinking, which arises from a desire to be in a harmonious relationship with the Universe, our Western linear thinking is oriented almost strictly toward the control of Nature and the conversion of natural resources into economic commodities—into money, the God of Western materialism.

Wendell Berry poses an interesting point with respect to these two patterns of thought: he believes that while natural processes may be cyclic, "there is within nature a human domain the processes of which are linear; the other, much older, holds that human life is subject to the same cyclic patterns as all other life."[9] If the two are contradictory, says

Berry, it is not so much because one is wrong and the other is right but because one is only partial and the other is complete.

Berry goes on to say that the concept of linearity is the doctrine of progress, which is supposed to bring us into a human-made material paradise. Within this concept, society discards old experiences as new ones are encountered. Although in our minds we never "repeat" the old ways or the old mistakes, in reality we repeat them constantly. We deny it, however, in our blind drive for material progress. We therefore never learn from history.

In Berry's vision there is but one definition of progress: onward and upward forever, an endless cross-country voyage of discovery. To return is merely to come back to the used, because progress means exploiting the new and the innocent.

Characteristic of the linear vision is the notion that anything is justifiable so long as and insofar as it is immediately and obviously good for something else. Linear thinkers require everything to proceed directly, immediately, and obviously to its perceived value. What, we ask, is it good for? And only if it proves to be immediately good for something are we ready to raise the question of its value: How much is it worth? By this we mean how much money is it worth, because if it can only be good for something else, then obviously it can only be worth something else. An excellent example of this type of thinking is portrayed in a paper by industrialist Marion Clawson, *Forests in the Long Sweep of American History*,[10] in which he starts out discussing forests and ends up talking about timber and trees as products—a resource to be converted into money.

Current dictionaries define "resource" in a strictly linear sense as the collective wealth of a country or its means of producing wealth: any property that can be converted into money. Linear thinkers therefore discount intrinsic value in everything touched, including human beings.

It's not surprising, therefore, that in our own culture the intrinsic value of Nature is still largely discounted. The same can be said of the intrinsic value of human beings, when our military capacity for the destruction of the "foreign enemy" takes magnitudes of precedence over the domestic welfare and tranquility of our domestic citizenry. Where does this kind of thinking lead us when we consider ourselves and one another only as "human resources"?

We can begin by looking at the education of our "resource managers." As soon as we demand, in this lifeless, linear sense, that education serve some immediate purpose and that it be worth a predetermined amount, we strip education of its intrinsic value, and it becomes mere "training." Such is the traditional training of foresters, range conservationists, fishery biologists, or game biologists, all of whom are trained in the traditional schools of "resource management" with which North America abounds. Once we accept so specific a notion of utility, all life becomes subservient to its use; its value is drained of everything except its "use," and imagination is relegated to the scrap heap.

This type of reasoning also makes difficult times for students and old people. Living either before or after their time of greatest social utility, it robs them of their sense of purpose. It also explains why so many species, both non-human and "primitive" humans, such as Indians in the Amazon Basin, are threatened with extinction. We perceive any organism not contributing obviously and directly to the workings of the dominant linear economy as having no value. Resource management threatens with extinction many organisms, including the organism of human society.

The only time one group of human beings makes another group of human beings extinct is when the first group sees itself as superior to the second group and wants—for nothing—what the second group has. In other words, in South America as in all parts of the world, the "civilized" peoples of a nation see indigenous peoples as subhuman—only a little above the animals with whom they share the wild habitat.

The reason for this attitude is that one cannot conquer a land, forcibly taking it from the indigenous peoples, and justify that conquest if the indigenous peoples are seen as equals. The conquered must therefore be viewed as subhuman. This view allows the conquerors to exploit resources at the expense of the conquered—even to the point of their extermination. Consider the following story about the Yanomami Indians:

Bitter disputes over gold and diamonds by miners, soldiers, and priests are endangering the lives of the Yanomami Indians, the largest primitive tribe in existence. The Indians are threatened by a gold rush mentality in the remote northern Brazilian territory of Roraima, a region about the size of Minnesota. Most of the mineral wealth lies buried where 9,000 Yanomamis live spread out in four groups along the savanna clearings of the tropical Amazon rain forest and its border with Venezuela. An equal number inhabit the Venezuelan side of the frontier.

Although it's believed the Yanomamis migrated from the Caribbean region thousands of years ago, evidence of their presence in Roraima traces back only 120 years because they burn their dead and drink a solution of the ashes.

Because the Yanomamis have little or no contact with the modern world, they have no immunity against common viruses and can easily die from flu or cold, as did the Native North Americans during colonial times. Disease is the main reason the number of Brazilian Indians shrank from five million when the Portuguese reached Brazil five hundred years ago to 220,000 today. Although armed violence has become a growing threat, it's bacteria and viruses that will ultimately kill the Indians.[11]

The great irony is that no one has asked the Yanomamis how they feel about being treated as subhumans. But then no one asked the Native North Americans or the African slaves how they felt, either.

This is but one example of a phenomenon taking place all over the world under many different guises. We humans are quite willing to make one or another group extinct if we covet the other's resources and can find a way to justify our covetousness! All we have to do in order to realize this is to witness history from the era of the Old Testament of the Bible to the present.

Threatened and endangered species result from linear vision. When we think in a linear way we look straight ahead fixedly with the notion that for an economic endeavor to be healthy it must be ever-expanding. In linear thinking we never look back, for our premise is that there can be no return. Linearity is above all the doctrine of possession. This doctrine is not complemented by one of relinquishment, replenishment, and sharing.

It should come as no surprise, therefore, that our concept of "use" does not imply wise use, or conservative use, or even good use. We simply trade quality in on quantity. Can it be any wonder that we find ourselves wallowing in our own waste and disposability?

Similarly, linear thinking means that we squander both time and life without respect for death. Through the lens of linear vision, death becomes accidental, the chance interruption of a process that might otherwise go on forever, and so it's an unacceptable surprise and always feared. After all, say the high priests of linearity, it is the length of life, the quantity, that counts; thus medical progress means to prolong life—regardless of its quality.

Linear vision flourishes in fear, ignorance, and contempt for the processes on which it depends. As linear thinkers, we do not, for example, see the forest for the trees, because in the face of these processes our concepts of linear, mechanical, expansionistic management are so unrealistic, so impractical, they have the nature of science fiction.

Processes are invariably cyclic, rising and falling, giving and taking, living and dying on ever-expanding ripples of time. Yet linear vision places its emphasis only on the rising phase of the cycle—on production, expansion, possession, youth, and life. It fails to provide for returns, idleness, contraction, giving, old age, or death.

Waste is thus a concept born only from a vision of economic linearity and specialization. According to this notion of life, every human activity produces waste, because every human activity is linear and specialized, and in order to be of social value must produce something of economic value. "This," says Berry, "implies a profound contempt for correct discipline; it proposes, in the giddy faith of prodigals, that there can be [everlasting] production without fertility, abundance without thrift. We take and do not give back, and this causes waste. It is a hideous concept, and it is making the world hideous. . . . "

Specialization and the Fate of Cultures

Although the genus *Homo* emerged "only" five to eight million years ago, it has become a remarkably adaptable and successful species. Unlike most species, which exist somewhere between five and ten million years before fading into extinction as other species take over, we modern humans have no immediate threat of extinction to face. Unless, of course, we as a species kill ourselves by making our home planet unfit for our own existence through pollution—something we are well on our way to doing.

In this sense, whatever crisis and transformation awaits humanity in the future, it is not one of individuals but of societies. We must therefore distinguish between a crisis and transformation in a species and in a society.

The human being as a species can continue living on Planet Earth for millennia, but human society is sick and in crisis. The culmination of the crisis may well cause the extinction of today's dominant social systems and the emergence of new ones—witness the old Soviet Union. The point is that human beings are generalists while human societies are specialists. The distinction between the two is both precise and critical.

A generalist, in either a biological species or a nonbiological system, can survive under a wide range of environmental circumstances, can use numerous kinds of energy, and can either fit itself to a wide variety of conditions or fit a wide variety of conditions to itself. A specialist, on the other hand, is fitted to a highly specific set of circumstances within its environment and can derive and use only certain kinds of energy.

Let's look at coyotes versus wolves. Coyotes are exceedingly adaptable, independent animals that can seemingly survive anywhere, including in the suburbs of Los Angeles, California. Coyotes roam the country singly, in pairs, and for part of each year as family groups. Ranging around alone, in pairs, or as family groups allows them to prey on a wide array of kinds and sizes of animals, beginning with grasshoppers (as pups) to prey as large as adult mule deer and yearling domestic cattle (when they reach adulthood). Coyotes are also adept at eating fruits, and in some parts of their geographical distribution they are called "melon wolves" because they steal from the farmers' fields.

As a generalist, the coyote can survive under a wide range of environmental conditions, from Texas to Alaska and from the Pacific Northwest to the Eastern Seaboard. Its arrival in Alaska and on the Eastern Seaboard within recent years is due primarily to the clearcutting of vast areas of dense forest. Our social activities have opened up thousands of square miles for the coyote to inhabit, areas that it can readily take advantage of because of its extraordinary adaptability. And because of its wide array of food items, the coyote can make use of a goodly variety of sources of energy.

Wolves, on the other hand, are social animals that live in packs. Compared with coyotes, their group life places limits on their ability to use habitats. Thus a far greater number of coyotes than wolves can live in Yellowstone National Park, because a pack of wolves acts as a single large organism and therefore requires a much vaster area in which to hunt. A pair of coyotes can live on rabbits and fruits in season, but a pack of five to seven wolves, each of which is much bigger than even a big coyote, acts collectively as a single large animal and in order to survive therefore requires prey the size of mule deer, elk, and moose.

A pack of wolves has a much harder time staying fed than does a pair of coyotes. It takes far more time, energy, and trials for a pack of wolves to select, chase, and bring down large prey at any time of the year than it does for a coyote, which at certain times of the year can do quite nicely on a diet of grasshoppers, meadow voles, and ripe berries.

As a specialist, the wolf is fitted to a narrow set of environmental circumstances and can survive only it if finds prey large enough to feed the pack as a whole. The wolf, therefore, has a limited range of prey items to which it is effectively adapted as sources of energy, and it can neither fit itself to a wide variety of conditions nor can it fit a wide variety of conditions to itself.

The wolf, as a highly *adapted specialist*, is vulnerable to extinction by societal desire, while the coyote, as a supremely *adaptable generalist*, is likely to out-survive humanity itself. This is particularly evident as the wolf's geographical range shrinks in the face of societal pressures on the landscape and the coyote's geographical range increases in concert with those same pressures. How does this concept apply to humanity and human society?

We as members of the the human species are about the most successfully-adaptable generalists on Earth. People live in the frozen tundra and along the sea ice above the arctic circle, throughout the temperate forests and plains, in the hot deserts, and in the depths of steaming tropical jungles. We live and reproduce on every continent and at every latitude between the two polar circles and beyond, and we have found cures for enough diseases to vastly increase our numbers and our longevity. In addition, we are generalists in the social sense. We have built and live in societies ranging from nomadic food-gathering tribes to sophisticated post-industrial civilizations, and from raw military dictatorships to "grass-roots" democracies.

Although we as individuals and as a species, like the coyote, are adaptable generalists, our modern societies are becoming more and more rigid specialists, like the wolf, as we allow ourselves to become professionally specialized. This was brought home to me with searing clarity while I was in graduate school, where I studied "natural history and ecology" because they were the broadest subjects I could find that included the greatest number of my many interests. The dean of the School of Science, however, admonished me to forget about natural history and ecology as "Indian lore," of which we had more than a century earlier supposedly learned everything we needed to know. He said that I should "specialize" and recommended strongly that I go into molecular biology.

I refused, because I knew society would someday learn it didn't know all it needed to about this "Indian lore." So I remained a generalist and have watched specialists come and go, come and go, while I'm still here doing what I love and loving what I do.

Keeping my own counsel has afforded me a certain insight into specialization in society. I have observed, for instance, that a politician who "creates" jobs and takes credit for his or her accomplishment seldom accepts equal responsibility for the built-in obsolescence of those same jobs. Yet the more specialized the jobs are, the more certain is their built-in obsolescence, so ultimately those people will again be out of work when the economy changes, when the need for the jobs disappears, or when the resources on which the jobs depend, such as old-growth forests, run out.

Because change is inevitable and because there are few "guaranteed" jobs for specialists, such as undertakers, over the long term, one is wise to remain adaptable. Nevertheless, specialists appear to have an advantage in the job market—which they perhaps do in the short run, while generalists have a corresponding disadvantage. But generalists have a great advantage in the long run because, rather than being rigidly set in their ways (as are most specialists), they are versatile and open to learning many things.

Such versatility allows generalists to flow with unforeseen changes and makes them rich in the experience of life; while specialists become encrusted in their specialities and are increasingly cut off from the experiences of life.

To the extent that individuals become rigid specialists, society becomes rigidly specialized. This specialization is increasingly apparent through the unfolding impact of the global division of labor and the polarization of global politics. In contrast, a Stone Age village and its neighbors could care for every basic need of its people. Short of such catastrophic disturbances as floods and volcanic eruptions, the Stone Age folk could cope with the vicissitudes of Nature.

Today, however, fewer than perhaps a dozen societies can produce enough food to supply the necessities of their own population, and the same can be said of energy, water, wood products, transportation, and communication—not to mention the myriad consumer goods most people seem to regard as their birthright. When societies are economically specialized and interdependent, they are more or less at the mercy of other societies for the items they lack. Japan, for example, offers high technology in exchange for almost everything else it needs to survive as a modern society. The other side of the coin is the nation of Gambia, West Africa, whose economy depends on the export of groundnuts. There a crop failure spells economic disaster.

The interdependence of societies in the political arena is much more obvious, because no country today, including the United States, thinks it can any longer assure its own materialistic defense without military allies, strategic bases, earth-circling spy satellites, and networks of collaborating intelligence agencies—all of which create and maintain what is increasingly apparent to be not peace but a balancing act of global terror.

The increasing specialization in almost all dimensions of contemporary societies, like that of a pack of wolves,

makes them more and more vulnerable to collapse from eco-
nomically-powerful competition and/or sudden changes in
the environment itself. Specialists are unstable and subject
to extinction (unemployment)—their usefulness comes and
goes—whereas generalists continually improvise, adapt, and
adjust to new ways.

Modern human societies are lured into specialization by
the linear thinking of quick monetary gains and materialistic
security. And today's societies, each strongly interdependent
on one another as they live side by side, have evolved into
an inherently precarious social system. When we add to this
already-precarious system the introduction of new technologies of production and communication, the system becomes
risky in the extreme, and the imminence of a system-wide,
social crisis should come as no surprise.

Since World War II, social specialization has been
global. Society has become specialized and interdependent
in the way it extracts resources from Nature, in the way it
cultivates Nature, in the way it uses energy, food, and raw
materials, in the way it builds dwellings and cities, and in
the way it disposes of its own wastes. This is an unstable
social system at risk of extinction. Another system could take
its place, however, because humanity itself is a generalist
and is not condemned to live and die in the super-specialized
societies it has created in the postwar era.

In the words of White Eagle: "Whatever man thinks he
becomes. What he sees in his surroundings, in his work, in
his religion; whatever it is he creates, he is in it. . . . Man is
his own jailer, his own liberator."

The Road to Social Extinction The evolutionary history
of life on Earth is one of species becoming increasingly specialized. With such specialization inevitably came extinction. But underlying the norm was a foundation of generalists
capable of merging themselves into a remarkably wide range
of environmental conditions. These generalists were consequently far less subject to either speciation or extinction. For

humanity, the lesson is clear. If we want our societies to survive, we must once again become flexible, adaptable generalists and build our societies accordingly. The threat is to contemporary societies. The challenge is to contemporary people. With this in mind, I am going to share a few of Mohandas K. Gandhi's ideas on national economic development, ideas that to me make impeccably good sense.

Gandhi looked forward to economic development, but he wanted to "prevent our villages from catching the infection of industrialism." He saw that industrialism led inevitably to the linear-visioned, unrestrained pursuit of material goods, which destroyed a person's purpose in life and all too often led to spiritual bankruptcy.

Gandhi realized that the economy, like the spinning wheel (the symbol of India's bid for freedom) was an organic whole, and that if economic growth was to take place, it must be in harmony with all aspects of the society. It must be holistic. If India tried to develop too rapidly—which in our Western sense means adopting industrial specialization—it would become linear in thinking and short-sighted in vision, getting out of kilter with itself, and negative consequences would follow.

Gandhi saw that if one did not tackle the major problems of the rural economy concomitantly with industrial development, industrial specialization would get too far ahead of agriculture, which would grind to a halt. This has already happened to some degree in a number of developing countries. "In the first decade of independence," observed *To the Point International* magazine, "not a single Black African country gave priority to agricultural investment, and expenditure on this sector represented only a tiny fraction of the total government disbursement. When industrialization did not deliver the goods . . . there was no agricultural base to fall back on."[12]

The same thing happened when I was working in Nepal in 1966–1967. The U.S. AID Mission's direction was to bring forestry into the modern era by our United States standards, ones inappropriate to the Nepalese culture and to the nature of the Nepalese forests. In reality, therefore, we helped the Nepalese to harvest their trees and destroy their forests for decades, or centuries, or perhaps forever.

Nation after Third World nation finds itself in this trap. Having committed themselves to rapid linear industriali- zation, they squander their foreign exchange and their na- tional natural resources on schemes of development unsuitable for their countries or for their cultures. When such schemes fail, they are left broke and hungry, often with a severely damaged environment—the legacy of travel in the "fast lane."

At this point, these Third World countries are left with only two options: One is to apply for assistance from Wash- ington or some other specialized, industrialized nation or from institutions like the United Nations, the International Monetary Fund, or the World Bank. To best serve their cus- tomers, such funding agencies as the World Bank need to place a high priority on learning the language of ecosystems that operate in various degrees of naturalness. Unfortu- nately, the agencies fail to do this, so the economic relief they proffer comes at a supremely high cost—the loss of self- direction and self-esteem of the indebted nation.

The second choice of these Third World nations is to exercise patience and adopt Gandhi's program of building or rebuilding self-sufficiency and self-esteem from the bot- tom up.

For whatever reasons, almost all developing nations have chosen and continue to choose rapid industrial spe- cialization. They simply trade in political imperialism for economic imperialism. India, for example, made this mis- take when, under Nehru, it turned its back on Gandhi's pro- gram and embraced rapid industrial specialization. Today India has little ability to distribute anything to its impov- erished masses from its relatively small but highly-advanced technical sector.

In Gandhi's view, if the individual, then the village, and

then the nation were brought step by step to economic self-sufficiency, it would be possible to attain and retain true political freedom for the whole. If, however, one got in a hurry and became economically dependent on another, it was at the expense of one's own liberty and freedom of choice. In order to protect its investment, for example, the World Bank has frequently dictated domestic environmental policy as a precondition for approving a loan, and has then commanded a supervisory role in the recipient's economy.

A Third World nation is thus exposed to grave risks when it opts to enter the international economic system. Once it has become reasonably integrated into the system, it may find that it has unwittingly imported such problems as inflation, the effect of foreign recessions, uncertainties in the price and supply of oil, sudden unemployment, or employment skewed toward the desires of foreign markets—to the detriment of its own economy. Now the leadership of the Third World nation is subject to even greater influence by foreign nations, and its economy is even more dependent on the debt-ridden international system, which seems to be on the verge of collapse.

The underlying problem is that today's world leaders want to build in a linear fashion from the top down, but without a solid, holistic foundation of human dignity and environmental sustainability that is cyclic in nature. This top-downness of industrial enterprise is propelled by a linear vision of the ability of human intelligence to transcend material limits and thus serve the powerful economic elite.

Although it is possible for some people to become so enthralled with the vision—or so dependent on the enterprise—that they see beauty in huge, belching smokestacks, dams in rivers, seemingly endless power lines, and dumps of toxic wastes that come with it, for the masses of humanity the crude, destructive, inequitable aspects of industry remain glaringly obvious. They too often are accepted and deemed necessary, however, as the price we pay for material progress. Such is the result of the linear vision.

Gandhi's plan for world order, on the other hand, is predicated on the voluntary cooperation and coordination of friendly states reaching out to one another with dignity, reaching out for mutual benefit in such a way that they can approach the same goal from different, even opposite, directions. Perhaps this is what President Woodrow Wilson meant when he said, "Friendship is the only cement that will ever hold the world together."

Put another way, if we in fact act as one another's keepers, society's internal guiding system can function properly and ensure that all the social components remain in harmony with one another. But if an external force, such as imperialism, or an internal force, such as premature industrial specialization, disrupts the balance, debilitating problems, such as urban drift, unemployment, hunger, crime, drugs, child and wife abuse and abandonment, civil disorders, terrorism, and general violence, become the norm.

Although the specialized, industrialized nations seem to have solved the problems of agriculture and mass production, they lack moral fiber and courage. They are rapidly despoiling the environment for short-term economic gain. And the inequitable distribution of wealth that is due to monopoly capitalism—and the now collapsed communism—threaten to plunge the global society into chaos. But through it all, we have a choice, because Gandhi's view of world order is built on a foundation of human dignity and harmony both within itself and with the environment on which human society depends.

Thus Gandhi would choose an ecologically sustainable environment that honors the cycles of Nature for the lasting benefit of everyone through the long haul, which means developing technology that is globally oriented and energy efficient. Instead, we are mired in a glut of quick, short-term profits for the immediate benefit of a tiny, powerful, linearly-thinking economic elite. This situation bears out Eduardo Galeano's observation that "Massive misery is the price poor countries must pay so that six percent of the world population may consume with impunity, half of the earth's generated wealth."

Economics, the Linear Trap Although linearity in economics became resolutely manifest with industrial specialization, it's not economics (which is linear, rigid, narrow of focus) but rather economists who think they somehow have the answers to the world's riddles, answers that have escaped theologians, scientists, and philosophers alike.

A result of such narrow, rigid linearity is one of the most insidious patterns of Western economic thought; the idea that whatever the immediate focus of one's attention might be—trees, cattle, people, corn, or soil—it has no value unless and until it is converted into money. Nothing, according to our economic system, has intrinsic value. Not even money itself.

The only value of anything seems to be its "conversion potential." This is often said of trees, for example. Clyde Martin of the Western Pine Association wrote in the *Journal of Forestry* in 1940 that "Without more complete and profitable utilization we cannot have intensive forest management. . . . When thinnings can be sold at a profit and every limb and twig of the tree has value, forest management will come as a matter of course."

An even better example is water. To understand value as "conversion potential" in the strict, linear, economic sense, let's look at water in the American West, because there water projects have been developed primarily to promote irrigated agriculture. What most people don't realize is that only a small part of the water used in the United States goes to towns and cities. The overwhelming majority of the West's water is used for irrigation.

In Utah, for example, eighty percent of the withdrawals of water go for irrigation; in New Mexico it's ninety percent. Further, the use of water for irrigation is inefficient at best. The United States Geological Survey found that a third of the amount of water delivered to irrigated farms was lost by seepage from canals. And this says nothing about the loss of water to the atmosphere through evaporation, especially in the arid southwest.

In spite of the obvious strain on both the quality and the quantity of the supply of water, the United States Bureau of Reclamation persists in its prodevelopment bias. "It is deplorable," says geology educator Luna B. Leopold, "that the government agency most responsible for managing water in water-short regions continues to be so insensitive to the hydrological continuum and the equity among claimants."[13] The Bureau's attitude is increasingly inexcusable.

Leopold points out that if we balance our withdrawals of water with Nature's capacity to replenish what we use, we can measure our use of water in such a way to protect the available long-term supply from being overtaxed.

We thus have two options for managing our use of water: One is to protect the availability of the long-term supply by disciplining ourselves to use only what is necessary in the most prudent manner. The other is to take water for granted and use all we want with no discipline whatsoever—as we now do—and then wonder what to do when we are faced with a self-caused shortage.

By using all the water we want in a totally undisciplined manner (because "unused water has no value"), we are both insensitive to the care we take of the world's water catchments and to the speed with which we are mining the world's supply of stored, available water. As D. J. Chasan put it, "One might suppose people would automatically conserve the only naturally occurring water in a virtual desert, but one would be wrong. Land and farm machinery have capital value. Water in the ground, like salmon in the sea, does not. Just as salmon are worth money only if you catch them, water is worth money only if you pump it."[14] And so we are damming, diverting, and channeling the world's rivers to "tame" and to "harness" them for short-term use by humans on the basis of poor economics and even poorer ecology. Would it not be much wiser to nurture the environment to ensure the availability of an adequate long-term supply of the life-giving water? There is, after all, no substitute for water!

Our water policy is largely in the hands of two goverment agencies who see the world in linear fashion. The United States Army Corps of Engineers is run by engineers who design and build structures to control flooding and to improve navigation, but the Corps also issues permits for the alteration of bodies of water, marshlands, and estuaries. This latter function brought the Corps of Engineers in contact with the Soil Conservation Service. The Service, which was originally a land-management agency, after World War II became another engineering organization.

Earlier, the policy of both agencies had been in the hands of agronomists, soil technicians, and managers of rangelands, but following the war most of the policy-making positions were filled by engineers. This change also took away the generalist, adaptable view of the Corps of Engineers and replaced it with a narrowly linear, specialized view. And the Corps has followed that route blindly ever since, regardless of ecological consequences.

One aspect of the engineering programs of both the Corps of Engineers and the Soil Conservation Service is the practice of "channel improvement" in streams and rivers. In this program the Corps of Engineers has carried out at least 5,000 miles of "improvements" and the Soil Conservation Service has handled more than 3,000 miles of changes. Such "improvements" lead to a straightening of a stream's channel and an alteration in its shape. In turn, straightening a stream's channel destabilizes it and downstream causes myriad effects like erosion of the banks, alterations of the channel's bed, degradation of the aesthetics, and changes in the composition of the plants and animals that inhabit the stream—changes that are often considered to be undesirable. And from these numerous "improvements," each planned on its own isolated rationale, comes the next change, a disaster of a larger order of magnitude: massive flooding, such as occurs in the lower reaches of the Mississippi River.

· According to Leopold, no studies have been conducted by either the Corps of Engineers or the Soil Conservation Service to determine the long-term effects, either on-site or downstream, of these alterations in the channel. These government agencies have no more interest in the intrinsic value of the long-term sustainability of the stream's health and dynamics than they have in the ecological future of the landscape. If the computed, but often unrealistic, cost-benefit ratio is on the side of short-term utility in the linear, product sense, economists tell the bulldozers to "rev up."

Defile Not the Land Because economists in our linear, capitalistic system refuse to accept intrinsic, ecological value as "real" value, we guide the use and management of our natural resources only by the cost-benefit analysis of their potential economic value when converted to something else, such as from trees to boards. This means that the only value economists can see is short-term specialization—a view that is killing the soils of Planet Earth.

Many cultures have emphasized the trusteeship of the soil through religion and philosophy. The Biblical Abraham, in his covenant with God, was instructed to "Defile not therefore the land which ye shall inhabit, wherein I dwell."[15] The Chinese philosopher Confucius saw in the Earth's thin mantle the sustenance of all life and the minerals treasured by human society. And a century later, the Greek thinker Aristotle viewed the soil as the central mixing pot of air, fire, and water that formed all things.

In spite of the durability of such beliefs, most people cannot grasp them because they are intangible. The invisibility of the soil is founded in the notion that it is as common as air and therefore is taken for granted as air is. Although to many people the soil seems "invisible" because it's part of the invisible present, when we think about it directly we nevertheless realize that humanity, indeed human society, is somehow tied to the soil for reasons beyond measurable materialistic wealth.

Even though we can justify soil protection economically, our ultimate connection with it escapes many people. One problem is that traditional, linear economics deals with short-term tangible commodities, such as fast-growing plantations of timber planted to maximize the production of woodfiber, rather than with long-term intangible values, such as the future prosperity of our children. But when we recognize that land, labor, and capital are finite and that every system has a carrying capacity, one that depends on natural or artificial support, the traditional linear economic system becomes more like a cyclic biological system.

In the late eighteenth century, Thomas Malthus proposed that the human population would grow faster than the soil's ability to sustain it, but agronomic advances in this century led many short-sighted leaders to dismiss this idea as simplistic and overly pessimistic. Today, however, Malthusian theory seems prophetic when one considers the trends in air pollution that poison the soil, overgrazing by livestock and the growing desertification, global deforestation and the loss of the soil's protective cover of vegetation and its vitality, and the ensuing famines.

Today forest managers often see the protection of the soil as a cost with no benefit. Those who analyze the soil by means of traditional linear economic analyses weigh the net worth of protecting the soil only in terms of the expected short-term revenues from future harvests of timber, and they ignore the fact that it's the health of the soil that produces the yields. This is so because the standard method for computing "soil expectation values" and economically optimal crop rotations commonly assumes that the soil's productivity always remains constant or increases but never declines.

In reality, however, reducing the productivity of the soil on marginal sites can push the expected present net worth of subsequent harvests of timber below zero. Given that reasoning, which is both short-sighted and flawed, it's not surprising that those who manage the land seldom see protection of its productivity as cost effective. But if we could predict the real effects of management practices on long-term economic yields, we might have a different view of the invisible costs associated with poor care of the soil.

One of the first steps along the road to protecting the fertility of the soil is to ask how various management practices affect the long-term productivity of the ecosystem, particularly that of the soil. Understanding the long-term effects of management practices in turn requires that we know something about what keeps the ecosystem stable and productive. With such knowledge, we can turn our often "misplaced genius"—as soil scientist Dave Perry rightly calls it— to the task of maintaining the sustainability and resilience of the soil's fertility. Protecting the soil's fertility is buying an ecological insurance policy for our children.

After all, soil is a bank of nutrient elements and water that provides the matrix for the biological processes involved in the cycling of nutrients. In fact, of the sixteen chemical elements required by life, plants obtain all but two, carbon and oxygen, from the soil. The soil stores essential nutrients in undecomposed litter and in living tissues and recycles them from one reservoir to another at rates determined by a complex of biological processes and climatic factors. In a forest, for example, the losses of nutrients in undisturbed sites are small, but some are lost when timber is harvested. Others may be lost through techniques used to prepare the site for planting trees, for reducing the hazard of fire, or for controlling unwanted vegetation.

So the resilience of forested sites following a disturbance like harvesting timber is at least partly related to the ability of the soil to retain nutrients and water and to maintain its structural and biologically functional integrity during the period in which plants are becoming reestablished. Beyond that, the health and fertility of the soil is reflected in the growth of the forest and the quality of the timber harvested now and in the future. This being so, we would be wise to reflect deeply on the observation of soil scientists V. G. Carter and T. Dale, who point out that civilized people despoiled their favorable environment mainly by depleting or destroying the natural resources, cutting down or burning most of the usable timber from the forested hillsides and valleys, overgrazing and denuding the grasslands that fed their livestock, killing most of the wildlife and much of the fish and other water life, permitting erosion to rob their farmland of its productive topsoil, allowing eroded soil to clog the streams and fill their reservoirs, irrigation canals, and harbors with silt, and in many cases using or wasting most of the easily-mined metals or other needed minerals. As a result, their civilization declined in the middle of its despoliation, or they moved to new land.[16]

With the above in mind, we need to pause and consider carefully the counsel in 1905 of the thinker George Santayana: "Those who cannot remember the past are condemned to repeat it." And if we are wise, we will ask: What are Nature's penalties for economically and ecologically disregarding the soil? One obvious penalty is loss of fertile topsoil.

In our concern for the topsoil we need only take the lessons of history, because although the birth of agriculture caused civilizations to rise, it was abusive, linear agricultural practices that destroyed the topsoil and thus caused the collapse and extinction of civilizations. And yet, with all the glaring lessons of history spread before us around the world, with all our scientific knowledge, and with all our technological skills, we insist on walking the historical path of agricultural ruin and impending social collapse.

The supreme irony is that even as we work to rid ourselves of all nuclear weapons on Earth and to establish a lasting peace among humans, we continue to commit genocide by ruining our environment. Through rain and snow, air-born pollutants reach the entire Earth from the tops of the mountains that pierce the clouds, through the vegetation, down into the soil, and down to the deepest recesses of the sea. As we continue to poison our environment, we destroy the stage—the soil—on which the entire human drama depends for life. Destroy the stage, and the drama is no more.

Soil scientist J. C. Lowdermilk addressed this point when he wrote, "If the soil is destroyed, then our liberty of choice and action is gone, condemning this and future generations to needless privations and dangers." To rectify society's careless actions, Lowdermilk composed what has been called the "Eleventh Commandment," which demands our full and unified attention and our unconditional embrace if human society is to survive:

> Thou shalt inherit the Holy Earth as a faithful steward, conserving its resources and productivity from generation to generation. Thou shalt safeguard thy fields from soil erosion, thy living waters from drying up, thy forests from desolation, and protect thy hills from overgrazing by thy herds, that thy descendants may have abundance forever. If any shall fail in this stewardship of the land thy fruitful fields shall become sterile stony ground and wasting gullies, and thy descendants shall decrease and live in poverty or perish from off the face of the earth.[17]

Beyond Topsoil Beyond our immediate disregard for the health of the world's topsoils, we must deal with other effects of our linear economics. One important effect is to cause the pollution of the world's air, which in turn pollutes not only the soil but also the waters, as reflected in lakes. An example of water pollution caused by linear thinking is a high glacial lake in the Rocky Mountains of northwestern Colorado.

A Native American hunter discovered the lake on a warm, sunny, mid-September afternoon in the year 1,000 A.D. The hunter's perception was a snapshot in time—a lake seen in a certain way, felt with a certain emotion, both of which were influenced by the particular set of circumstances that created his mood on that particular afternoon. Although the hunter didn't know it, however, the peculiar chemistry of the lake's water, a chemistry created through innumerable chemical, physical, and biological interactions over time, added materially to the clarity of the water and to its abundant life. The hunter, for his part, merely observed what to him was a perfect lake.

Centuries passed, and in the year 1829 a fur trapper discovered the lake. As the years unfolded, the lake became known to other trappers and received a name. Again, to the trappers, who also saw but a snapshot in time, the lake was perfect, its clarity and teeming life a wonder to behold.

Then, on August 5, 1960, personnel of the State Department of Fish and Game analyzed and characterized the chemistry of the lake's water. What the personnel of the Department couldn't possibly know was that the water's chemistry was already different from what it had been when the first Native hunter discovered the lake in the year 1000, or even when the trapper discovered it in 1829. Neither did the personnel of the Department know that airborne industrial pollution had been seriously affecting the lake for the previous fifty years or so.

So from the fifth of August, 1960, all future change in the lake's water will be measured against the standard established by the first chemical analysis of the lake's water, as though on that day the lake was the best it had ever been or the best it would ever be. What is seldom considered, however, is that the lake's chemistry, its thermal dynamics, and its community of plants and animals are interdependent and over the millennia had been changing, albeit gradually and without the changes being perceived by humans, to arrive at the particular condition recorded at the moment of the measurement. Once the water's chemistry has been described, like a snapshot in time, any change from that characterization is likely to cause concern, because our perceived standard of pristine purity has changed.

By the late 1800s, however, on the eastern seaboard of the United States, the industrial revolution had already begun, with all its unintended so-called "side effects" pouring into the air, effects to be viewed later by many human beings as pollutants belching into the atmosphere. Over the next several decades the types and amounts of atmospheric pollutants on the eastern seaboard increased. This buildup resulted in more pollutants being borne aloft, to be scrubbed from the air each winter by falling snow, and each winter they accumulated in the snowpack only to be released into the lake with each spring's thaw.

Finally, by the tenth of September, 2000, when the lake's waters will be reanalyzed, the chemistry will have been so altered by the human-introduced airborne chemicals that its water may be lifeless or the medium for different life. Thus, forty years after the water's chemistry was first character-ized, not only the lake's original chemical composition, as measured in 1960, may be extinct but also the life it once nurtured.

Here one might ask, "But can't we rehabilitate the lake and bring it back to its 'original' state?" No, we can't, be-cause society, through industrial pollution, has released into the Earth's life-support systems concentrated forms of en-ergy far in excess of Nature's ability to recycle them in the foreseeable future. But if we humans cleaned the world's air—all of it—and kept it free of our human-introduced pol-lutants, the lake, given enough time, perhaps centuries, may in a relative sense approach a state similar to its "original" state (the state of the water's chemistry on the day it was first characterized).

Somehow, we humans must all become conscious of the fact that in the wink of an eye we can alter irreparably what it took Nature hundreds, or thousands, or even millions of years to create. Once we have polluted Nature's purity, we simply cannot undo what we have done or even redo what Nature did originally. Nature alone may be able to do that, and then only in a relative manner. Such a feat takes time, however, far more time than we either have in one life span or are willing to allow beyond our lifetimes.

We may thus cause the extinction of the lake's chemistry and may unconsciously bring forth a new creation, a new chemistry, one that could in a few years translate into a sterile, lifeless lake—not the creation we wanted. I say this because human society is only now beginning to come to grips with air pollution, amidst much informed denial of the problem and foot-dragging from the industrialized nations, especially the United States.

Consider, for example, that controls on emissions will strike at the economic heart of all industrialized nations, which derive their power principally from the combustion of fossil fuels. In the end, therefore, if we continue on our present course with our foot-dragging, our unwillingness to change our thinking, and our unwillingness to control ourselves and to master the greed of our own behavior, we may ultimately kill the soils and the waters of the world. In some places we already are but a step away from such disaster.

Thinking about this scenario, as it is happening today in the high lakes of the Rocky Mountains and elsewhere in the world, I remember flying over Lake Erie some years ago and seeing it bright orange from chemicals discharged into its water by unconscious, unthinking human beings. Let's look for a moment at Lake Erie:

Its fisheries gone and the quality of its water worsening, Lake Erie, the twelfth largest lake in the world, was used for a century as a cesspool into which everything, from raw sewage to solvents, was poured. The lake became increasingly "eutrophic," which means its mineral and organic nutrients increased, thus reducing the dissolved oxygen and producing an environment that favored plant life over animal life. The eutrophication came about because the growing populations of Detroit, Cleveland, Toledo, Erie, and Canadian towns along the lake's northern shore dumped their personal and industrial wastes into the lake. And with the eutrophication came mats of slimy, decaying algae, and a shortage of oxygen so acute that by the late 1960s the lake was declared officially dead.

The lake was not "dead," however; it was teeming with organisms—but the "wrong" kind. Those organisms still thriving were "nuisance species," including algae, which gave the water an obnoxious flavor and odor, and "junk fish," species for which human society had found no economic use.

Over the last thirty years or so, the lake has been "cleaned up," but some of the damage caused by pollutants and human activities, such as overfishing, seems irreparable. Blue pike, for example, a favorite sport fish unique to Lake Erie, is considered to be extinct. Exotic species of fish, such as coho and chinook salmon, help keep the lake clean but were introduced artificially and thus tend to change the balance of populations of native organisms.

And the chemistry of the lake's original water has been altered through increased amounts of potassium, calcium, and sodium from the runoff waters from urban, suburban, and rural lands. Lake Erie's original chemistry is extinct. Today, Lake Erie is a different lake, one whose water has been redesigned with the cultural chemistry of human society. And so it is that lakes, which once evolved to the cyclic, rhythmic beat of Nature's sun-powered baton, now complete their death throes in response to the artificially-high levels of energy dumped in them by a society using fossil and nuclear fuels.

I have in this chapter given you some idea of the reason humanity has so often designed its world by exploitation. Now we must examine our own heritage to see why we in the "New World" have continued to design our own environment by the exploitive modes of the "Old World."

6
OUR EUROPEAN HERITAGE

Although our European ancestors had already lost their identity and their sense of place in and of Creation before they invaded North America, the Native North Americans knew who they were and where they belonged in and of Creation. Native North Americans survived largely by hunting and killing. In their world life was always balanced on an exceedingly fine line between earthly existence and non-existence—the hunter and the hunted. To survive in such a violent world, they reconciled themselves with Creation by means of their myths and rituals—their metaphors of Creation—and through their spiritual connection with the Creator, of which they were but a manifestation. They lived their myths through enacted rituals that remained in harmony with their changing environment. They understood that "their Universe" was always in creation, always changing, and never fully created, never static or absolute; they accepted Creation as the constant in their lives and adapted themselves to it through the continuity of their myths.

The ancestors of most of us, on the other hand, came from afar, from the pastoral scenes of Europe, and they saw not a land to be understood and nurtured but a wild, untamed continent to be conquered. They beheld the vast riches of the land in the form of products from millennial processes, such as fertile soil for farming, forage for livestock, timber for building, clean water for irrigation, clean air, and abundant wild animals to be commercially hunted and trapped. Later, they saw gold and silver to be mined. These products seemed to our ancestors both limitless and free for the taking. That someday environmental consequences would result from their exploitation of the land was not part of their thinking. Why? Because they came from "civilized" countries with "civilized" myths and rituals and felt that they were being thrust rudely into an "uncivilized" continent inhabited by "savages" and wild beasts, the conquest of which was their duty.

Our ancestors did not understand that their myths belonged to another place and another time in the evolution of human society and were incompatible with those of the indigenous peoples of the New World—or with the New World itself, for that matter. The myths of the Native North Americans belonged to the land they inhabited, whereas those of our ancestors belonged to a land halfway around the world. But, in line with a perfectly human tendency, our ancestors' first inclination was to *survive* in the wild, unknown continent and then to seek the familiar and comfortable by trying to force their myths from an "old" known world onto a "new" unknown world.

At best, our European ancestral myths had already through long tradition become rigid and so were inharmonious with the land, with the indigenous peoples, and with the reality of constant change; at worst, they were on a collision course with the survival of human society as we know it on Earth. And somewhere along the way, we have forgotten who we are.

As the Native North Americans, in keeping with their myths, viewed the land as something that could not be owned and considered themselves to be an inseparable part of its spiritual harmony, so the Europeans, in keeping with *their* myths, sought to conquer, harness, subdue, and own the land. And, with a few exceptions, they probably neither understood nor cared about the Native North Americans' values or points of view, because, according to Genesis, humans were given dominion over the world, and the Europeans viewed "savages" as little more than wild beasts.

This idea, as mythologist Joseph Campbell points out, is "not simply a characteristic of modern Americans but is the biblical condemnation of nature, which . . . [our forebears] inherited from their own religion and brought with them, mainly from England. God is separate from nature, and nature is condemned of God." In other words, Nature is here to be exploited. We are here to master Nature and, as masters, to improve Her ability to function.[18]

Native North Americans, on the other hand, had lived on and with the land for more than ten thousand years. They viewed the land and all it contained as a "Thou," something holy and to be revered; whereas our European ancestors viewed the same land and all it contained—including the indigenous people—as an "it," simply an object to be exploited. The Europeans therefore invaded the New World and saw the land as a vast unlimited commodity to be exploited for their own short-term private gains.

They dominated the land, squandered its resources, slaughtered its indigenous people and its commercially-exploitable wild animals, and polluted its soil, water, and air in less than four hundred years, because they lacked a spiritual connection with Nature. Their connection was only with the potential for economic conversion of the commodities Nature produced.

These sturdy forebears brought their European science and technology to the New World and relied on these, as they had in the past, to solve their social problems. What they failed to understand, however, is that science and technology are human tools and as such are only as constructive or destructive, as conservative or exploitive, as their users. Science and technology have no sensitivity, no experience, no morals, and no conscience. It is neither scientific endeavors nor technological advances that affect the land, including its people; what ultimately affects the land are the thoughts and values of the people who create and use tools like science and technology.

Although many examples of our human insistence on trying to control Nature through science and technology can be cited, I choose instead to share highlights from Professor Robert Bartlett's 1988 article about North Dakota: "Adapt or get out: The Garrison Diversion project and controversy." This article captures succinctly the unchanging rigidity of our traditional European heritage that comes almost solely from a linear-product mentality. In fact, Bartlett begins his case study by quoting a 1955 suggestion of native North Dakotan Carl Kraenzel that the solution to the difficulty of living with limited water in the Plains is to "adapt or get out." Bartlett says wryly, "The phrase, 'technology can solve many problems,' could become North Dakota's epitaph."[19]

Thirty years after Kraenzel's declaration, says Bartlett, even after the environmental movement, the energy crisis, major changes in the developmental policies for the nation's water, and the economic and agricultural recessions of the 1970s and 1980s, controversy continues over the construction of the Garrison Diversion Unit, a huge, federally-financed irrigation project in North Dakota that was begun in 1889 and is only twenty percent completed.

Accepting the existing conditions of the environment and adapting to them is still not a readily accepted strategy for dealing with Nature's blueprint imposed by life on the Plains. Clearly, European Americans have difficulty adapting to either environmental circumstances or evolving ideas. In fact, the social order established by settlers in North Dakota after 1880 was, from the very beginning, incompatible with

the ecological limitations of the land. And little progress has
yet to be made in tailoring North Dakotan life to the reality
of Nature's blueprint and limited resources.

North Dakotans have hotly debated the issues of forcing
the ecosystem, working against Nature, irreversible environmental damage, long-term operating costs, and the irretrievable commitment of resources. Like most Westerners living
in arid regions, the people of North Dakota have long assumed, almost unquestioningly, that we can overcome the
ecological limitations of scant rainfall through the science-
based technology of managing water.

The beliefs that the magic cure for all environmental-
economic ills is somehow locked within the scientific-tech-
nological complex, and that all we humans have to do is turn
the key, has been held "so strongly, so widely, and for so
long," Bartlett declares, "that it is an article of faith in the
North Dakotan civic religion." And it persists even in the
face of much evidence to the contrary.

The same can be said of logging the old-growth forests
and the extinction of the spotted owl in the Pacific Northwest.
The same can also be said of deforestation, which is spread-
ing across Canada and throughout the tropics like a cancer
as loggers cut the remaining old-growth forests at an exponential rate. The same can be said as well of water in the
American Southwest and of oil in the Alaskan Arctic.

An escape from the shackles of our European heritage,
a culture emphasizing a rigid human arrogance toward Nature, does not appear imminent for the landscape of North
Dakota or elsewhere in North America. Professor Donald
Worster put it well:

> History is always easier to understand than it is to
> change or escape. In the case of the West, a reversal of
> past trends must be regarded as a small possibility—
> and nothing more than that. Long the mythic land of
> new beginnings, it is now a region heavily encased in
> its past. What has been done there with the water and

land over the past century and a half has had consequences for the people as well. It has handed them a
fate, and there will be no quick release from it.[20]

As with most environmental limitations to activities desired by humans, the Garrison Diversion project for North
Dakota had its origins in the conscious rejection of the need
for humans to adapt to Nature's preexisting circumstances.
The untested assumption of human arrogance that people
can solve most or even all problems largely through science
and technology is ingrained in North Dakota. Historically,
the people have been motivated by the belief that they can
somehow escape the dictates of Nature, that they cannot only
overcome them, they can also create an economy that is not
bound by them.

The great irony of our European heritage is that we project the blame for our failures onto everyone and everything
outside ourselves, but we seldom turn the searchlight inward, where all too often lies the cause of all our problems:
our unbending, arrogant, materialistic motives. Because the
people of North Dakota cannot get what they want environmentally and therefore economically, for example, they feel
a sense of disadvantage, exploitation, and betrayal, in which,
according to Bartlett, their political culture has come to be
characterized as that of a victim.

By subscribing wholeheartedly to the myth of technological salvation, North Dakotans have for nearly a century
avoided the need to change and to adapt institutions and
politics to new and different times—a common political fail-
ing. Citizens have translated the failure of technology to deliver as expected into a myth of political deception,
treachery, and selfishness. The political elites claim that the
national politics of interest-group liberalism have betrayed
them; the state of North Dakota had in the 1940s pinned its
hopes on those politics. And the people have yet to accept
and face the problem of intellectual rigidity and the unwillingness to adapt.

As Worster states, a change in thinking from the domination of Nature to the *accommodation* of Nature will be difficult to achieve anywhere in American culture, and nowhere will it be more difficult to achieve than in the parched reaches of the West. Yet just because people must adapt to the physical realities of limited water in the American West does not mean that the West should not have been settled or that water should not be managed. The West, says writer Wallace Stegner, has splendid, inhabitable parts for a limited population that is willing to live within Nature's rules of sparseness and mobility. The original sin, Stegner believes, was not only the unrestrained engineering of water but also essentially a sin of scale, because anyone who wants to live in the West has to manage water to some degree. When Stegner says the sin was one of scale, he means that scale was a measure of human arrogance.[21]

Besides a presumptuous rejection of Nature, our European heritage is encrusted in a rigid adherence to traditions and traditional ways of doing things, not to mention a determined resistance to change at any cost. Such thinking and behavior is a patent refusal to accept our responsibilities to the future in the face of necessary change.

Instead, we pass on the ecological cost of our arrogance to the generations to come. The 1986 statement by engineering educator James C. Fletcher about the space program is an excellent example of the arrogance of the moment: "There simply is no way, in our system of government, to get a long-term national commitment. Neither the President, Congress, nor the Budget Director can commit their successors." Of course they can commit them; ecologically, we commit the future all the time. But just because the president, congress, or the budget director commits their successors to this or to that, regardless of the nobility of the commitment, doesn't mean that commitment will be honored.

This lack of commitment is an old and traditional tune of our European heritage, one that many of us have heard for years, both in and out of the government. It says that whatever it is it "can't" be done, that there are no options, so there is no responsibility attached to my actions when I resist change. But as The Buddha said more than 2,000 years ago, "Doctrine is like a raft that carries you to the opposite bank. But who would be so foolish as to carry the raft on his shoulders and go on dragging it over dry land simply because it was useful on the water?" Thus far in our history, I think, we the American people have been so foolish because we have insisted on dragging our out-of-place, out-of-date European heritage over dry, barren land.

Perhaps because we continue to drag with us many of our outmoded doctrines, we tend to see the world as black and white, right or wrong—either/or. This duality of view often keeps us from seeing the unity of all things, which means this *and* that as two sides of the same coin.

7

DUALITY AND THE WESTERN MYTH

Duality is a linear concept of this versus that, of black versus white, of right versus wrong, of good versus bad, where never the twain shall meet. But is this really so, or is it only an appearance of reality? To me, such linear duality is only an appearance.

Consider, for example, the Chinese symbol of *yin* and *yang*, which is a continuum, a cycle, or a circle in that each cause and each effect has embodied within it the completion of its own cycle—often expressed as its apparent opposite (Fig. 4). Another way of looking at this notion is to remember that for anything to exist it must be in dynamic relationship to something else (Fig. 5A) and that every relationship is cyclic and is constantly changing (Fig. 5B).

If, on the other hand, we view the world as a linear sequence of discrete entities, such as opposites, we would

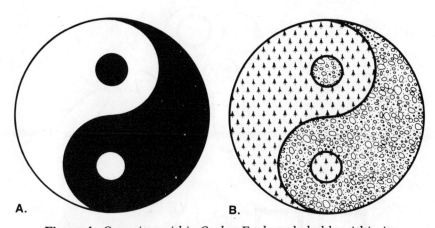

A.   B.

Figure 4. *Opposites within Cycles:* Each cycle holds within its dynamic motion the seeds of its apparent opposite. A, Yin and Yang: In Chinese thought, everything is cyclic. This notion is expressed in a symmetric arrangement of the dark *yin* and the bright *yang*. The rotational symmetry forcefully suggests a continuous cyclic movement: As the *yang* returns cyclically to its beginning, the *yin*, attaining its maximum, gives place to the *yang*. The two dots symbolize the idea that each time one of the forces, *yin* or *yang*, reaches its extreme, the seed of its opposite is already contained within it. B, Above and Below Ground: In this symbol the aboveground portion of the forest (tree crowns) and the belowground portion of the forest (tree roots and soil) are shown in a dynamic cycle. The dots represent the idea that old-growth forests recycle nutrients into the soil and that the soil in turn gives up the nutrients to the next forest.

see yellow on one side of a piece of paper and blue on the other side of the same piece of paper (Fig. 5C), but we would be forgetting that the two sides of the paper are united by the four edges where the yellow and blue blend to form green (Fig. 5C). Hence, each piece of paper is a continuum. In fact, everything is a cyclic continuum of unity.

Let's consider three other examples. First, let's look at *good*, as it is usually depicted—white, versus *evil*—black (Fig. 6). Here *good*, pure white, is epitomized at 12 o'clock, but becomes more and more the gray of ambivalence as it moves

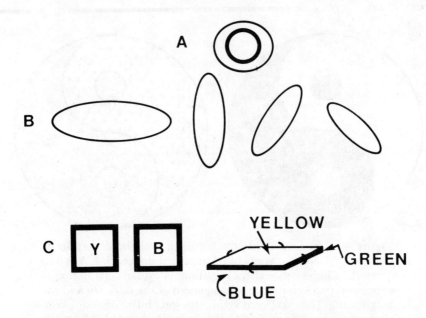

Figure 5. *Dynamic Relationships:* Nothing can exist in a vacuum. For anything to exist, it must be in dynamic relationship with something else (A), and every relationship is a cycle that is changing constantly (B). But the world seen through the lens of a linear sequence of discrete entities, such as opposites, would be a world of fragmentation where the yellow on one side of a piece of paper and blue on the other side of the same piece of paper would never meet (C).

towards 3 o'clock until at last it epitomizes *evil*, pure black, at 6 o'clock. If we continue, however, pure *evil* moves towards the gray of ambivalence at 9 o'clock and finally reaches the epitome of *good* at 12 o'clock. Thus *good* and *evil* are both only a perception and only an appearance of what is, which we individually interpret somewhere along the ever-changing continuum of unity.

The British philosopher James Allen clearly revealed the nonexistent duality of either/or when he wrote:

Circumstances . . . are so complicated, thought is so deeply rooted, and the conditions of happiness vary so vastly with individuals, that a man's *entire* soul condi-

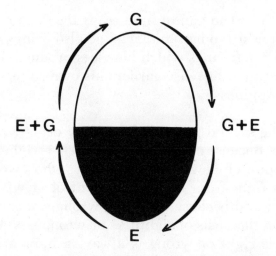

Figure 6. *Good and Evil:* The relationship between good and evil is dynamic. Here, good is epitomized at 12:00 o'clock but becomes the gray of ambivalence at 3:00 o'clock, only to epitomize evil at 6:00 o'clock. Pure evil, 6:00 o'clock, becomes the gray of ambivalence at 9:00 o'clock and finally the epitome of good at 12:00 o'clock. Although I used an oval to exaggerate the physical points in this figure, I used the notion of a clock to explain the functional dynamics.

tion (although it may be known to himself) cannot be judged by another from the external aspect of his life alone. A man may be honest in certain directions, yet suffer privations; a man may be dishonest in certain directions, yet acquire wealth; but the conclusion usually formed that the one man fails *because of his particular honesty*, and that the other prospers *because of his particular dishonesty*, is the result of a superficial judgment, which assumes that the dishonest man is almost totally corrupt, and the honest man almost entirely virtuous. In the light of a deeper knowledge and wider experience, such judgment is found to be erroneous. The dishonest man may have some admirable virtues which the other does not possess; and the honest man obnoxious vices which are absent in the

other. The honest man reaps the good results of his
honest thought and acts; he also brings upon himself
the sufferings which his vices produce. The dishonest man likewise garners his own suffering and
happiness.[22]

The second example of duality deals with right versus
wrong. Because everyone—*everyone*—is right from his or her
own point of view, the question is, "who's wrong?" If everyone is right from his or her point of view, then no one is
wrong; and because no one is wrong, we cannot argue any
case on the basis of rightness or wrongness. Whether something is right or wrong is always a human judgment, and
judgments can deal only with appearances, not with reality.
Everyone loses when issues are "settled" by judgments of
right or wrong, because, again, judgments can deal only with
appearances, and everyone has the "right point of view" from
his or her own point of view (Fig. 7).

If you study Figure 7 you'll note that the four persons,
labeled as A, B, C, and D, are each standing at a different
corner of a small city park and that each of them has a clear
view of a different flower growing directly in front of him or
her. Note also that the tree growing in the middle of the park
either partly or completely obstructs the views of the other
flowers from the place at which each person is standing.

Now, if each person is asked to characterize her or his
view of the park, who has the right view? Who sees the park
clearly and completely? No one. So if you haven't seen the
park and want a description of it, ask all four people about
their points of view, put them together in a composite, and
you will come as close as you can to "seeing" the park without visiting it in person and without exploring it in its en-
tirety.

This figure illustrates that everyone is right from her or
his own point of view and that each point of view is different—not wrong, only different—regardless of the subject
under discussion. But I find the concept of "differentness"

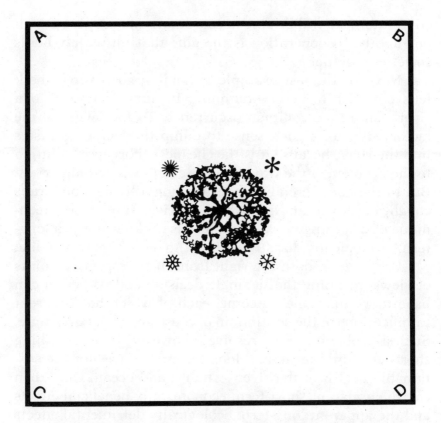

Figure 7. *Four Viewpoints:* Each of four viewpoints offers a different point of view. Four persons, labeled as A, B, C, and D, are each standing at a different corner of a small city park, and each of them has a clear view of a different flower growing directly in front of them. The tree growing in the middle of the park either partly or completely obstructs the views of the other flowers from the point at which each person is standing.

difficult to get across in a society that stresses the "rightness" or the "wrongness" of everything. If we insist on the duality "right versus wrong," we'll always be in competition with one another because we'll always be misjudging appearances. If, on the other hand, we can agree that everyone is right from his or her point of view and that each point of view is only a different perception along the same cyclic continuum, we will be able to coordinate and cooperate with one another. Cooperation is the glue that ultimately holds societies together.

Now for the last example of duality, good versus bad: let's consider a factory dumping its toxic wastes into a river—an all-too-common occurrence. To the owner of the factory, it makes good sense to dump the factory's wastes into the river, because it is the cheapest short-term solution to the problem of the way to dispose of unwanted materials. But to the commercial crabber making a living from crabs caught in the estuary into which the river empties, the technique of disposing of waste materials in the water is a long-term, ecologically disastrous threat to her or his way of life.

Once again, both are right from their respective points of view—meaning that a single decision and its action can have more than one outcome, each of which has different ramifications in the continuum of cause and effect over time. Such a problem can be resolved, however, by establishing short-term, mid-term, and long-term objectives for the sustainable health of the river, estuary, and ocean. Only then can the apparent short-term economically-beneficial effects and the apparent long-term ecologically-detrimental effects be viewed with sufficient clarity to see the differences between the points of view in a way that may allow us to resolve the issue in a way that achieves the objectives.

Is duality real? If we focus on the overriding principle of Universal Unity, there is no duality, because there is no duality in the principle. But if we focus only on the apparent results of the principle in action, we perceive duality because we've lost sight of the unifying action of the principle. Looking only at the effect, the symptom—which is what humanity usually does—is to lose sight of the unifying Principle of Evolution, because the unifying action of the principle is both cause and effect, creation and extinction, in simultaneous, dynamic relationship along the cyclic continuum of our ever-expanding, ever-changing Universe. To me, therefore, the duality of opposites has disappeared into the transcendent

Unity of infinite relationship, the great Cosmic cycle of Creation.

As I said before, however, we continue to drag with us many outmoded doctrines from our European heritage. In so doing, we tend to see the world as black and white, right or wrong—either/or. This duality of view often keeps us from seeing the unity of all things, so we focus on one part of Nature's equation to the exclusion of the rest. When, for example, we focus solely on economic products to the exclusion of the ecological processes that produce the products in the first place, our cultural decisions often introduce the cause of one or more extinctions into the ecosystem. And these decisions, almost always an expedient of linear economics, or politics, or both, become the "trilogy of extinction."

8

PURPOSELY-CREATED EXTINCTION

For millennia—ever since our first, conscious perception of the horizon beyond life—we have been discussing creation and extinction, life and death—at least, our own. Over time, the term "extinction" was used most often in discussing the evolution of plants and animals, including human beings. The concept of extinction seemed fairly simple; it had but one face: it meant that a form of life came into being, existed for a time, and then ceased to be. And because people tend to think of time, life, and death as linear—since we seem to have time only once—we view birth, death, and in between as discrete points along the linear continuum of time. In this sense, creation is conceived of as but a flicker, and extinction as forever.

Extinction is, however, thrusting itself into our consciousness as a much more complicated matter than heretofore assumed. From today forward, the many faces of extinction will become reflected more and more clearly in society's mirror as contemporary Americans are forced to recognize their society's purposely-caused extinctions of both species and ecological processes in the name of short-term economic/political expediency.

The ominous reflections of these extinctions signal the creation of a world in which society as we know it is in imminent danger not only of forming the "Museum of Extinctions" but also of becoming its curator. Unless we reverse the growing problem of global pollution, we doom ourselves as a species to the selfsame museum.

The Trilogy of Extinction

George Horace Latimer wrote: "It's good to have money and the things that money can buy, but it is good [also] to check up once in a while and make sure you haven't lost the things that money can't buy."

Despite Latimer's admonition, we are today moving through an accelerated process of losing many things that "money can't buy," such as our spirituality, the quality and liveability of our environment, and our dignity as human beings. We are also losing an ever-increasing number of fellow travelers on our planetary home in space. Such losses come about because we are progressively linear and materialistic in our view of the world and in our measures of success. We have accomplished all of this through the introduction into human culture and society of economically-oriented, purposely-created extinction.

The motive behind this introduction is something called "conversion potential," which, as I said earlier, is oriented almost completely toward the control of Nature and the conversion of natural resources into economic commodities— into the God of Western materialism: money. Conversion potential dignifies with a name the erroneous notion that

Nature has no intrinsic value and must be converted into money before any value can be assigned to it. All of Nature is thus seen only in terms of its conversion potential. It is this distorted, funhouse-mirror view of Nature that gave birth to the trilogy of extinction: intellectually-created extinction, the economics of extinction, and manifested extinction.

Intellectually-Created Extinction

The trilogy of extinction begins in the human mind as a tiny worm of blindness that distorts wholeness into saleable parts and relegates the "leftovers" to the trashbin. Old-growth trees are a case in point.

In Nature's forest, old trees often develop root rot, which so weakens them that they are easily blown over by strong winds. This is how Nature *reinvests biological capital* in the soil, which in turn nurtures and grows the trees of tomorrow's forest. In the mirror of our linear, materialistic, human-centered society, such wholesome reinvestment is seen only as "economic waste."

Neither seeing nor understanding the life and processes of a fallen old-growth tree as Nature reinvests it in the soil of the forest floor, economists and people of the timber industry at large continue to seek ways of eliminating such "wasteful loss of woodfiber." To them, trees blown over by the wind just lie on the ground rotting and are "good to nobody."

This concept of economic waste drives the corporate/political planning system to liquidate all possible old-growth trees because those in the system think of them simply as "free profit that will be wasted if not cut and used." And there is no plan to ever again allow trees to reach old-growth status; when they are cut, they are gone—not only the large live tree but also the large snag, which is a standing dead tree, and the large fallen tree. So "intellectually-created extinction" is a person's conscious thought coupled with his or her purposeful plan to eliminate something from a particular area. The effect of an intellectually-created extinction too often makes a potentially-renewable resource into one that is definitely finite.

In addition, the capitalistic idea of getting the maximum profit out of all resources—be they renewable or nonrenewable, such as fossil fuels—with the minimum investment is used not only to dictate but also to justify the unmitigated corporate/political exploitation of our home planet. In this vein, the purposely-planned permanent liquidation of every available old-growth tree, without recompense and without replacement, to feed the corporate/political machine's appetite for free profit constitutes the "intellectually-created extinction" of the world's old-growth forests.

The Economics of Extinction

Intellectually-created extinction through the process of economic planning is the precursor of the economics of extinction. It leads to the completion of the trilogy in the concept of manifested extinction. The economics of extinction has corporate and political greed as its soil and soul. The economics of extinction is thus the epitome of the materialistic, utilitarian view of the world, a view that totally disregards the sanctity of life and its ecological/spiritual functions.

The motto of the economics of extinction is *Profit over all!*—even if it means the loss of most of the world's species of plants and animals and the ecological functions they perform. Liquidation pays, even unto the purposeful extinction of a species; conservation costs, and cost is unacceptable to profiteers.

In North America the "profit over all" motto is therefore the guiding force of those in the timber industry who justify the liquidation of as much of Nature's remaining old-growth forests as humanly possible. They then use this same motto to justify the conversion of the liquidated forests into economically-designed crop-like plantations of young trees to be harvested—theoretically, at least—over and over and over into the distant future, like fields of corn. But trees are only one part of a forest, the only part to which our distorted vision assigns "conversion potential." By converting a forest into a repetitive plantation, the rest of the forest is destroyed, its soil impoverished, and its myriad organisms and processes dismissed as useless junk and impediments to the sanctity of the profit margin.

In 1908 President Theodore Roosevelt, concerned about the "profit over all" attitude in general and that of the timber industry in particular, convened the first-ever meeting of all the governors of the states to address the topic of the environment. His opening address to the conference is as pertinent today as it was eighty-three years ago. He began:

> I welcome you to this Conference at the White House. You have come hither at my request, so that we may join together to consider the question of the conservation and use of the great fundamental sources of wealth of this Nation.
>
> So vital is this question, that for the first time in our history the chief executive officers of the States separately, and of the States together forming the Nation, have met to consider it. . . .
>
> This conference on the conservation of natural resources is in effect a meeting of the representatives of all the people of the United States called to consider the weightiest problem now before the Nation; and the occasion for the meeting lies in the fact that the natural resources of our country are in danger of exhaustion if we permit the old wasteful methods of exploiting them longer to continue.

What Roosevelt went on to say is as important today as it was in 1908: "Just let me interject one word as to a particular type of folly of which it ought not to be necessary to speak. We should stop wasteful cutting of timber; that of course makes a slight shortage at the moment. To avoid that slight shortage at the moment, there are certain people so foolish that they will incur absolute shortage in the future, and they are willing to stop all attempts to conserve the forests, because of course by wastefully using them at the moment we can for a year or two provide against any lack of wood."

Roosevelt's argument was that any right-thinking parent strives to leave his or her child reasonably prepared to meet the struggle of life and a family name to be proud of. "So this Nation as a whole," said Roosevelt, "should earnestly desire and strive to leave the next generation the national honor unstained and the national resources unexhausted. . . . "

Even in Roosevelt's time, intellectually-created extinction led to the economics of extinction, which claimed the hearts and minds of those individuals who sold their souls to the corporate/political machine. Thus are the thoughts of the human mind translated into action *against* Nature. Now, almost a century later, we see the trilogy of extinction nearing completion with the visible loss of not only species but also whole ecosystems.

Manifested Extinction

How does intellectually-created extinction, which leads to the economics of extinction, translate into manifested extinction? When for example, the old-growth forests in the Pacific Northwest are liquidated, no more old trees will stand as living monarchs (Photo 6), to die and stand as large dead trees (Photo 7), and to topple as large fallen trees (Photo 8) and lie for centuries decomposing, providing a kaleidoscope of habitats, and performing their myriad functions as they recycle and reinvest their biological capital into the soil from which they and their compatriots grew. As the trilogy of extinction is consummated in the forest, the standing large dead tree and the large fallen tree, which are only altered

Photo 6. *A Forest Monarch:* A live, old-growth Douglas fir (right foreground) and a decomposing, fallen Douglas fir, which has been on the ground for well over a century. (U.S.D.A. Forest Service photograph by Jerry Franklin.)

states of the live old-growth tree, will go the way of the oldest living thing on Earth, the old-growth monarch of the forest: down the economic hall of extinction.

And with the old-growth forest shall go such species as the northern spotted owl (Photo 9) and the marbled murrelet, which have evolved in concert with that particular habitat. In fact, the owl and the murrelet have adapted to particular features of that habitat.

The northern spotted owl nests in tall, broken-topped old-growth Douglas fir trees. The marbled murrelet, a sea-bird, nests on carefully selected large, moss-covered branches at least a hundred feet up in old-growth trees, with other branches close overhead to protect the nest site. The murrelet's nest tree is located several miles inland from the coast, where the murrelet feeds. Being so specialized in the selection of their reproductive habitats, neither owl nor mur-

Photo 7. *The Standing Dead:* A large standing dead old-growth ponderosa pine, which has stood in northeastern Oregon for several years. In the lower foreground note the woodpecker holes in the snag. (Oregon Department of Fish and Wildlife photograph.)

Photo 8. *The Fallen Monarch:* A large, fallen old-growth Douglas fir. The man standing next to the fallen tree is six feet seven inches tall.

relet is capable of adapting to the rapid changes wrought by the liquidation of the old-growth forest.

And now comes an interesting twist to the story. It is not only species of plants and animals that will become extinct with the liquidation of the old-growth forests; so will the "grandparent trees." As young trees replace liquidated old trees in crop after crop, the ecological functions performed by the old trees, such as creation of the "pit-and-mound" topography on the floor of the forest with its mixing of mineral soil and organic top soil, become extinct processes. Why? Because there are no more grandparent trees to blow over.

The "pit" of pit-and-mound topography refers to the hole left as a tree's roots are pulled from the soil (Photo 10), and "mound" refers to the soil-laden mass of roots, called a "rootwad" (Photo 11), suddenly projected into the air above the

Photo 9. *Northern Spotted Owl:* This owl is tied closely to some of the habitat characteristics produced only by old-growth forests in the Pacific Northwest. (Oregon Cooperative Wildlife Research Unit photograph by Gary Miller.)

Photo 10. *Blow Ye Wind:* Pit-and-mound topography caused when an old tree blew over in a severe wind.

floor of the forest. The young trees that replace the grandparent trees are much smaller than the old trees and different in structure. They can't perform the same functions in the same ways.

Of all the factors that affect the soil of the forest, the roughness of the surface caused by falling grandparent trees, particularly the pit-and-mound topography, is the most striking. It creates and maintains the richness of species of plants in the herbaceous understory and affects the success of tree regeneration.

One way uprooted trees enrich the forest's topography is in creating new habitats for vegetation. Falling trees create opportunities for new plants to become established in the bare mineral soil of the root pit and the mound. With time, the fallen tree itself presents habitats that can be readily colonized by tree seedlings and other plants. Falling trees

Photo 11. *Once I Was Rooted:* Rootwad of an old-growth Sitka spruce along the Oregon Coast. For scale, note my wife Zane, five feet six inches, standing at the bottom right of the picture.

also open the canopy, and the opening allows more light to reach the floor of the forest (Photo 12). In addition, pit-and-mound topography is a major factor in mixing the soil of the forest floor as the forest evolves.

The extinction of the grandparent trees changes the entire complexion of the forest through time, just as the function of a chair is changed when the seat is removed. The "roughness" of the floor of the forest, which over the centuries resulted from the cumulative addition of pits and mounds and of fallen grandparent trees (Photo 13), will become unprecedentedly "smooth"—without pits and mounds, without large fallen trees.

Water moves differently over and through the soil of a smooth forest floor, one that is devoid of large fallen trees acting as reservoirs, storing water throughout the heat of the summer, and holding soil in place on steep slopes (Photo 14).

Photo 12. *The Open Canopy:* An opening in the forest caused by the fall of two old-growth giants. (U.S.D.A. Forest Service photography by James M. Trappe and the author.)

Gone are the huge snags and fallen trees that acted as habitats for creatures wild and free. Gone are the stumps of the grandparent trees with their belowground "plumbing systems," which guided rain and melting snow deep into the soil.

This plumbing system of decomposing tree stumps and roots comes from the frequent formation of hollow, interconnected, surface-to-bedrock channels that drain water rapidly from heavy rains and melting snow. As roots rot completely away, the collapse and plugging of these channels force more water to drain through the soil matrix, reducing soil cohesion and increasing hydraulic pressure, which in turn causes mass soil movement. These plumbing systems cannot be replaced by the young trees of plantations.

Suddenly the artistry and the ecological sustainability of Nature's ancient forest has vanished, and with its banishment go the lifestyles of a special breed of logger, log-truck

Photo 13. *When Trees Fall:* Fallen high-elevation old-growth Douglas fir trees. The Douglas fir with the bark on (center) fell as a live tree in a recent windstorm. The whitened Douglas fir was a standing dead tree for many years before it blew over and fell across the live tree, perhaps in the same windstorm. Large fallen trees add the diversity of "roughness" to the floor of the forest.

driver, and mill worker, perhaps never to be replaced. Where once stood Nature's mighty forest in the parade of centuries now stands humanity's pitiful, ecologically-sterile economic plantation—the epitome of the greed embodied in the corporate/political motto "profit over all." Now is the trilogy of extinction complete.

A Lesson in a Box

The trilogy of extinction—beginning in secret with the hidden intellectually-created extinction, passing through the hidden economics of extinction, and completed with the visible manifestation of extinction—is a result of the linear, product-oriented thinking of our Western society. Such thinking is based on the linearity of economic and statistical theory, neither of which account for the novelty of Nature's

Photo 14. *Of Contours, Trees, and Soil:* Remains of fallen old-growth Douglas fir lying along the contour of a gentle slope. Note the soil held in place by the presence of the fallen tree (lower-right corner of picture). This old tree is saturated with water and acts as a reservoir throughout the year. Pencil is used to indicate scale. (U.S.D.A. Forest Service photography by James M. Trappe and author.)

creative processes, because neither economists nor statisticians understand Nature. And Nature in turn cares not a whit about the lack of understanding of economists or statisticians.

Linear economics and statistical theory focus on the wrong end of the biophysical system. They not only omit the novelty of Nature's creative processes but also omit humanity itself. This omission was recognized by Albert Einstein in 1931 when he wrote:

It is not enough that you should understand about applied science in order that your work may increase man's blessings. Concern for man himself and his fate must always form the chief interest of all technical endeavors, concern for the great unsolved problems of the organization of labor and the distribution of goods—in order that the creations of our mind shall be a blessing and not a curse to mankind. Never forget this in the midst of your diagrams and equations.

The upshot is that we are focusing on the wrong end of the system in our attempt to "manage" it, be it a forest, a grassland, an ocean, or our society. "Management," after all, is only a metaphor through which we justify our impact on the system, whatever system it is. The concept of management allows us to focus on the desired economic product rather than on the ecological processes that produced the product in the first place. In "forestry," therefore, we see only the trees, not the forest.

What, you might ask, has focus got to do with anything? Well, if you walk to the door of your living room and stop to survey the room, you see everything in your living room in focus and in relationship (the forest). But now, if you walk to the coffee table in the center of the room, pick up the newspaper, and begin to read a story on the front page (the tree), your focus on the story causes everything else in the room to effectively disappear from view—to go out of focus.

This narrowness of focus brings us to "a lesson in a box"—a box of cake mix, that is. A box of cake mix? Yes, a box of cake mix.

A critical ecological lesson lies inherent in making a cake from "scratch," and if I were teaching a course in ecology, every student would have to learn how to make a cake from scratch. Because then she or he would know what ingredients go into a cake, what they do there, why they are important, and why the cake comes out of the oven as it does.

Today, however, few people know how to make a cake from scratch. Instead, they buy a box of cake mix and erroneously think they have purchased a cake—which, of course, they have not. They have bought a box of some of the ingredients for a cake, but they don't know what those ingredients are, where they came from, what proportions they are in, what their quality is, who or what put them into the box, and whether or not everything is as it should be inside of the box. They are taking all these things on faith.

So you buy a box of cake mix, bring it home, and dump the contents into a bowl. Is there an instant cake in the bowl? No. Why not? Where is the cake? I don't know. Well, what's in the bowl? A dry, powdery mixture of some of the ingredients for a cake.

If you now read the instructions on the box, you will find that you must add two eggs, a half-cup of oil, one and a half cups of water, and stir. Now do you have a cake in the bowl? No. What do you have? You have the batter, a gooey blob, which consists of all of the ingredients, now in the bowl. But where's the cake? Why don't you have a cake?

If you go back to the instructions on the box, they will tell you to heat the oven to 375 degrees Fahrenheit, and when that temperature has been reached, to insert the gooey blob, which you have been instructed to transfer to a cake pan, and to bake it for forty minutes.

When the forty minutes have passed, you open the oven and withdraw the pan. Is there a cake in the pan? Yes. Why? What happened in the oven that did not happen in the bowl when you first emptied the contents of the box into it? Well, first of all, you didn't have all the necessary ingredients in the box, so you had to add some. But even then something was missing: heat. It was the heat of the oven that caused the chemical interactions to take place among the ingredients, interactions that in turn caused the cake to come into being. The heat was the catalyst driving the chemical-physical processes that "created" the form and function of the cake. Heat was thus basic to the "formation" of the cake.

The point is that you can understand a cake, including what happens when an ingredient is omitted, only when you make one from scratch, because only then can you see all the ingredients and their interrelationships among one another before and after being heated. A cactus, a grass, a shrub, and a tree are much the same as a cake. Each is but the physical manifestation of the chemical-physical interactions among, in their case, a seed, soil, water, air, sunlight, climate, and time.

Thus as a bakery produces cakes, so a forest produces trees. But as a cake does not make a bakery, so a tree does not make a forest. A bakery is housed in a building with electricity, water, ventilation, sewage disposal, an owner, a baker, a bookkeeper, a sales person, delivery trucks that maintain a supply of ingredients, and so on. And part of the profits from the bakery must be reinvested in it to ensure that it functions properly if it is to continue producing cakes for sale. Now consider that if a bakery is the sum total of the chemical-physical constituents that combine to make the cakes, so a forest is the sum total of the chemical-physical constituents that combine to make the trees.

Suppose you enter the bakery as a customer with only one thing on your mind: to buy a cake. At that moment your thinking is not only linear but also focused only on the product you want to purchase. If, however, the bakery can produce only seventy-five cakes a day and if seventy-six customers, each intent on getting his or her own cake, show up, self-centered competition rules, tempers flare, and the polarization of duality sets in—mine versus yours, right versus wrong. And if one person buys two or even three cakes, for whatever reason, real trouble ensues.

So it is in a forest. Each timber company enters the forest as a customer intent only on securing as many trees for itself as possible, at the least cost, to maximize its own profits in the shortest possible time. Thus, while timber companies and "environmentalists" fight over who is going to get the last old-growth tree, for whatever reason, society loses sight of the forest and the need to understand the complexities of its processes, because all the focus is on the tree.

What society has forgotten, however, in its linear, competitive drive to harvest trees, is that the quality and the quantity of the ingredients—seeds, soil, water, air, sunlight, climate, and time—and the interactions of the chemical-biological processes among them constitute the forest, which produces the trees. This is the "lesson in a box"—the error of focusing solely on the product while ignoring, even disdaining, the processes that produced the product to begin with. What, you ask, is the moral of the lesson in a box? The moral is: focusing on the products one would exploit to the exclusion of the processes that produce them is the major cause of extinctions world-wide.

Extinction as a Moral Issue

We have made the extinction of species a moral issue when it really is a biological issue, a condition of creation. And we have ignored the extinction of processes and habitats. Extinction of any biologically-oriented phenomenon is as much a biological issue as is creation, and it is neither good nor bad, right nor wrong, moral nor immoral. The morality of the issue attaches not to extinction as an act but rather to the choice one makes about whether or not to cause an extinction and for what reason.

Consider that humanity purposely caused the "eradication equals extinction" of smallpox as a marvelous feat of modern medicine. Was that choice moral or immoral? Why? By the same token, if a mosquito in the old-growth forests of the Pacific Northwest were on the brink of extinction, would we halt logging? How about the northern spotted owl or the marbled murrelet? How about indigenous peoples, such as the Indians living in the rain forests of the Amazon?

Where is the line of morality drawn? Where is the balance in the milieu of social values?

The morality of the issue lies not in the manifested biological act but in the *intent* residing in one's soul. Las Vegas, in southern Nevada, is not only built in a very fragile desert where no city should exist but also is made up of the people who squander more water than people anywhere I've ever been. And they can least afford it.

Nevertheless, when my wife, Zane, and I took morning walks in Las Vegas, the gutters of the streets almost always ran with great streams of water, some of which extended for a quarter of a mile or more. The excess water comes from uncontrolled irrigation systems used solely to keep household and corporate lawns green. In addition, numerous artificial lakes and ponds and countless open swimming pools all squander water. But rather than conserving water, the city and the county coveted the water of others who lived in the north and tried to figure out ways of getting that water, very much against the wishes and the will of those to whom the water "belonged."

The intent of the "water grab" in Las Vegas was to maintain the building boom unabated and uncontrolled for as long as possible, even if it meant the extinction through loss of its habitat of such species as the endangered desert tortoise, or a city doomed to run out of water, perhaps sooner than anyone thought. I suggest that the *intent* of the "developers" in Las Vegas is no less damning ecologically and no less immoral consciously than was Sadam Hussein's directive to pump oil into the Persian Gulf or to set Kuwait's oil wells on fire as a "justifiable" act of war, which was based on and fueled by greed.

In turn, the extinction of a species is almost always caused by the destruction of its habitat, the morality of which stems from the *intent* of the destroyers. Although we seldom think of habitats becoming extinct, that is exactly what happens when habitats are so altered they no longer can function in a way that sustains a particular species—or group of species, as in the tropical rainforests of the Amazon. For our purposes, however, a more local story of habitat destruction will serve to show why species become extinct:

The last known dusky seaside sparrow died in captivity in 1987 at Florida's Walt Disney World, where scientists had once hoped to save the species from extinction by cross-breeding it with similar sparrows. "As far as we know there are not any more," said Megan Durham of the U.S. Fish and Wildlife Service. "This marks the extinction of the species. No female or evidence of reproduction in the wild has been seen since 1975, and this bird was more than 12 years old."

Once plentiful in Brevard County, Florida, where it lived in marshland along the St. Johns River, the dusky seaside sparrow fell victim to human-caused destruction of its habitat. The bird's sole habitat was ten square miles of marsh near Titusville, a marsh directly in the path of advancing development from the Cape Canaveral space complex. Although similar but different habitat was available nearby, the dusky seaside sparrow refused to move. Its stick-close-to-home character made it unique among North American birds and a favorite with visiting watchers—and spelled its demise when its tiny habitat was usurped unilaterally for the Cape Canaveral space complex.[23] The dusky seaside sparrow was just a little bird in a tiny habitat. So what difference does its loss make? Besides, the Cape Canaveral space complex is more important. Is it really?

Let's examine an example of a species on the brink of extinction because its habitat has been systematically destroyed in society's myopic pursuit of profits. The California condor once graced the sky of southern California, riding the thermals on its ten-foot wingspan. The sky is now empty of this majestic bird.

Personnel of the United States Fish and Wildlife Service have captured the last condor to give it a stay of extinction, but at the cost of its dignity. And what about our dignity? Is not our dignity linked with that of every living thing that shares the planet with us? How can our dignity be intact when we unilaterally choose to erase even one form of life from the earth? Extinction is forever, and the species we make extinct have no voice in that decision.

It is difficult for me to write about the condor because I am also writing about myself and society as a whole. Like me, the condor is far more than simply one of God's creatures. Both the condor and I also represent ecological functions without which the world will be impoverished. True, someone else may be able to take over my individual functional role, but what creature can take over that of the last condor? And we are more than simply creatures that perform ecological functions; we represent the health of the ecosystem—I as an individual in a much smaller way than does the last condor.

As the condor becomes extinct, its ecological function becomes extinct, and both the condor and its function become extinct because the habitat required to keep the condor alive has become extinct, through its alteration to serve the economic gains of society at the cost of the condor's existence. All this means that the whole portion of the ecosystem of which the condor was once a part must now shift to accommodate the condor's annihilation. Do we know what this means in terms of the ecosystem? No!

What about the hundreds or thousands of species the industrialized West and Japan are making extinct around the world through the motive of "profit over all," which inevitably leads to the trilogy of extinction through the destruction of habitats? How will the ecosystem respond on a global basis to these cumulative losses? What repercussions will human society face as the ecosystem adjusts to their absence? How much of the world must we humans destroy before we learn that we are not, after all, the masters of Nature but exist at Her courtesy?

Viktor Frankl, a psychiatrist who survived the Nazi death camps of Auschwitz and Dachau, understood the feeling of extinction. He could remember the men who walked through the huts comforting others, giving away their last piece of bread. They may have been few in number, said Frankl, but they offered sufficient proof that everything can be taken from a human being but one thing: the last of the human freedoms, the freedom to choose one's attitude in any given set of circumstances, to choose one's own way.[24] Can the California condor choose its own way behind its prison bars, or is that right also usurped through human arrogance?

Frankl quoted a fellow prisoner, who said, "There is only one thing that I dread: not to be worthy of my sufferings." The condor, by its nature, is worthy of its suffering. The question is: what have we as a society learned from its suffering?

We have relegated the condor to death row in part-payment for our iniquities and transgressions. Then, to salve our social conscience, we have plucked it from the sky and put it behind bars, and we continue to destroy its habitat. Now we will spend money on breeding programs and perhaps purchase a small reservation on which to free a few individuals, should they survive.

Would it not be more honest simply to restore the remaining condors to the dignity of freedom, to watch them become extinct in the majesty of the sky, and to accept responsibility for our human failings? How else can we grow in consciousness of the effects we cause with our greedy ways than to watch the sky slowly become empty of a child of millennia, a creature that took from the beginning of our planet to perfect, to watch the sky become empty by an act of humans, not of God?

If we as a society were called before the throne of judgment today, how would we answer the questions of each species' intrinsic value in the Universal balance, of the trusteeship we each inherited as custodians of our home planet for those who follow? I don't know, but I think a good place to start is to restore the condors to their birthright, the freedom and dignity of the sky. Then perhaps our consciousness will be raised a little, and their suffering and ours will have value.

And should the condors survive, their survival might lead to a time in history when human society and condors can live together. But the question remains; who makes this decision, and based on what motive?

Questions about morality, human society, and the environment are becoming more urgent in their need to be recognized, asked, and faced, because, when all is said and done, we will find that the morality of an issue lies embodied in the questions we ask. After all, the questions we ask are but the outer reflections of the inner harborings of our souls— our individual notions of morality, which are among the many faces of extinction.

It's Our Choice

A human social system is governed by the same Universal Laws that quite literally "grew us" and that govern the survival and evolution of all living things. This is true even though a human society is composed of individually conscious and unique beings, each of whom possesses *free will*. We have, in the short term, compounded this simple statement, however, because we have superimposed our human *will* onto Nature's cycles and balances in the biosphere.

That the Universal Laws govern human beings and their societies the same as they govern Nature was not understood, or perhaps even considered, when our European ancestors arrived in the New World. So it is little wonder that those ancestors spoke grandly over the decades and centuries of "clearing the land" and of "busting the sod," of "harnessing the rivers" and of "taming the wilds." And in keeping with this mentality, they begrudged the predators a right to life— and in the process became what they were against: the most voracious predators the Earth has ever hosted. And yet they only did the best they knew how in their time and their place in history. How could they have done otherwise?

We stand today at a different time and a different place

in history. We are present *now*, and we are making history. Yet even we, at the dawning of the twenty-first century, fail to understand and to accept that the world functions perfectly, that only our *perceptions* of the way the world functions are imperfect. What distorts our perception is that we focus only on that portion of the world we intend to exploit, the products, and we ignore the ecological processes that produce those products. This warped sense of Nature as a mechanical being gave rise to the platform of "deep ecology."

A group of Norwegian environmentalists, primarily the philosopher Arne Naess, introduced the term "deep ecology" in the early 1970s. The term is meant to characterize a way of thinking that approaches environmental problems at their roots in such a way that the problems can be seen as symptoms of the deepest ills of our present society. To me, however, a better term is *sacred ecology*, which clearly connotes "spiritual ecology," that of the "root" cause. And dealing with the root cause demands a fundamental shift in thinking.

The idea of deep or sacred ecology contrasts with "shallow ecology," which I think of as *material ecology*, because it merely addresses the symptoms themselves through technological quick fixes, such as the installation of pollution-control devices and other regulations theoretically imposed on industry. It does nothing, however, to heal the problem.

Those who adhere to the concepts of sacred ecology seldom criticize the concepts of material ecology as being unnecessary but say instead that in themselves the mere treatment of symptoms is insufficient. Although "new" technologies and reforms in our current political system are much easier to implement than are any fundamental changes in our thinking and our materialistic sense of values, these "material solutions" and the people who propose them are clearly avoiding the heart of the problem. This avoidance of the real issues faced by human society—those seated in spiritual bankruptcy, for which there is no Chapter 11 protection—may ultimately cause the collapse of our social system.

A good example of avoiding the heart of an issue is the

sentiments of the "turtle-shell artisans," craftsmen who include handicapped Japanese survivors of the World War II atomic bomb blasts. They complain that the United States government is "driving them to extinction" by naming the marine hawksbill turtle as an endangered species whose bodily parts it is illegal to sell or to own.

The Japanese people, explained Bunki Nakakoga, president of the Nagasaki Tortoise Shell Federation, have a "special feeling" toward turtle-shell products. "America," he said, "has only a 200-year history, yet your country is going to destroy a 400-year-old technique." But critics of the turtle-shell industry see the conflict as just one more example of Japanese refusal to acknowledge or to accept moral, biological limits on resources from parts of the globe not under Japanese jurisdiction. This attitude of allowing a species to be exploited to extinction to save an industry for a little while longer is described as "village morality," in which one thinks only about one's own village (Fig. 8). Hence the notion of a *linearly-oriented materialistic machine* as our personal and social metaphor.

There is a marked difference between the unified diversity of Nature and the vast array of possibilities offered us by our society, many of which make no sense at all. This lack of sense may be caused in part by our having chosen not only for ourselves but also for our world the linear metaphor of a machine, which has many parts but, in the way of machines, has neither internal intelligence nor moral sense to guide it. In addition, the parts are unaware of either their purpose or their functions. And while we can usually find or make one or more "spare" parts for a machine, we cannot do so with Nature. So if the hawksbill turtle becomes extinct, it is extinct. There is no way to reproduce one, no matter how noble the reason.

Thinking like machines is only one step away from *living like machines.* Such a synthetic lifestyle not only alienates us from ourselves and from one another but also alienates us from Nature. In addition, such a mechanistic lifestyle

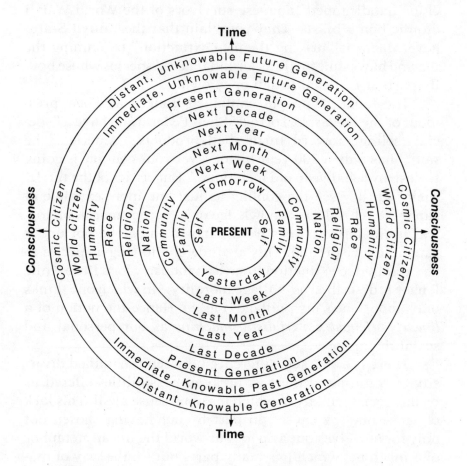

Figure 8. *A Scale for a World View:* The degree of our self-concern determines the scope of our world view. As can be seen from this figure, the closer we are to the present the more narrow and self-centered our views of the world are. Conversely, the farther we project into the future or into the past, the wider and more other-centered our views must become. Thus the legacy we leave to the generations of the future depends on the scope of our view of the world.

leads to economic problems through the separation of social classes and to philosophical problems of the duality of thought in terms of either/or, right/wrong, and so on. Our synthetic, linear, mechanical thoughts and lifestyles pit us against Nature, which makes our lives increasing complicated beyond the total complexity of Nature's diversity.

And it is precisely because of our mechanistic thinking that we contend we can have more and more of everything simultaneously if only we can control Nature—manage Her, as it were. In so doing, we save the pieces we value and discard those we don't. We are thus simultaneously simplifying the biosphere and separating its parts by purposely discarding and accidentally losing pieces of it. We are redesigning our home planet even as we throw away Nature's blueprint in the form of both species and processes. In short, we focus so narrowly on the *products* that we are destroying the *processes* that produce them.

We in Western culture have become so linear and mechanical in our thinking and so irrational in our knowledge and the use of it that we have forgotten that everything is defined by its relations to everything else. In the end, we must both understand and accept that everything—*everything*—is a relationship that fits precisely into every other relationship and is changing constantly. The paradox is: the only constant in life is change, and everything is in the process of becoming something else.

As human beings of Western culture, the way we deal with and fit into this pattern of constantly changing relationships is by thinking. We must thus recognize that any human influence on the landscape or in the biosphere—positive or negative—is a product of our own thoughts, because our thoughts, after all, precede and control our actions. We do nothing without first having the thought to do it. This means that the problem of pollution, for example, is neither in the soil, in the water, or in the air, but in our minds (the cause); the problem only manifests itself (the effect) in the soil, water, and air.

We cannot, therefore, find a solution through science, or technology, or the activities of land management without changing our thinking, because all these things, which lie outside of ourselves, are the results of our thoughts. The only possible solutions to our social/environmental problems lie within us. Until we turn the searchlight inward to our own souls and consciously change our thinking, our motives, and our attitudes, we will only compound our problems.

A charming story, which illustrates how truly our outward situations mirror our minds, concerns the man who was given permission to see both heaven and hell while still alive. He chose to visit hell first. To his surprise, he found an enormous gathering of people at a feast. They were seated at a long table covered with every imaginable delicacy. Yet the people, all lamenting loudly, appeared to be starving to death.

As the man studied this strange scene more closely, he observed that the handles of their eating utensils were so long that they were unable to bring the food to their mouths. So the man left with sorrow in his heart and went to visit heaven.

In heaven he found an almost identical scene: the same eating utensils with handles much too long for the people to reach their own mouths. But the people of heaven were laughing and rejoicing, because rather than choosing to try to *feed themselves*, as were those in hell, the people in heaven chose to *feed one another*.

In the final analysis, the choice of our behavior is ours. We must therefore accept that by our thoughts, which we put into actions, we are *creating* a "new" world through the *extinction* of our concept of the "old" world. Stated differently: with each decision we make about the way we choose to behave today, we are creating our own futures. We can thus design our world in such a way that culture both creates its own harmony and is in harmony with Nature.

III
CULTURE AS CREATIVE HARMONY

In a union of beauty and ugliness, beauty always triumphs in the end: in obedience to a divine law, Nature invariably returns to the better; it strives ceaselessly toward perfection.

—RODIN-GSELL

9

HOW WE SEE TODAY'S
OUTER LANDSCAPE

As human beings we are continually changing the landscape in which we live. The ways in which we change the landscape depend on the level of our consciousness of the effects we cause when our thoughts are translated into decisions, which are in turn translated into actions. In the beginning, for example, humanoids (creatures resembling humans) had relatively little impact on the landscapes in which they lived. Their impact increased as they evolved languages, cultures, and societies, because through these devices they could participate with Nature in more intensely organized ways. Today the human species has essentially altered the landscapes of the entire world through airborne and waterborne pollution and through the unbridled exploitation of Nature's bounty.

Human society changes the dynamics and the design of

every landscape with which it interacts, and it has been doing so for thousands of years. The history of England is an example. About 330,000 years ago, 310,000 years before the "Native North Americans" arrived in the "New World" across the Bering-Chuckchi platform from Siberia, the early human-like creature *Homo erectus* was already living in what today is England, which was at that time attached to the European continent. As the Pleistocene Epoch drew to a close between 12,000 and 10,000 years ago, the ice withdrew, though not in a single smooth recession. During this time, Paleolithic (old stone-age, earlier than 12,000 years ago) cultures of "modern humans" (*Homo sapiens*) occupied the warmer places in the south of what today is England, where they seem to have had an ecological impact with their selective dependence on wild horses and reindeer for food and raw materials.

As the climate ameliorated, the trees that had survived the glaciation in southern Europe and the Caucasus gradually returned to the once-glaciated areas until climax-stage mixed deciduous forest was established about 8,000 years ago.

Then about 7,000 years ago, that part of the European continent that today is England separated from the mainland. Mesolithic (middle stone-age, between 12,000 and 5,000 years ago) hunter-gatherers still inhabited the newly-formed island, and they remained until the coming of agriculture about 5,000 years ago.

The earliest cultural landscapes of the area—those purposely manipulated with fire—were formed in the middle to late Mesolithic period, between 7,000 and 5,000 years ago. As far as we know, that first cultural landscape came from the conversion of a mixed deciduous forest into a mosaic of high forests, open-canopy woodlands, and grassy clearings with fringes of scrub and bracken fern, patches of wet sedge, and bogs of peat. Among these habitats, groups of late Mesolithic peoples without knowledge of crop-based agriculture moved about gathering food.

The coming of agriculture from Asia around 5,000 years ago was one of the great turning points in western Europe, the beginning of the Neolithic culture (new stone-age, which began with the advent of agriculture). For Neolithic people, the advent of agriculture was not gradual. Instead, the full complement of agricultural tradition and myth probably came as a fully developed package from the East, even if accessory hunting persisted. The model of the earliest agriculture in western Europe is a mosaic of small clearings, which were abandoned as the fertility of the soil became exhausted or the weeds became too bothersome. As new clearings were made, abandoned ones reverted to forest.

In contrast, with the Neolithic agriculturalists of England, Native North Americans arrived in the New World only about 20,000 years ago. They had neither the cultural technology nor the time to alter their environment as much as did peoples of Europe. When the British landed in the New World, therefore, they perceived a much wilder continent than the one from which they had come.

Today, through the exploitation begun by our European ancestors and ever-advancing exploitation technology, the landscapes of the North American continent are vastly different from the way they were when the Europeans first invaded the shores of the New World about 400 years ago. But over that amount of time the landscapes would have changed even if the continent had hosted only the aboriginal peoples.

The Landscape as Nature's Kaleidoscope

Although landscape is usually thought of as a finished product in the sense of a view or vista of scenery or as that aspect of the land characteristic of a particular region, the idea of a landscape as finished is static and incomplete. When I think of a landscape, I think of a dynamic kaleidoscope of all the elements and all the scales of relationships and events focused for an instant, this instant, in the center of the Universe.

I say "the center of the Universe," because I am here participating in Creation as an active observer. I therefore stand at the exact center of the Universe, because as an individual human being, I am the center of all interdependencies; all interdependencies radiate from me and come back to me. As I am the center of the Universe, so are you; so is everything in Creation. The center of the Universe is therefore everywhere and nowhere.

In considering a landscape, think first of the dynamic *geological processes*, which evoke every conceivable scale of time, space, and relationship that formed the land and the resultant *macroclimate* (the prevailing climate of the times as it affects the continent). In turn, the geological processes and the climate act together on the *parent materials* (the original rock from which a particular soil is derived in a particular location). The result is the *topography* of the area. These are the long-term ecological limits, which control and define a landscape in space through the long reaches of time (Fig. 9).

Geological processes constantly alter the surface of the Earth. One process is the collision of the oceanic plates with the continental plates as the former moves under the latter, thrusting the Earth's crust upward into folds and buckles, which form ranges of mountains. These mountains have a profound impact on the overall climate of the area. They determine the amount and pattern of precipitation that falls in a given time, and they dictate the accompanying temperature. They determine when, where, and in what way the precipitation falls.

The type of parent material or rock of which the mountains are composed determines not only the way they will erode but also the type of soil that will be formed as a result of being exposed to a particular climatic regime over time. The effect of climate over time is known as weathering. The initial formation of the mountains, their sizes, shapes, and

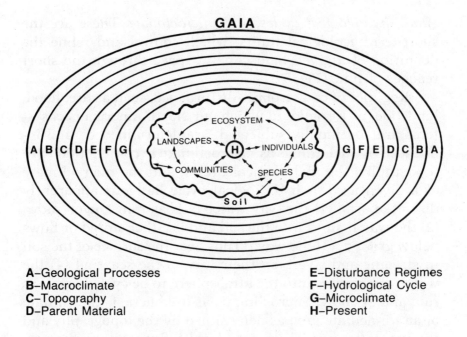

A–Geological Processes
B–Macroclimate
C–Topography
D–Parent Material

E–Disturbance Regimes
F–Hydrological Cycle
G–Microclimate
H–Present

Figure 9. *Relationships Among Ecological Processes:* Ecological processes integrate value-neutral relationships. The outer rings stand for long-term limits on relationships: geological processes, macroclimate, topography, and parent material. The inner rings are short-term limits: disturbance regimes, the hydrological cycle, and the microclimate. Soil is the exchange "membrane" between the abiotic long- and short-term limits and the biotic constituents of the world. The biotic components are the individuals, species, communities, landscape, and ecosystem. The ball in the center of the figure is the present moment on the landscape.

the types of parent materials of which they are composed determine part of the pattern of weathering and erosion. The prevailing climate also determines part of the pattern of weathering and erosion. Taken together, climate and weathering form the resulting topography or the physical features of the particular place or region at any given point in time.

In addition to and within the control of the long-term ecological limits, there are such dynamics as *disturbance re-*

gimes, hydrological cycles, and *microclimate*. These are the short-term ecological limits, which control and refine the definition of a given landscape in space through the short reaches of time (Fig. 9).

Regimes of catastrophic disturbance, such as fire, flood, landslide, or tornado, to which our North American ecosystems are continually subjected, are determined by and influenced by such things as macroclimate in conjunction with topography, the hydrological cycles, and the microclimate of a given area. A hydrological cycle has four apparently discrete parts: (1) the way water falls as rain and/or snow, (2) the way it sinks into the soil and is either stored or flows below ground, (3) the way it runs over the surface of the soil in streams and rivers on their way to the sea, and (4) the way it evaporates into the atmosphere to be cycled again as rain and/or snow. Microclimate, as used here, is the climate of an immediate area as determined by the topography and the vegetation, which exert a local influence over the macroclimate, the prevailing climate of the times.

Between the nonliving long- and short-term ecological limits of a landscape and the living components of the landscape (its plants and animals) lies the *soil* (Fig. 9). The soil is a combination of both nonliving and living components of the landscape. It is an exchange membrane, much like the placenta through which a mother nourishes her child. The soil, which is derived from the parent materials laid down by the geological processes, is built up and enriched by the plants that live and die in it. It is also enriched by the animals that feed on the plants, void their bodily wastes, and eventually die, decay, and return to the soil as organic matter.

And then there are the *individual* living organisms, which collectively form the *species*, which in turn collectively form the *communities* that spread over the land. These organisms, through the exchange medium of the soil, are influenced by the short-term ecological limitations even as they themselves influence those same limitations through their life cycles (Fig. 9). The dynamic interactions of communities and soil are controlled and influenced by the long-term ecological limitations that collectively form the *landscape*. And it is the landscape that we humans arbitrarily delineate into *ecosystems* as we try to understand the dynamic interactions between nonliving and living components of our world (Fig. 9).

To gain a sense of the dynamic nature of a landscape through time, we'll take a peek at the changes wrought in the central portion of the United States—that which today is the Great Plains. Our view begins as the last glacial stage, the Wisconsin, named after the state, reached its maximum development and then receded into history.

While the glacier was at its maximum, temperatures lowered on the North American continent, and arctic plants grew as far south as what is now Virginia, Oklahoma, and Texas. Coniferous (cone-bearing) trees like pine and spruce grew in what is now the Great Plains, along with some deciduous (leaf-shedding) trees.

As the last glacier receded and the climate warmed, the deciduous forest began to take over from the coniferous. The center of the continent continued to warm and dry, and fire began to play an increasingly important role in shaping the vegetation. Although the coniferous forest became confined to the cooler climates of the Rocky Mountains and westward, the grassland in the center of the continent expanded and withdrew as temperatures waxed and waned. During times of warmer temperatures the deciduous forest retreated eastward and grassland filled the area—and vice versa. Because the climate continued to warm and dry, wind-driven grass fires increased and helped the grassland eventually take over from the trees and shrubs to form the Great Plains of today.

So, although climate was a factor in the evolution of the grasslands that greeted the early European explorers in the

center of the North American continent, so too were the vast-
ness and the flatness of the Great Plains and the annual fire-
carrying dieback of the grasses.

When thinking about landscapes in the Pacific Northwest, I am often reminded of the fires, both large and small,
that over the millennia shaped the great forests I knew as a
youth. And later in life, as I studied the interactive connec-
tions between animals and forests, I found the recurring
cycles of the birth, growth, and death of individuals, the
waxing and waning of habitats and of plant and animal communities, and the evolution of species that eventually returned again to the distant unknown.

What seems clear to me now is that the Universal cycles
are not perfect circles, as they so often are depicted and as
I always thought they were. They are rather a coming together in time and space at a point where one "end" of a
cycle approximates—but *only* approximates—its "beginning" in a particular place. Between its beginning and its
ending, a cycle can have any configuration of cosmic happenstance (Fig. 10).

Further, Nature's cycles are most "real" and discernible
to me as they pertain to and influence living organisms, those
beings with which I share the gift of life. Beyond that, in the
nonbiological reaches of the cosmos, cycles become more and
more abstract as they extend either backward or forward
into the continuum of time. Thus while cycles give dimension, context, and texture to the landscape, they are more
real to me in the living here and now than they are when
they penetrate into the formation of the short- and long-term
ecological limiting factors as they affect any given place on
Earth (Fig. 10).

In discussing the attributes of a landscape, we must be
aware of all of the factors that have come together to create
a particular place as we perceive it, not just the events themselves but also the cycles in which the events are embedded.
In addition, it soon becomes apparent to those viewing a

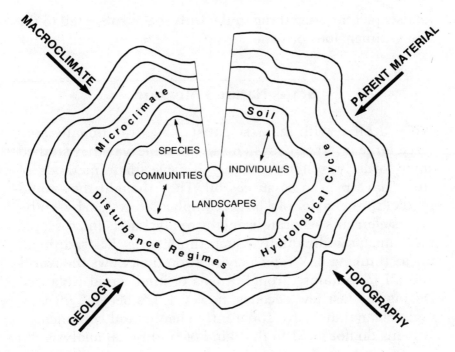

Figure 10. *The Shape of Cycles:* Cycles are not perfect circles. Cycles are a coming together in time and space at a point where one "end" of a cycle approximates its "beginning" in a particular place, but only approximates it. Between its beginning and its ending, a cycle can have any configuration of cosmic happenstance. Cycles are most "real" and "knowable" as one progresses from the geological processes (outer rings) toward the individual living organism (the center). Nonbiological cycles become more and more abstract as they extend either from the soil to geological processes or backward or forward into the continuum of time.

The long-term limits on cycles are the geological processes, macroclimate, topography, and parent material. The short-term limits on cycles are disturbance regimes, the hydrological cycle, and the microclimate. Soil is the exchange "membrane" between the abiotic long- and short-term limits and the biotic constituents of the world. The biotic components are the individuals, species, communities, landscape, and ecosystem. The ball in the center of the figure is the present moment on the landscape.

landscape that everything in the Universe is subjected to the many dimensions of scale.

Scale, Nature's Measure

When dealing with scale, scientists have traditionally analyzed large interactive systems in the same way they studied small orderly systems, mainly because their methods of study have proven so successful. They thought they could predict the behavior of a large, complicated system by studying its elements separately and by analyzing its microscopic mechanisms individually. Such thinking is the traditional linear thinking of Western civilization that views the world and all it contains through a lens of intellectual isolation. During the last few decades, however, it's become increasingly clear that many apparently chaotic and complicated systems do not yield to that kind of traditional analysis.

Instead, large, complicated, interactive systems like components of landscapes and even landscapes themselves seem to evolve to a critical state in which even a minor event starts a chain reaction that can lead to an unpredictable, monumental change—often to catastrophe.

Although such systems produce more minor events than they do catastrophic ones, chain reactions of all sizes are an integral part of the systems' dynamics. The mechanism that leads to minor events is the same mechanism that leads to major events. And because such systems are open (which means they can be influenced by such things as the gravitational pull of the moon) they never reach a stable state but rather evolve from one semi-stable state to another.

Not understanding this, however, analysts trying to figure out why catastrophes happen have typically blamed some rare set of circumstances, some exception to the rule, or some powerful combination of mechanisms. So when a tremendous earthquake shook San Francisco, geologists traced the cataclysm to an immense instability along the

San Andreas fault. When the stock market crashed on "Black Monday," 1987, economists pointed to the destabilizing effect of trading through the mechanization of computers.

Although those factors may well be causative, systems as large, complicated, and dynamic as the Earth's crust, the stock market, and the ecosystem can break down not only under the force of a mighty blow but also at the drop of a pin. Large interactive systems perpetually organize themselves to a critical state in which a minor event can start a chain reaction that leads to a destabilizing breakdown. After the breakdown the system will begin organizing toward the next critical state, and so on (Figs. 11 and 12).

Another way of approaching this is to ask the question: "If change is a Universal constant so nothing is static, what is a natural state?" In considering this question, we soon begin to realize that "the balance of nature" idea in the classical sense (disturb Nature and She will return to Her former state when the disturbance is removed) fails to hold. Although we usually perceive the pattern of vegetation on the Earth's surface to be stable, particularly over the short interval of our lifetimes, in reality the landscape and its vegetation are in a perpetual state of dynamic unbalance with the forces that sculpted them. When these forces create novel events that are sufficiently rapid and large in scale, we perceive them as "disturbances."

Perhaps the most outstanding evidence that an ecosystem is subject to constant change and disruption rather than in a static balance comes from studies of naturally-occurring external factors that dislocate ecosystems. For a long time, says Dr. J. L. Meyer of the University of Georgia, we failed to consider influences outside ecosystems. Our emphasis, she says, was "on processes going on within the ecosystem" even though "what's happening [inside] is driven by what's happened outside." Ecologists, she points out, "had blinders on in thinking about external, controlling factors"[25] like the short- and long-term ecological factors that limit cycles.

Climate appears to be foremost among these factors. By

Figure 11. *The Perpetual Reorganization of Large Systems:* . Large, interactive systems perpetually organize themselves to a critical state, at which point a minor event can start a chain reaction that leads to a catastrophe, after which the system will begin organizing toward the next critical state, and so on. Here a forest can burn and become a grassland, which in turn starts organizing itself—through successional stages—toward a forest again, which may someday burn again, and so on.

Figure 12. *The Reorganization of a Grassland:* A grassland becomes a shrubland. Here a perennial grassland is overgrazed and becomes a desert shrubland, which, if not too severely damaged, starts organizing itself—through successional stages—back toward a grassland or, if overgrazing continues, toward a desert dominated by bare ground and cacti.

studying the record laid down in the sediments of oceans and lakes, scientists know that climate, in the words of Dr. Margaret B. Davis of the University of Minnesota, has been "wildly fluctuating" over the last two million years, and the shape of ecosystems with it. The fluctuations take place not only from eon to eon but also from year to year and at every scale in between. "So you can't visualize a time in equilibrium," asserts Davis. In fact, says Dr. George L. Jacobson, Jr. of the University of Maine, there is virtually no time when the overall environment stays constant for very long. "That means that the configuration of the ecosystems is always changing," (Fig. 13) creating different landscapes in a particular area through geological time (Fig. 14).

With this notion of perpetual change in mind, consider that all of us can sense change—the growing light at sunrise, the gathering wind before a thunderstorm, the changing seasons of spring's new leaves, summer's swaying blossoms, autumn's golden harvest, and winter's stark, naked trees and chilling winds. Some of us can see longer-term events and remember more or less snow last winter compared to the snow of other winters or that spring seemed to come early this year.

But it is an unusual person who can sense, with any degree of precision, the changes that occur over the decades of his or her life. At this scale of time we tend to think of the world in some sort of "steady state," and we typically underestimate the degree to which change has occurred. We are unable to directly sense slow changes, and we are even more limited in our abilities to interpret their relationships of cause and effect. This being the case, the subtle processes that act quietly and unobtrusively over decades are hidden and reside in the "invisible present."

It is the invisible present that is the scale of time within which our responsibilities for Planet Earth are most evident. Within this scale of time, ecosystems change during our lifetimes and the lifetimes of our children and our grandchildren. To see how scale works, let's examine some of the

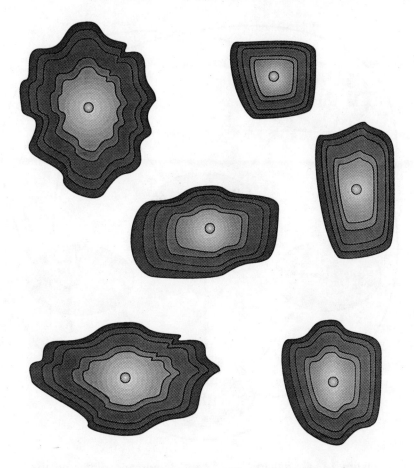

Figure 13. *Ecological Snapshots:* These are ecological snapshots in time. The configuration of a given ecosystem and landscape is always changing. Each is viewed geologically as an ecological snapshot in and through time.

geological history of Zion National Park in the state of Utah.

Where today the deep canyons and massive walls of stone enthrall visitors (Photo 15), 245 million years ago a sea in which lived marine fishes covered the area of Zion. Over a period of roughly 35 million years, about 1,800 feet of sediments were deposited on the floor of the sea, along the coastal plain, and along the inland streams.

As the climate warmed, the sea changed into a gigantic

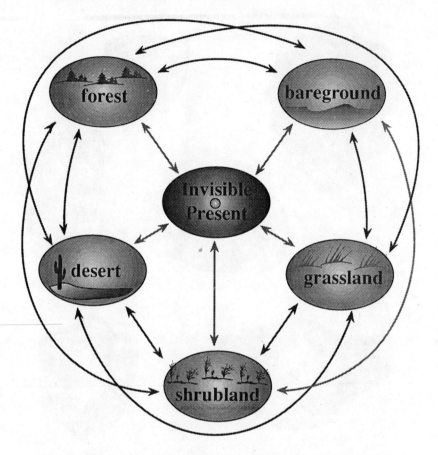

Figure 14. *A Changing Landscape:* Landscapes differ on the same acreage through geological time. Changes in the long- and short-term limiting factors affect a particular area and create myriad different landscapes and ecosystems through geological time. The ball in the center of the "invisible present" represents the here and now with the ongoing "invisible" changes we cannot detect.

swamp. Here, 210 million years ago, crocodile-like plant-eating dinosaurs swam in the sluggish streams whose floods carried drifted trees on their swirling waters from distant forests to form log jams. Here too, small, fragile dinosaurs hunted along the streams' banks. As the climate once again became moister during the next 40 million years, the swamp

Photo 15. *The Great Wall:* Canyon wall at Zion National Park, about 1,500 or 2,000 feet high.

became a lake and the sand, silt, and clayey mud of the streams and the swamp gradually hardened into rock.

The lake for a time had fish living in it, but then some

of its waters became shallow and eventually disappeared. And existing streams spread silt and sandy mud over the sediments deposited on the lake's bottom. Toward the end of this 40-million-year interval the climate began to dry, and in a short space of time, geologically speaking, the now-intermittent streams deposited more sediments.

Then, about 170 million years ago, the ancient sea, the swamp, the lake, and the intermittent streams became buried beneath a desert of marching sand dunes of the "Navajo Time." This now-hostile environment had little life associated with it, and the few hardy plants and animals that did exist often died during the great storms, which blew clouds of hot, dry sand into dunes. As the dunes were built, destroyed, and built again, some of the plants and animals became entombed and are the rare fossils of today in what is now the Navajo Sandstone, which ranges from 1,500 to 2,000 feet thick. Although the source of the sand eroded away 150 million years ago, evidence indicates that the source had been a region of highlands in what is today the state of Nevada.

For a brief period following the creation of the Navajo Desert, flood waters carrying suspended sediments buried the dunes in deposits of red mud, after which the climate returned to more desert-like conditions.

Again the climate changed, and 145 million years ago a vast, shallow sea once more covered the area, drowning the Navajo Desert. Now the once-sterile desert with its cap of red mud became the floor of the sea and the home of sea lilies (crinoids) and of shellfish. When the warm, teeming waters retreated, they left behind, buried in limey silt, shells that produce the present fossils.

Over the millions of years, in response to changing environmental conditions, various materials were deposited in the sediments. The Zion area experienced shallow seas, coastal plains, a giant swamp, a lake, intermittent streams, and a desert filled with massive wind-blown dunes of sand. While the shallow seas covered the area, mineral-laden waters slowly filtered down through the layers of sediment. Minerals like iron and calcium carbonate were deposited in the spaces between the particles of silt, sand, or mud, cementing them together, turning them into stone. And the weight of each layer caused the basin to sink and maintained its surface at an elevation near sea level. This process of deposition-sinking-deposition-sinking continued layer upon layer until the accumulation of the successive sediments became 10,000 feet thick!

Geologists believe that Zion was a relatively flat basin with an elevation near sea level from 245 million years ago until the last shallow sea dried about 10 million years ago. At that time, Zion was a featureless plain across which streams meandered lazily as they dropped their loads of sediment in sandbars and floodplains.

Then, in an area extending from Zion to the Rocky Mountains, a massive geologic event began. Forces deep within the Earth's mantle started to push upward on the surface of the Earth. The land in Zion rose from near sea level to as much as 10,000 feet above sea level.

Zion's location on the western edge of the uplift caused the streams to tumble off the Colorado plateau, flowing rapidly down a steep gradient. The Virgin River, for example, drops more than four thousand feet from the northeast corner of Zion National Park in Utah to Lake Mead in Arizona, 145 miles away; in comparison, consider that the upper Mississippi River drops only 210 feet from Lake Itasca, in Minnesota, to Grand Rapids, Minnesota, also a distance of 145 miles.

And because fast-flowing water carries more sediments and larger boulders than does slow-moving water, these swift streams in Zion began eroding down into the layers of rock, cutting deep, narrow canyons. In the ten million years since the uplift began, the North Fork of the Virgin River has not only carved Zion Canyon but also has carried away a layer of rock nearly 5,000 feet thick, a layer that once lay above the highest existing rock in Zion National Park.

The uplift of the land is still occurring, so the Virgin River is still excavating. The river, with its load of sand, has been likened to an ever-moving strip of sandpaper. Its grating effect, coupled with the steepness of the Colorado Plateau, has allowed the river to cut its way through the Navajo Sandstone in a short time geologically speaking.

The cutting of Zion Canyon created a gap in the solid layer of resistant sandstone, and the walls of the canyon relaxed and expanded ever so slightly toward this opening. Because rock is not very elastic, this expansion caused cracks, known as pressure-release joints, to form inside of the canyon's walls. These cracks run parallel to the canyon about fifteen to thirty feet inside the walls. They occur throughout the Navajo Sandstone (Photo 16).

The grains of sand that form the Navajo Sandstone itself were once driven bouncing across the desert by the wind, only to be caught within the steep face of a dune, where they became buried. Over time, the cement of lime tied grain to grain creating the stone of sand.

Today, however, the process is reversed, and a new cycle has begun. The layer of siltstone and sandstone directly beneath the Navajo Sandstone is softer and more easily eroded than is the Navajo Sandstone. Thus, as the walls of Navajo Sandstone are undermined by the erosion of this softer material, water from rain and snow seeps into the joints, where it freezes in winter, wedging the walls of the joints ever farther apart.

In addition to freezing, the water, one drop of rain at a time, one melting flake of snow at a time, aided by chemical action, dissolves the cement. The structure gradually weakens. A last grain of sand holding the undermined wall in place moves, and the massive piece of rock falls, breaking away along the line of least resistance, leaving the graceful sweep of a huge arch sculpted in the face of the cliff a thousand feet above the floor of the canyon (Photo 17). And so is revealed yet another vertical face previously hidden as a crack or pressure-release joint inside the wall. Below, the

Photo 16. *Inside the Canyon Wall:* The arrow points to the pressure-release joint inside the canyon's wall.

rock, shattered by the fall, gradually returns to sand and is once again blown hither and yon by the wind or carried toward the sea by the restless Virgin River.

In the end, Zion, cemented together grain by grain over millions of years, is being dissolved over millions of years one grain at a time by the persistence of water from snow and infrequent thunderstorms. But while Zion undergoes its inevitable changes, it is the home for 670 species of flowering

Photo 17. *When Gravity Knocks:* The arrow points to the place where a massive piece of rock has fallen and revealed another vertical face of the cliff.

plants and ferns, 30 species of amphibians and reptiles, 125 species of resident birds, and 95 species of mammals. Gone, however, are the wolf, the grizzly bear, and the native big-horn sheep, extirpated within the last hundred years by the invading European-American settlers. Thus are tipped the scales of change, of creation and extinction in all of its dimensions.

10

INNER VS. OUTER LANDSCAPES

Until we shift the focus of our attention from the products of the outer landscape to the process of the inner landscape of our soul, we will continue to destroy our external environment. "The movement to a lasting society cannot occur without a transformation of individual values and priorities. . . . Materialism simply cannot survive the transition to a sustainable world," according to Worldwatch in 1990. There should be no surprise in this, because all material things created by humanity, including jobs, have built-in obsolescence. This means simply that the more deeply and clearly we analyze the problems our world is facing, the more we realize that the crisis is not "out there" somewhere but is within us.

It is a personal, inner crisis of the human spirit that manifests itself as a collective outer crisis of social morality. The health, vitality, and honesty of our own personal inner landscapes governs the authenticity with which we treat our-

selves, one another, and Planet Earth in the collective outer
landscape called society. In other words, our crisis is spiritual bankruptcy.

Authenticity is the spiritual voice of the heart, which
each of us seeks and to which each of us responds. "Authenticity" is the condition or quality of being trustworthy or
genuine. It is the harmony between what one thinks, says,
and does and what one really feels—the motive in the deepest
recesses of one's heart. One is authentic only when one's
motives, words, and deeds are in harmony with one's attitude.

One's attitude is the visible part of one's behavior, but
one's motive is hidden from view. Emerson wrote, "Your
attitude thunders so loudly that I can't hear what you say."
And it's when visible behavior is out of harmony with motive
(bespeaking an ulterior motive) that attitude points to a hidden agenda, an ulterior motive. It's this lack of inner harmony between motives and deeds that is currently plaguing
human society with a projected sense of inauthenticity.

It's the ulterior motive, perceived as a crime by the public at large, that causes a lack of trust based on a lack of
authenticity. "Commit a crime," wrote Emerson, "and the
earth is made of glass. . . . Some damning circumstance always transpires." Quite simply, the lack of authenticity results from our failure to respond individually and
collectively to cultural evolution. The Scottish philosopher
Carlyle summed up our choice about the authenticity of the
individual when he said, "Change yourself, and then you will
know there is at least one less rascal in the world."

Cultural Evolution

Ulterior motives are those self-serving motives that are perceived by the public at large as being negative or dishonest.
Such motives often come about when someone is resisting
changing his or her set of values to meet changing social

conditions brought about by cultural evolution. Cultural evolution is the collective change in societal values stemming
from a shift in the collective social consciousness. In general
terms, a social system is catapulted into the throes of evolution when it has reached a sufficient level of complexity,
has self-reinforcing feedback systems among its components,
is exposed to a sufficiently rich and constant flow of energy,
and when its normal functioning is drastically disturbed by
a collective shift in social consciousness.

Although culture is learned from the past, modified in
the present, and passed on to future generations, cultural
evolution does not follow so quiet and orderly a course. As
I have said elsewhere in this book, evolution occurs in leaps
of turmoil during which an old, rigidly-adapt*ed* species or
system is swept away and replaced by a new flexibly-adapt-
able one. Thus, as a cultural system becomes destabilized, it
can respond to a small (perhaps peripheral) movement like
the environmental movement of the 1960s by amplifying it
and making it the dominant factor in further cultural evolution.

It would be nice to think that if society learned one important thing from the decade of the 1960s, it was that one
cannot unilaterally destroy the "establishment" without of-
fering a viable replacement, that before an old paradigm can
be cast out there must be a new one to fill the void. But
cultural evolution doesn't work that way.

Each new paradigm—each new leap of evolution in culture—is built on a sudden shift of insight, a quantum leap
of intuition, which carries forward with it only a modicum
of old ideas. Those who cling to the old way and fight against
change demand irrefutable proof that change is needed. The
irony is that the old way also began as the new way and was
also challenged to prove change was necessary or even desirable.

The personal and social trap of an old rigid paradigm is
that any system of belief that has become comfortable has
also become self-limiting. At this point new data—whatever

somehow countermands the accepted, established view—cannot fit into the old way of thinking, which has grown rigid with tradition and hardened with age. It is therefore periodically necessary to crack open the old if a new thought form is to enter and grow, moving both the individual and society forward in a leap of cultural evolution, the offspring of which is a renewed sense of authenticity.

Moving forward may be difficult for those whose belief system and personal identity are invested totally in the old paradigm; they see no reason to change. For those who subscribe to a new paradigm, moving forward is easier because there is something toward which to move—a new vision. But rallying to a new paradigm also can be physically dangerous to limb and life, for too often we charge others with being "wrong," implying that we ourselves are "right." Neither claim is correct, of course, in a world that is neither black nor white.

There comes a point in the history and evolution of every individual and society when change is necessary if that individual or society is to continue to evolve. And it all begins or ends with the willingness of the individuals—who collectively are society—to change. If the willingness to change is absent, as it almost always is, there comes a personal or social crisis that takes the initiative out of the hands of the individual or society and thrusts them forward unceremoniously, kicking and screaming along the evolutionary path.

Consider, for example, Jesus, a supremely gentle man, who preached the love of God above all else and the moral imperative of love, mercy, justice, and faith among all people. Jesus refused to knuckle under when challenged by the Pharisees of Jerusalem and by the administrators of the mighty Roman empire. For his courage and faith, he was crucified. But when the Roman empire began to crumble under the weight of internal dissension and corruption, the followers of the original twelve disciples emerged from the catacombs and converted the emperor himself to their new faith.

Then there was the Buddha, who found enlightenment under the bodhi tree. The Buddha's words and example transformed many parts of the ancient Hindu civilization during a time of social turbulence and dissatisfaction. Over the decades, the Buddha's teachings have been carried throughout much of the Orient.

Centuries later, a few idealists with the courage to live their dreams of freedom, equality, justice, and brotherhood rejected the King of England and united thirteen colonies into a union of greatly different values, social structures, and economies, and from that union grew a new nation.

And within my lifetime there was a humble man named Gandhi who told the British that they could steal everything from him and even kill him, and then they would have his dead body, but not his obedience. It was, of course, Gandhi's obedience that the British needed in order to enslave his spirit and keep India in slavery. But Gandhi, a free man in his heart and in his mind, challenged the might and the treachery of the British Empire with truth and love. And in the end, the British consummated India's freedom, because force, violence, and brutality simply could not stand against truth, love, and determined peaceful nonviolence.

And there were others, such as Adolf Hitler, Joseph Stalin, Sadam Hussein, and Ronald Reagan, who brought out the dark side of human society. Their time was brief, however, because truth and love always win in the end.

All of these people, saints and sinners, intellectuals and soldiers, armed with only an idea and the courage to act on it, could topple dominant regimes whose corruption festered internally. There have been others who toppled lesser foes but who nonetheless changed the world.

But how, asks Ervin Laszlo, who is with the United Nations Institute for Training and Research, does all of this apply to the present condition of humanity and human society? The answer, he says, is that we are entering an epoch of critical instability, which, unlike past epochs, is global in extent. Our world is so highly specialized, so thoroughly interdependent, and so economically enmeshed that a tremor of instability in any part of the global house of cards will spread rapidly, destabilizing most societies.[26]

Unless we cause a global nuclear holocaust or poison ourselves with pollution, humanity will survive, but the social crisis we face is unprecedented in dimension and will mark the end of an epoch. The types of social, economic, and political organizations that have been created in modern times will undergo major and sudden change like the one that has already happened in Eastern Europe, including the change in the old Soviet Union. And the outcome will neither be determined by nor predicted by any past social experience with respect to the way the new social order will function.

The quiet time in the United States since the last burst of cultural evolution is over. We have again sailed into a maelstrom set in motion in the United States largely by the administration of President Ronald Reagan, whose backward policies of fear, terror, and greed set the stage for the crisis, and we must ride it out with the ship.

There are those, however, who have consciously prepared for the crisis and will live through it. This despite the fact, as Jonathan Swift said, that "when a true genius [or visionary] appears in the world, you may know him by this sign: that all the dunces are in confederacy against him."

These are the people who have the foresight to "read the handwriting on the wall" and to act on it with courage. They see the close of the twentieth century as the end of the dominant old social system and the opening of the twenty-first century as the freedom to create a new and better social order. They look ahead, prepare, discuss, and perfect their ideas, and they wait patiently to implement them. They possess the inner vision, the knowledge, and the courage to act for the good of the whole when their inner knowing tells them the time is right. They will hold the helm of cultural evolution and give it the direction they can by asking bold new questions, those that guide the evolution of society for the good of society and of Planet Earth. And here the watch-word is "balance."

On the Eagle's Wing

If our human society is to survive the future, we must strike a balance in all we do. I use the metaphor of an eagle to depict social balance for two reasons. First, because so many nations, such as the United States, Germany, Austria, Mexico, and the Roman Empire, have used and still use the eagle as their national symbol, and second, because an eagle cannot fly unless its wings are balanced. Put too much weight on one wing or the other, and all an eagle can do, regardless of its might, is spiral downward until it crashes—as did the Roman Empire, as did Germany twice, and even as our social system is doing today.

To avoid such a crash we must balance ourselves between linear thinking and cyclic thinking, because in order to produce and to maintain our society we need both. Cyclic thinking is in harmony with the environment and in tune with our spirituality, but even though we "do not live by *bread* alone," we must have bread. Linear thinking is therefore necessary to produce the material products that maintain the physical aspects of human life and society. Society is thus the body of the eagle, cyclic thinking is one wing, and linear thinking the other. For the eagle to fly straight and true, the wings must be in balance.

With this imperative of social balance, the main question that needs to be asked in terms of the future is: How do we balance ourselves, the human animal, with the spiritual and material energies of Planet Earth? Although I don't have THE answer, I have an idea to share with you.

This idea is that humanity looks at the world in which it lives from an angle that is 180 degrees off. We are, for example, concerned today in our heightened ecological awareness with the things we are losing from the environment, such as biodiversity. But we need in addition to be far more concerned with the things that we are *introducing* into the environment, things with which it is not adapted to cope, such as our exploding human population, which in turn causes the losses. What any culture, including ours, introduces into its environment and the attitude with which the introductions are made is determined by the mythological view with which it sees its place in and of Creation.

Mythology and Lifestyle

The underpinnings of social values and therefore chosen lifestyles are rooted in cultural myths. A people's thoughts and values, which are based on their cultural myths, translate into their lifestyles, and it is the cultural underpinnings of their chosen lifestyles that ultimately affect the land they inhabit.

Most Native North Americans, for example, survived largely by hunting and killing. They lived in a world where life was always balanced on a fine line between the hunter and the hunted. To survive in such an unpredictable world, they reconciled themselves with Creation through their myths and rituals and through their spiritual connection with the Creator. Their lifestyles reflected a spiritual Creation, because they lived their myths through enacted rituals, which remained to a large degree in harmony with their changing environment.

Another and very different set of cultural myths was brought to this country by the European invaders, largely from the pastoral scenes of Europe. When they arrived in the New World, they saw not a land to be understood, adapted to, and nurtured but a wild, untamed continent to be conquered. They came from "civilized" countries with "civilized" myths and lifestyles and felt that they were being rudely thrust into an "uncivilized" continent inhabited by "savages" and wild beasts, the conquest of which was their duty.

What Europeans did not understand, however, was that their myths and lifestyles belonged to another place and another time in the evolution of human society and were incompatible with those of the indigenous peoples of the New World, or with the New World itself, for that matter. The myths and lifestyles of the Native North Americans belonged to the land they inhabited, whereas those of the Europeans belonged to a land halfway around the world.

The Native North Americans, in keeping with their myths, lived with the land and considered themselves to be an inseparable part of its spiritual harmony—something that could not be owned. The Europeans, in keeping with their myths, sought to conquer, harness, subdue, and own the land.

Native North Americans, on the other hand, had lived on and with the land for more than ten thousand years. They viewed the land and all it contained as a "Thou," something holy to be revered, whereas the invading Europeans viewed the same land as an "it"—simply an object to be exploited for short-term private gains.

At best, the European's ancestral myths and lifestyles became rigid through a long tradition of ecological exploitation and so were incompatible with the land, with the indigenous peoples, and with the reality of constant change. At worst, they were on a collision course with the survival of human society as we know it, because although we are wise in our own eyes, we are blind to the truth that we neither govern nor manage Nature. We *treat* Nature wisely or unwisely for good or for ill, but we do not control Her. We do something to Her, such as overpopulating Her, and She responds, and in Her response lies the lessons we are loath to learn. Which brings us to lifestyle.

Lifestyle is commonly defined as an internally consistent way of life or style of living that reflects the values and attitudes of an individual or a culture. We in Western civilization have made lifestyle synonymous with "standard of living," which we practice as a search for ever-increasing material prosperity. If, however, we are to have a viable, sustainable environment as we know it and value it, we must reach beyond the strictly material and see lifestyle as a sense of inner wholeness and harmony derived by living in such a way that the spiritual, environmental, and material aspects of our lives are in balance with the capacity of the land to produce the necessities for that lifestyle.

Whether a given lifestyle is even possible depends on "cultural capacity," a term that is an analogue for "carrying capacity," which is the number of animals that can live in and use a particular landscape without impairing its ability to function in an ecologically-specific way. If we want human society to survive the twenty-first century in any sort of dignified manner, we must have the humility to view our own population in terms of local, regional, national, and global carrying capacities, because the quality of life declines in direct proportion to the degree to which the habitat is over-populated.

If we substitute for "carrying capacity" the idea of "cultural capacity," we have a workable proposition for society. Cultural capacity is a chosen quality of life, the quality that can be sustained without endangering the environment's productive ability. The more materially-oriented the desired lifestyle of an individual or a society, for example, the more resources are needed to sustain it and the smaller the human population must be per unit area of landscape. Cultural capacity, then, is a balance between the way we want to live, the real quality of our lifestyle and of our society, and the number of people an area can support in that lifestyle on a sustainable basis. Cultural capacity of any area will be less than its carrying capacity in the biological sense.

Cultural capacity is a workable idea. We can predetermine local and regional cultural capacity and adjust our population growth accordingly. If we choose not to balance our desires with the land's capabilities, the depletion of the land will determine the quality of our cultural/social experience and our lifestyle. So far, we have chosen not to balance our desires with the capabilities of the land, because we have equated "desire, need, and demand" as synonyms with every itch of "want." We have lost sight of ecological reality.

If we desire to maintain a predetermined lifestyle, we must ask new questions: (1) How much of any given resource is necessary for us to use if we are to live in the lifestyle of our choice? (2) How much of any given resource is it necessary to leave intact as a biological reinvestment in the health and continued productivity of the ecosystem? and (3) Do sufficient resources remain, after biological reinvestment, to support our lifestyle of choice, or must we modify our lifestyle to meet what the land is capable of sustaining?

"Necessity" is a proposition very different from the collective "desire, want, need, demand" syndrome, so arguments about the proper cultural capacity revolve not only around what we think we want in a materialistic/spiritual sense but also around what the land can produce in an environmentally-sustainable sense. Cultural capacity is a conservative concept, given finite resources and well-defined values. By first determining what we want in terms of lifestyle, we may be able to determine not only if the Earth can support our desired lifestyle but also how we must behave with respect to the environment if we are to maintain our desired lifestyle.

To see how this works, let's examine a few examples of cultural capacity. On September 21, 1989, Hurricane Hugo flattened most of South Carolina's beachfront. Since then, houses have been rebuilt and stand once more "eave to eave" as testimony of American's determination to live by the sea. The result is that so many people are trying to buy so little remaining land that a standard city lot may sell for as much as $500,000.

Today, nearly half the American population lives within an hour's drive of a coast. By the year 2010, predicts the National Oceanographic and Atmospheric Administration, nearly sixty percent, or 127 million people, will live in the coastal zone, including the shores of the Great Lakes, Puget Sound in the state of Washington, and along the shores of such rivers as the Columbia.

Pollution and destruction of habitats, problems faced in every coastal region of our nation, are fueled both by unchecked growth of the population and by an increasing desire on the part of many Americans to live by the sea or some other shore. The Pacific Northwest, just now beginning to feel the pressures of a growing coastal population, which began on the eastern seaboard at end of World War II, hopes to avoid both the overcrowding and the building in hazardous areas that has plagued such states as South Carolina.

In Oregon, the demographics of the coastal population are changing with the influx of retired persons, many of whom have some environmental awareness. Nevertheless, as people build their dream homes by the sea and along other shores, they fill in wetlands, cut down forests, and cause the erosion of the beaches, thus making changes that threaten the very environment that drew them to the coastal areas in the first place. This is a clear example of grossly exceeding the cultural capacity of a chosen area.[27]

The decline of the Hawaiian paradise is a prime example. The United States Fish and Wildlife Service, the Hawaii Department of Land and Natural Resources, and The Nature Conservancy of Hawaii made the decline the subject of a joint report that took a decade to prepare.

Until people found the Hawaiian Islands, perhaps one new species evolved every ten thousand years. This number is significant because the Hawaiian Islands surpass even the Galapagos Islands, off the coast of South America, in the number of species that evolved from a single ancestor. In Hawaii at least fifty species have evolved from a common ancestor.

Beginning in the 1700s the islands became a crossroads for Pacific travel, and early seafarers introduced domestic pigs, goats, horses, and cattle onto the islands as sources of fresh meat. But even within the last fifteen years the introduction of foreign species of plants and animals has increased dramatically.

Besides the obvious introductions of domestic animals, less expected imports had affected the islands: bird malaria and pox, both of which are carried by mosquitos, have had a severe impact on native Hawaiian birds. Brown tree snakes, which have devastated the native species of birds on Guam, have six times been intercepted on flights to Hawaii.

The banana poka, a passion-flower vine, which is kept in check in its native South America by the feeding of insects, has no such controlling mechanisms in the islands. Consequently, since arriving in Hawaii it has smothered 70,000 acres of forests on two islands and is threatening larger tracts.

To date, nearly two-thirds of Hawaii's original forest cover has been lost, including half the vital rain forests. Ninety percent of the lowland plains, once forested, have been destroyed. Of 140 species of native birds, only 70 remain, and 33 of those are in danger of extinction. Eleven more species are beyond recovery. As of November 1991, 37 species of plants native to Hawaii are listed as federally endangered; within two years 152 more species will be proposed for federal listing. Among the state's rarest species of plants are 93, including trees, shrubs, vines, herbs, and ferns, each of which has only about a hundred known surviving individuals. At least five species have been reduced to just one individual.

The cause of the decline is twofold: (1) the cumulative effect of people's careless, unplanned, unbalanced conversion of the land from Nature's design to society's cultural design in the form of agriculture, ranching, and residential use, and (2) our introduction of non-native species of plants, insects, and mammals.

The results include the loss of the forests, which once intercepted and generated rainfall and protected the coral reefs and beaches from siltation caused by the erosion of soil. Forest loss, coupled with the extinction of native plants and animals, affects every level of the islands' economy and cultural heritage, such as the generation of unique materials for clothing, textiles, ornaments, canoes, and scientific study. Because its cultural capacity has been grievously exceeded, Hawaii has become largely a paradise lost.[28]

Thus, when the arguments are over, it must be remembered that if we are to remain within our cultural capacity we must make our desired societal lifestyle the eagle's body. Then the Earth's ability to sustain that particular cultural capacity is one wing and the size of our human population is the other. And today, the wing on which rides the human population is far too heavy for the eagle of our desire to long remain airborne.

Equity and Balance

There's another balancing act we impose on the eagle: that of balancing ourselves within ourselves and within the outer world. Every human being, for example, has a dual polarity of masculine and feminine in his or her psychological makeup. It's one of our tasks in life to balance this polarity so that we may see the world in the reality of unity rather than the illusion of combat between both the inner and the outer genders.

Many societies began by worshipping the Goddess, "Mother Earth," the feminine giver of life. As culture evolved, particularly the Judeo-Christian culture, the Goddess was slain and replaced by the God. Today our society is patriarchal. The feminine is banished and in psychological exile, and now our masculine society makes war within itself, among its neighbors, and on the feminine, because the masculine pole is one of action and of absolute control through combat.

The results of banishing the Goddess are everywhere to be seen: deforestation; desertification; erosion; pollution of the air, water, and soil; human slavery in all its many social forms; and ceaseless wars that lay waste the world for all living things. Consider, for example, that President George Bush was willing to spend billions of dollars to wage a war in the Persian Gulf over oil, but was unwilling to spend one-tenth of that amount of money to take care of his own citizens' medical needs, housing needs, or educational needs, let alone the needs of a sick, polluted environment, caused largely by the proliferation of the military-industrial machine—the masculine God of War.

Well, you might say, the United States isn't just masculine anymore: look at all of the women in the work force. Yes, more women are in the work force today, but are they allowed to succeed if they are "feminine"? In my experience, they must be tough and competitive and be able to "fit" themselves into a masculine combat zone. Are they paid equally for equal work? In my experience, the answer is no. Do they have equal chances for advancement? Again, the answer in my experience is no. Golda Meir spoke the social truth when she said, "To be successful, a woman has to be much better at her job than a man." This is still true!

Why this insistence on masculine domination? It has to do with fear and its companion of control. The person who harbors the most fear also harbors the most need of being in control of his or her external environment, and the need to be in control is always fed by the need for the "inequity of enemies."

When, for instance, the invading Europeans conquered the Native Americans, they could not "see," let alone acknowledge, that the Native Americans were just as human as they themselves were. Had the Europeans acknowledged that truth, they could never have justified the wholesale murder of the natives and the stealing of their land.

The same principle holds for the Africans degraded as slaves. If white Americans ever admit that black Americans are their equals, which in every way they are, then whites would have to treat them as such, which means going beyond their fears of being out of control. And that, in turn, means sharing control of their mutual social destiny—something whites in America are not ready to do.

I can make the same case for every racial minority in every country in the world. I can make the same case for women, for city folks versus rural folks, for valley-dwelling folks versus hill-dwelling folks, for rich folks versus poor folks, and for "civilized" society against "wild" Nature, *ad infinitum*. It isn't a question of who's better than whom, it's a question of who's more afraid of whom. It's a question of who's so afraid of being out of inner control that they must have outer control at any cost—even unto the denigration of fellow human beings, the unmitigated abuse and extinction of nonhuman creatures, and the flagrant rape of Planet Earth.

A wonderful example of inequity is the case of those people living in the city versus those living in the country, which took place in my home town of Corvallis, Oregon, a number of years ago. I read in the local newspaper that a farmer had been arrested and fined for throwing garbage on somebody's lawn in town. As I read the article, I had difficulty believing what I was reading, because "all men [people] are created equal," according to the Constitution of the United States, but in everyday life some people are a lot more equal than others. The story went like this:

Joe City, who lived in Corvallis, took his garbage out to the country and dumped it on Bill Rural's property near Bill's house. Although Bill didn't see Joe dump his garbage, he found a bill in the garbage with Joe's name and address on it. So Bill picked up all Joe's garbage and drove into Corvallis, where he dumped it onto Joe's front lawn. Joe went to the police and complained.

Even though Bill said that the people of Corvallis were continually dumping their unwanted garbage on his land and that in this case he could prove it was Joe's garbage, Joe had legal standing and Bill did not. Bill was arrested and fined, but *nothing* happened to Joe—something that sent a clear message of inequity to Joe, to Bill, and to everyone else. In other words, it was okay for the city folks to dump their garbage with legal impunity on the property of the rural folks, but not vice versa.

Note that everything I've said is built on a foundation of inequity, of someone or something being superior to someone or something else. The perceived superiority is the dominance of the masculine pole over the feminine pole, of conquest and control over relationship and nurturance. This is not to say that the masculine pole is negative while the feminine pole is positive, but it is to say that masculine and feminine are different and that masculine and feminine are each only one wing of the eagle.

Inequity clearly carries over into those agencies whose missions are to uphold and fulfill the legal mandates on public lands for the good of the landowners—the public. But we see everywhere the appalling lack of evenhandedness, the pressure of this special-interest group or that special-interest group, and the bending of people within the agencies to this or that political pressure. There was a time, however, when equity counted for something; as Thucydides said of the Athenian code, "praise is due to all who . . . respect justice more than their position compels them to do."

Agencies and individuals responsible for the welfare of our nation's natural resources have functions that are prescribed by law but not necessarily specified by law. A wide range of administrative discretion is therefore not only permitted but also allocated by legislative bodies. Although this is as it should be, the system lacks a guiding precept that "public service" means service to the whole of the public with a sense of balance, equity, and sustainability.

These agencies and individuals are often under political pressure from self-seeking special-interest groups, whose pressure results in dedicated public servants being captured not only by the history of their organization but also by the fear and political weaknesses of their superiors. This means these same public servants are subjected to conflicting demands and receive no assurance or ethical governance from the public or any overseeing body. The result is that our system of managing the nation's natural resources has neither an ethical standard or "ethos" nor a sense of balance or equity.

Ethos is a Greek word meaning character or tone, and in the context of managing land it is best thought of as a set of guiding beliefs, which in the land-management agencies of the United States Government are all too often absent. In phrasing this guiding direction, a distinction needs to be made between ethos and policy.

Policy can be written in explicit terms and *can be* in the form of an order—the letter of the law. Ethos, on the other hand, is implicit and includes a guiding set of human values—the heart of the law—that is understood but cannot as such be written out. Yet ethos can be translated into policy should one wish to do so. We are, however, as Leopold wrote in 1933, confronted by a contradiction: "To build a better motor we tap the uttermost powers of the human brain; to built a better countryside we throw dice."

The United States Forest Service is an excellent example of an agency not fulfilling its legal mandate in order to bolster industrial greed and to avoid change. The Forest Service has told Congress that it cannot guarantee the sale level of timber in the Pacific Northwest unless Congress protects the Service from court review of the environmental soundness of its plans to harvest timber on public lands.

The statement brought an immediate rebuke from the environmentalists, who subsequently won an injunction barring the sale of timber on 66,000 acres of habitat of the threatened northern spotted owl because the Forest Service had violated the environmental laws again and again. Regardless of what laws were, are, or will be broken, John H. Beuter, deputy assistant secretary of agriculture and an economist, insisted that "the only way we can be realistic" about any level of sales of timber is for Congress to guarantee that the sale can be made despite environmental challenges. This means getting out the cut at any cost, even if the Forest Service continues to break the law and to jeopardize the owl's ability to survive extinction.

This all came about because United States District Judge William Dwyer, of Seattle, Washington, cited in his legal opinion "a remarkable series of violations of environmental laws" that have pushed the northern spotted owl to the brink of extinction, causing it to be listed officially as threatened, and that continue to push it closer and closer to extinction by "a deliberate and systematic refusal by the Forest Service and the Fish and Wildlife Service to comply with the laws protecting wildlife."[29]

"The problem," wrote Dwyer, "has not been any shortcoming in the laws, simply a refusal of administrative agencies to comply with them. This is not the doing of the scientists, foresters, rangers, and others at working levels of the agencies. It reflects decisions made by higher authorities in the executive branch of government."

In a sense, the agencies are doing what the legislature has directed them to do, but anyone who has been in government knows that administrative discretion—throwing the dice—is both wide open and often redefined in midstream to suit the current administration's political aims. This type of "discretion" both permits and encourages the buckling of individuals under political pressure from special interest groups backed by whichever administration is currently in political power.

Although an agency may sense the need for balance and equity, its personnel are often under pressure not only from groups outside the agency with special interests but also from their own supervisors. These supervisors are in turn usually pressured by officials in the administration who derive their position of authority not from experience or expertise in the management of resources but from one or another of the political decisions.

The result of such behavior is a striking disregard for the public interest and a net loss of the local, national, and

global wealth, both intellectual and monetary. Yet the allocation of advantage to the few at the expense of the many
persists in spite of the growing alarm over pending shortages,
a weakening social structure, increasing pollution, and ongoing, irreversible degradation to the quality and quantity
of our resources. Keep in mind that in most instances Congress itself has set and continues to set the stage for the social
and environmental degradation the world is currently experiencing. This is done not only by writing legislation that
favors one or another special interest but also by giving no
counteractive instructions for the protection of the public.

Thus the public, lacking information and insight, fails
to react, and even when reaction does come, it's only after
considerable damage has already befallen both society and
the environment. The public has, for example, begun to perceive that our societal commonalties, such as clean air and
clean water, affect everyone on Earth.

It thus falls to the citizenry to express the ethos and to
create and maintain the equity of both the governed and the
government. If the citizenry becomes divorced from concern
for the common good, then its government follows the same
path. Citizens can become increasingly divorced from concern if they are uninformed, if they fail to see the consequences of neglecting the general welfare, and if they are
given no insight into the operational details of the way their
own interests and those of their children are being taken care
of and protected. While they may be late in expressing their
ethos, it is the public that forces a largely self-serving Congress to take heed.

Nevertheless, if our society is to survive the centuries, it
must be designed with the unwritten assumptions of justice,
mercy, and equity for the common good. Democratic governance by the will of the people is effective and responsive
only so long as there exists an ethos in the administration—
a set of guiding beliefs in decision making, translated
through policy—even though unwritten into law. This ethos
is the intuitive "gut feeling" that the resources of the nations

and of the planet are worthy of respect and care—husbandry, if you will—and that they are essential to our long-term well-being.

Democratic guidance is effective only when equity—justice, mercy, and fairness to all—remains available and is not submerged in private or narrow interests. Such equity among human beings and between humanity and Nature depends on balancing the wings of the eagle. So it is that the battle for wholeness and balance—between masculine and feminine, between God and Goddess, between action and inaction, between conquest and nurturance, between inequity and equity, between materialism and spirituality, between humanity and Nature, and within and among human societies—is to be fought in each of our hearts.

I say this because we sometimes think we have made great strides overcoming racism, sexism, human arrogance, social inequity, and the despoliation of Nature, but to me these prove to be largely outer fluff. I see and I feel very little change in basic attitudes, in those agendas of fear hidden deep in our hearts.

Until our attitudes are in harmony with our actions and our actions are in harmony with our attitudes, there will be little real progress in social change, because laws and policies do not and cannot change attitudes. Only people on an individual basis can do that.

Until we face squarely the balancing of the masculine and the feminine poles and therefore the unification of humanity within itself and between itself and Nature through the granting of inner equity, justice, and mercy for all, we will continue to weaken and to destroy human society. Divided in combat, it cannot long survive the ages. Thus, in the end, we see the inner landscape of our being reflected on the outer landscape of the Earth, first through the questions we ask and second through the manifested results of those questions.

11
THE QUESTIONS WE ASK

Each question is a key that opens a door to a room filled with mirrors, each one a facet of the answer. Only one answer, however, is reflected in all the mirrors in the room. If we want a new answer we must ask a new question—open a new room with a new key.

We keep asking the same old questions—opening the same old door and looking at the same old reflections in the same old mirrors. We may polish the old mirrors and hope thereby to find new and different meanings out of the old answers to the same old questions. Or we might think we can pick a lock and steal a mirror from a new and different room with the hope of stumbling onto new and workable answers to the same old questions.

The old questions and the old answers have led us into the mess we are in today and are leading us toward the even greater mess we will be in tomorrow. We must therefore look long and hard at where we're headed with respect to the quality of the world we leave as a legacy. Only when we are willing to risk asking really new questions can we find really new answers.

One ostensibly new way of viewing the old problem of continual development is expressed in Norwegian Prime Minister Brundtland's report for the World Commission on Environment and Development. It calls for "sustainable development," which juxtaposes two mutually exclusive concepts—that of "sustainability" and that of "development."[30] "Sustainability" is the language of balance and limits over time, whereas "development" is the language of expansion, of ever-expecting more in some limitless fashion. Brundtland's report thus attempts to see the problem as one of paradox.

If this is the paradoxical way we are going to view the world, says philosopher Ivan Illich, then some of the pressing questions of today are: "After development, What? What concepts? What symbols? What images?" To find an alternative language, to find something that works for today in terms of the future, Illich suggests that we return to the past to discover the history around which were invented the mythological "certitudes" that undergird our current thinking. These certitudes encompass "need," "growth," "development," and the like, and together form the organizational core of our modern experience.[31]

The answer to a problem is only as good as the question and the means used to derive an answer. Science does not always ask good questions. Professor Walter McDougall, of the University of California at Berkeley, has in fact declared that "Big Science" has become destructive to the scientific endeavor as a whole. That's the case because the lure of large grants in fields aimed at predestined results is deadly to that most important ingredient in science: the ability to ask a "free" and unrestrained new question. The overall goal of scientific endeavor must remain the pursuit of pure knowledge, which by definition demands that the pursuit be totally unencumbered and forever open-ended.

To keep the search for truth on its own credible track, we must first recognize that we tend not only to form a single hypothesis but also to become so attached to it that any criticism of or challenge to our methods raises all our ego defenses. This means that the moment a person has derived what seems to be an original and satisfactory explanation for a phenomenon, at that instant the attachment to his or her intellectual child springs into existence. And the more the explanation grows into a definite theory, the more near and dear it becomes. Then comes the massaging (as I've often heard it called in government agencies) of the theory to fit the data and of the data to fit the theory.

In addition, we tend to become "method-oriented" rather than "problem-oriented" in our thinking and therefore in many of the questions we ask. It's important to recognize that we become method-oriented in our questions, because we tend to think that through our experiments—our methods—we are learning the *Truth* about Nature when in fact we are learning only about our experimental designs—again, our methods—and our assumptions and expectations.

It's impossible to accurately "represent" Nature through science, because scientific knowledge is not only a socially-negotiated, rigid construct but also a product of the personal lens through which a scientist peers. Scientists may attempt to detach themselves from Nature and to become "objective," but they are never completely successful. They are part of Nature and must participate with Nature in order to study Nature.

As well, every scientist sees through his or her lens but dimly, first because we cannot detach ourselves from Nature and second because all we can judge as fact are our own perceptions, which are always colored by our personal lenses. We may polish and wipe them as we will, but appearance—not reality—is all we can ever hope to see, and so it is appearance to which we often unknowingly direct our questions.

The truth about scientific research is that nothing can be proven—only disproven; nothing can be known—only unknown. This being the case, we can never "know" anything in terms of knowledge. We can "know" it only in terms of intuition, which is the knowing *beyond* knowledge and which is inadmissible as evidence in modern science. Whatever truth is, it can only be intuited and *approached*, never caught and pinned down.

The irony is that knowledge, which is external to a person, is not "knowable," and intuition, which is internal to a person, is not knowledge and therefore is not subject to disproof. Intuition is inner sight—individualized, inner knowing—for which proof is unnecessary and explanation impossible. Knowledge, on the other hand, is a collective outer experience of humanity's and society's subjective judgments about things, the Truth of which cannot be known and therefore is explainable only in the illusions of its appearance.

Thus the actual objects of our inquiries, the formulations of our questions and definitions, and the mythic structures of our scientific theories and facts are social constructs. Every aspect of our scientific theories, facts, and practices—including "scientific method" itself—are but expressions of contemporary socio/political/economic interests, cultural themes and metaphors, personal biases, and personal/professional negotiations for the power to control, albeit minutely, the scientific knowledge of the world.

Over the twenty some years that I worked in science I learned that Truth is an inner phenomenon of faith, which is absolute but unshareable and unprovable. Illusion, on the other hand, is an outer phenomenon of knowledge, which is shareable but only relative and disprovable—the social construct of science.

Facts that scientists construe to be *statistically true* statements about Nature, say Bruno Latour and Steve Woolgar, are demonstrated to be concrete, deified, magic outcomes of the social process of fabricating statements about the world so as to distinguish order from chaos.[32] Thus, instead of scientific consensus being achieved when the "facts" reach the state of "speaking for themselves," scientists come to a consensus when the political, professional, and economic costs of refuting them make further negotiation untenable.

There is, however, no single reality, but rather a multiplicity of realities, the representation of which depends on one's position in the process of negotiating an acceptable social view of reality. Thus, regardless of the question, the reproducibility of the experimental design and methods does not mean that the results represent anything about Nature. The reproducibility of the experimental design shows merely that a particular negotiation of reality is reproducible under a certain set of conditions. Thus, the results of every experiment may be valid, if unprovable, only because the experimental design tells us nothing about the results. It tells us only that the reproducibility of the experimental design is socially acceptable according to a consensus of scientific opinions.

If, therefore, we are going to ask intelligent questions about the future of the Earth and our place in the scheme of things, we must be free of scientific opinions based on "acceptable" interpretations of scientific knowledge. In addition, we would be wise to consider the gift of Zen and approach life with a beginner's mind—a mind simply open to the wonders and mysteries of the Universe.

A beginner sees only what the answers might be and knows not what they should be. If, on the other hand, I become an expert, I think I know what the answers should be and can no longer see what they might be. The beginner is free to explore and to discover a multiplicity of realities, while the expert grows rigid in a self-created prison of a single pet reality, which often turns into an obsession to be protected at any cost. Thus the beginner understands the question better than does the expert.

We must, if we are going to ask intelligent questions, be open to multiple hypotheses and explanations, and we must be willing to accept a challenge to our ideas in the spirit of learning rather than as an invitation to combat. One of the most important scientific questions we can ask is: "How *small* and *elegant* an experiment can I perform?"[33] The greatest triumphs in science are not, after all, triumphs of facts but rather triumphs of new ways of seeing, of thinking, of perceiving, and of asking questions.

Such triumphs of vision and of thought come not only through knowing which questions to ask but also through a willingness to risk what most people think of as failure. The avoidance of risk, says University President Harold Shapiro, is, in the end, "an acceptance of mediocrity and an abdication of leadership." We must beware of giving in and of "raising the flag of failure" too soon, because if we don't immediately achieve our stated objective society is quick to judge something as a failure.[34] But true success or failure is a personal view and lies not in the event itself but in the *interpretation* of an event. When Thomas Edison's ten thousand experiments with a storage battery failed to produce results, for example—and society would surely have deemed that a failure—he said, "I have not failed. I've just found 10,000 ways that won't work." This same line of reasoning is implicit in Winston Churchill's famous commencement speech: "Never, never give up! Never, never give up!"

Before we can get fundamentally new answers we must be willing to risk asking fundamentally new questions. This means that we must look long and hard at where we're headed with respect to the quality of our environment and to the legacy we are leaving the children of the world. Remember that the old questions and the old answers not only have gotten us to where we are today but also are guiding us to where we will be tomorrow.

Heretofore we have been more concerned with getting politically-right answers than we have been with asking morally-right questions. Politically-right answers validate our preconceived economic/political desires. Morally-right questions would lead us toward a future in which environmental options are left open so that generations to come may define their own ideas of a "quality environment" from an array of possibilities.

A good question, one that may be valid for a century or more, is a bridge of continuity among generations. We may develop a different answer every decade, but the answer does the only thing an answer can do: it brings a greater understanding of the question. An answer cannot exist without a question, so the answer depends not on the information we derive from the illusion of having answered the question but on the question we ask.

In the final analysis, the questions we ask guide the evolution of humanity and its society, and it's the questions we ask, not the answers we derive, that determine the options we bequeath to the future. Answers are fleeting, here today and gone tomorrow, but questions may be valid for a century or more. Questions are flexible and open-ended, whereas answers are rigid, illusionary cul-de-sacs. The future, therefore, is a question to be defined by questions.

With the foregoing in mind, consider the two questions I'm now posing: (1) What is *necessary* environmentally, spiritually, and materially for us, and for our children, and their children, to have a quality lifestyle? and (2) What do we mean when we speak of sustainability?

What Is Necessary Environmentally, Spiritually, and Materially for Us, Our Children, and Their Children, to Have a Quality Lifestyle?

As an admittedly—even *proudly*—materialistic society, we tend to ask ourselves over and over such questions as: What do I want? How much do I want? How much can I get? How fast can I get it? How can I get it for little or nothing? We have evolved into the "me, now, I never have enough, I want it for nothing" generation. Such social immaturity has posed some interesting problems for land managers who feel they are somehow mandated to meet the "public demand" for products. "Meeting the public demand" has long been the timber industry's cry of justification for the unbridled exploitation of the world's old-growth forests.

Our materialistic societal appetite has reached a compulsive, addictive state in which to *want* is to *have* to have! We have made synonyms of "desire, want, need, and demand," and in so doing we have lost sight of the ecological reality of both the present and the future. The equating of desire, need, and demand with every itch of "want" becomes clear when you consider mail-order catalogs, which I call "torture books," because I didn't know I "needed" something until I saw it in the pages of a catalog; now all of a sudden I just can't live without it. And the catalogs are relentless!

Society's present collective "wants, desires, needs, and demands" have already outstripped the world's capacity to supply them, and this is without even taking into account the "wants, desires, needs, and demands" of the coming generations. Nor does it take into account the incredibly stupid waste of global resources in war—any war for any reason.

If we as consumers continue to insist on feeding our insatiable appetites and on destroying incredible amounts of precious resources in war, we will surely destroy the Earth even without the use of nuclear weapons. Greed takes a little longer than war, but the result is the same.

The questions we're asking now are unwise questions because they're based on greed. To date, for example, we ask: What is the absolute *maximum* that we can get out of Nature, and what is the absolute *minimum* that we must legally leave behind for whatever reason? If human society is to survive, however, the time has come to ask different questions: How much of any given resource is *necessary* for us to use if we are to live in a reasonably comfortable lifestyle? How much of any given resource is *necessary* to leave intact in Nature as a biological reinvestment in the health and continued productivity of the ecosystem for the benefit of both ourselves and the generations to come?

"Necessity" is, in this sense, a very different proposition from the collective "want, desire, need, demand" syndrome. If we are wise enough to curb our appetites and to embrace the concept of *necessity* instead of *want*, the Earth still has, I believe, enough resources to nurture us while we relearn how to nurture the Earth. Nurturing the Earth brings us to the concept of sustainability.

What Do We Mean When We Speak of Sustainability?

Before we can effectively discuss the impact of lifestyle on the environment, we must consider the idea of "sustainable development" as outlined in the 1987 report of the *World Commission on Environment and Development*, which calls for juxtaposing two mutually exclusive concepts: that of "sustainability" and that of "development." Sustainability is the language of balance and limits. Development is the language of expansion, of expecting ever more in limitless fashion.

In the short term, sustainable development seems like a viable concept, but in the long term, sustainability and development will prove to be mutually exclusive, because continual development, as sustainable development would be practiced, must ultimately exhaust the land and its resources. To understand how this works, one has only to witness the British drive for colonial expansion, which came about because continual development was not ecologically-sustainable within the limited confines of the British Isles. To continue development beyond the ecological exhaustion of their land, the British had to subjugate other cultures and steal their resources.

Like England, the Earth is an island, and over the long run development is no more sustainable globally than it was in Britain. If we in the United States insist on practicing sustainable development so that we don't have to change our economic values, the time will come when we, like the British, must subjugate other peoples or other planets and steal their resources.

Sustainability, on the other hand, demands that if a global human society is to be sustainable, continually-increasing development, which exhausts one resource after another, must cease. While sustainability does not exclude the extractive use of resources, it does demand a balanced approach to their extraction and use. This means that the economic divesting of resources from any ecosystem must be at least balanced by the biological reinvestment of resources in that selfsame system, regardless of the economic impact on the profit margin—something that is not now happening. The concept of balance is important because we live between two spheres—the atmosphere (air) and the lithosphere (soil), and if we destroy either one, we will be the authors of our own extinction (Fig. 15).

If, for example, we imagine sustaining our current ex-

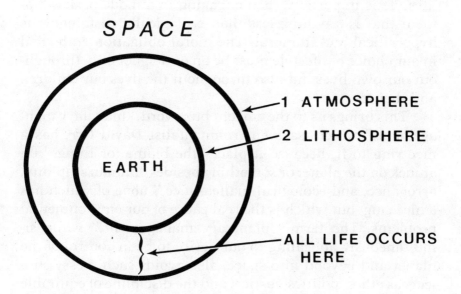

Figure 15. *Between Two Spheres:* We live in the middle, between two spheres—the atmosphere (air) and the lithosphere (soil).

pansionist approach to economics (continually-increasing development) into the future, we soon bump into environmental crises and see the need to re-frame the old economic paradigm—that continued growth (development) can solve all social problems. The old question—"How do we balance development and conservation?"—is replaced with the new question—"Can we have the one without the other?" The new question is critical, because conservation implies duration over time through wise use—that is, the sustainability of whatever is being conserved.

We now assume, in our strategies to raise material prosperity, that ever-expanding development is necessarily and ethically good because it results in the production of more material goods, thus making life "better" than it presently is. But if the importance of development is only to allow us to achieve ever-higher levels of material prosperity, then sustaining environmental degradation only to accommodate development is unethical. If, however, a whole and harmonious lifestyle is important, then engaging in a mode of development that is anything less than ecologically sustainable is hypocritical and immoral. The moral obligation embodied in our choice of lifestyle must be an option not only throughout our own lives but also throughout the lives our children and theirs.

This brings us to the current buzzword, "planetary management," which, says environmentalist David Orr, has a nice ring to it, because it places the blame for things run amuck on the planet or something besides "human stupidity, arrogance, and ecological malfeasance," none of which has a nice ring, but which is the real cause of our environmental problems. The term, "planetary management," while simultaneously appealing to our desire to be in control of the planet and beyond into space, also avoids such messy subjects as ethos, politics, justice, and the discipline of equitable distribution and of moral choice. In addition, management is a mechanical concept, one that we like because it reinforces our belief that we either are or can be in control of Nature.[35]

Because management is a mechanical concept, our plans to manage the Earth are founded on the belief that ignorance is a problem that can be solved with science and technology, which we conceived of, ironically, as being both linear and largely mechanical. But there is much to learn about the Earth, and there are many good reasons to believe that its complexities are permanently beyond our comprehension. Thus the salient point is not our knowledge but our *ignorance*, because only our ignorance can be proven. Our knowledge rests before the jury of tomorrow!

Ideally, management means knowing what's manageable and what's not and having the wisdom to leave the latter to manage itself. The ideal notwithstanding, our insistence on managing what cannot be sustainably managed—a tree farm—while leaving unmanaged what could be managed sustainably—a forest—is one source of the problem. Additionally, our lack of will to control our materialistic appetites, expansive economies, exploitive technologies, and exploding population is causing us to unintentionally redesign the Earth. That we *must* redesign the Earth is a given, simply because we exist. How we go about redesigning the Earth is another issue.

In redesigning the Earth, sustainability is a dimension in the scale of time, a dimension we ignore at our peril as we consider how we will treat our available resources. The paradigm within which our decisions are made today in economics, agriculture, and the determination of yields in forestry is based on a *timeless* view of reality. This economic view of quantitatively-constant values, such as the notion of the unchanging biological fertility of the soil, is both mechanistic and ecologically naïve.

Further, such concepts of sustained yield in timber, sustained yield in finances, and sustained growth in economics are all efforts to deny the existence of time. Evolution, in this view, is reduced to a mechanical process without any place for the novelty of change; it is a clockwork world with no capacity for a creative process. It allows only reversible and qualitiless locomotion, like a train running endlessly back and forth on a track.

The consequences of this perspective for economists is that, in their view of resources, soil, water, air, sunlight, and climate are ignored because they are considered to be "free" and their degradation thus imposes no "costs." "Free" in this sense means they belong to no one and thus to everyone, so their quick exploitation makes sense; otherwise, their perceived short-term economic value will be lost.

So it is that the timber industry, having nothing invested in the growing of the old-growth trees, sees the old-growth forest as free and so all too often ignores the degradation of the land caused by logging. The timber industry contends the wood fiber it harvests is a product of the air and sunlight, and it ignores the qualitative depreciation of the biological capital of the soil.

The timber industry also tends to ignore the creative evolution of the forests they harvest, evolution that is ongoing in the genetic, ecological, and cultural sense. Norman Jacob, as founder of the Pacific Institute for the Study of Cultural and Ecological Sustainability, puts it this way: the "normal" forests of industrialists and the "perfect" markets of economists are timeless, qualitiless, mechanical, and strictly fictional constructs of what in reality is a timeful, qualitative, and organic world.

In a qualitiless world devoid of change and without novelty, efficiency of use in resources is an attractive concept, because it is easy to "know" what is best in a predictable, objective, static, and mechanical world. In such a world, the perspective of relationship in space and the irreversible quality of time do not exist, so "experts" can "tell it like it is" instead of admitting they are "telling it as they perceive it."[36] The economic goal thus becomes the homogenization of the creative, evolutionary process through objectivity, whereas human subjectivity, which at best is only a clear perspective from one point of view, is summarily invalidated.

Although the computer has become a metaphor for our

linear understanding of such things as economics, forestry, and many other fields of endeavor, including science, we still have to contend with our human subjectivity. We still have to deal with the fact that when we optimize one set of circumstances we do not necessarily optimize another.

In a world seen as linear and locomotive, a world in which something goes forward and backward like a train along the same straight track, optimization appears to make sense and is often thought to be somehow synonymous with sustainability. In reality, however, we can neither "optimize" nor even choose what is "best" ecologically, because we live in an evolving world where change and novelty preside and our perceptions are but a kaleidoscope of what *appears to be* at any given point in time.

It is therefore sometimes better to do what is satisfactory, what will suffice, or even what is deemed mediocre, if that is the most we can do and feel intuitively good about it in our humanly subjective way. It is better *not* to "know" what is "ecologically optimum" or what is "ecologically best" in a dynamic world where the only certainty of the present is the uncertainty of the future. When we insist on optimizing or doing what we intellectually "know" is best ecologically, it is inevitably from a economic/political point of view, which is almost always counter-intuitive and ecologically unwise. If, however, we honor our intuition, we will find the place where culture meets Nature and both are mutually sustainable.

12

WHERE CULTURE MEETS NATURE

Today, human society stands at a threshold in its history. We, who think ourselves the pinnacle of earthly creation, are killing the very placenta that nurtures us with our economic myopia and our technological shortcuts and quick fixes. What we are doing to our home planet is but a reflection of what we are doing to ourselves. If we as a society, as a species, choose to smother in our own wastes, we will be the cause of our own demise.

Consider, for example, that the Canadian federal government has been forced to close, at least for several years, large areas of British Columbia's coastal seabed to the harvesting of crabs, prawns, and oysters. The forced closures are due to high levels of dioxin and furans—toxic chemical compounds that not only can cause cancer and birth defects but also have penetrated deeply into the muddy bottom of the ocean floor. These poisons are produced by British Columbian pulp and paper mills in their chlorine-bleaching process used to make paper white and are discharged with impunity into the rivers, estuaries, and open ocean.[37]

Keep in mind that everything, from driftwood to human garbage and poisons, ends up in the sea—the great receptacle of the Earth. Because we perceive the seas of the world to be vast and incorruptible, we take them for granted. In the last analysis, however, the deadliest of all human errors, our arrogance, always produces something invisible and unthinkable until it manifests in crisis proportions. But we don't have to make choices that bring about such disastrous effects. Our choices are not cast in concrete. If what we do the first time doesn't work, we can choose to choose again and create some other outcome.

If we choose to move toward a biologically-adaptable landscape, whatever we do will take the utmost in courage, foresight, and faith. With the right attitude, any mistakes we make may become the wisdom of the future, because mistakes, which are simply misjudgments, stimulate the questions we ask and attempt to answer. But we must act while the Earth still has the strength and the resilience to survive in the face of ongoing errors, and while there still is an ecological "margin of safety" to allow a few more mistakes from which to learn.

To make sure that those who follow us have a chance to correct our errors and to learn from them, we must always remember that all we have to give the next generation is options. An option spent foolishly for short-term economic gains at the expense of long-term ecological sustainability is an option foreclosed. The foolish, greedy expenditure has become a condition of impoverishment, such as liquidating the ancient forests for whatever rationalized reason, because whatever the "other choice" was, it is no more.

Liquidate the ancient forest, and its large old-growth trees are gone. That's obvious. What is not obvious, however, is that a vast array of other options, both visible and invisible, are gone as well.

Each time we make a decision dealing with natural resources, therefore, we must ask: How will our decision either maintain or enhance the options for the future? If we elect to spend this option, what is the choice that will replace it for the next generation?

The generations to come have no choice but to respond to our decisions, which will have become their inherited circumstances. And because the decisions we are making today are inexorably creating the circumstances of the future, in sober reality the future is today.

The whole first part of this book has been necessary to set the stage for another discussion: about the way we can create and maintain a culturally-sustainable environment as a legacy for the future. Such a legacy requires a firm foundation, which in turn must rest on solid cornerstones.

The Cornerstones of a Culturally-Sustainable Environment

The cornerstones of a culturally-sustainable environment for the future are: (1) the choice of introductions, (2) policy, (3) biodiversity, and (4) patterns across the landscape.

The Choice of Introductions

We introduce thoughts, practices, substances, and technologies into the environment, and we usually think of those introductions in terms of development. Development of any kind is therefore the collective introduction of thoughts, practices, substances, and technologies in a commercial strategy to use or extract a given resource. Whatever we introduce into the environment in the name of development will consequently determine how the environment will respond to our presence and to our cultural necessities. It is therefore to our social benefit to pay close attention to what we introduce.

Introduction of a foreign substance, process, or technology has a much greater impact on an ecosystem's ability to function than does taking something away. Consider the effects of some of the things we have introduced into the environment, because these things represent both our sense of values and our behavior. Our initial introduction is our pattern of thought, which determines the way we perceive the Earth and the way we act toward it—either as something sacred to be nurtured or as only a commodity to be converted into money. Because our pattern of thought determines the value we place on various components of an ecosystem, it's our sense of values that determines the way we treat those components and through them the ecosystem as a whole.

In our linear, product-oriented thinking, an old-growth forest is an economic waste if its "conversion potential" is not realized—that is, the only value the old-growth trees have is their potential for being converted into money. Such notions stimulated Professor Garrett Hardin to observe that "Economics, the handmaiden of business, is daily concerned with 'discounting the future,' a mathematical operation, that under high rates of interest, has the effect of making the future beyond a very few years essentially disappear from rational calculation."[38] Unfortunately, Hardin is correct. Conversion potential of resources counts so heavily because the economically-effective horizon in most economic planning is only five years away. Thus, in our traditional linear economic thinking, any merchantable old tree that falls over and reinvests its nutrient capital into the soil is an "economic waste" because its potential was not converted into money.

New equipment is therefore constantly being devised to make harvesting resources like trees ever more efficient. The chain saw, for example, greatly speeded the liquidation of old-growth forests world-wide. Possessed by this new tool, the timber industry and the forestry profession lost all sense of restraint and began cutting forests faster than they could regrow. Further, no forested ecosystem has yet evolved to cope ecologically with the massive systematic and continuous clearcutting made possible by the chain saw and the purely economic thinking behind it.

In our search for "national security" and cheap energy, we are introducing concentrated nuclear waste into many ecosystems, an introduction the impact of which is both global in scale and complex in the extreme. And there is no safe way to introduce the concentrations we are creating. The melt-down of the nuclear reactor at Chernobyl was not potentially so dangerous as was the buried nuclear dump that blew up near Chelyabinsk, in the southern Ural Mountains, in late 1957 or early 1958. The land around Chelyabinsk was dead, and will be for perhaps centuries, over an area of roughly one thousand square kilometers. All that was left standing after the explosion were chimneys.

We have not the slightest idea how to deal safely with the concentrations of nuclear wastes we are introducing into the world. Yet instead of committing our efforts to producing safe, clean solar and wind energy, we cling steadfastly to unsafe, dirty nuclear energy and create thousands of tons of nuclear waste annually through the military-industrial complex and peacetime technology. If we continue this course, the biosphere will eventually adapt to high, generalized concentrations of radioactivity, but most life as we know it will not be here to see that adaptation take place.

Our management of the world's resources is always to maximize the output of material products—putting into operation the "conversion potential." In so doing, we not only deplete the resource base but also produce unmanaged and unmanageable "by-products," often in the form of hazardous "wastes." In unforeseen ways, these "by-products" are altering the way our biosphere functions. In reality, there is no such thing as a "by-product;" there is only an unintended product, which more often than not is undesirable.

Because of unforeseen and usually undesirable effects from many of our introductions, we must shift our thinking from managing for particular short-term products to managing for a desired long-term condition on the landscape, an overall desired outcome of our decisions and actions. To illustrate, we'll examine two very different examples of introductions and their long-term effects. The first example is suppression of fire; the second is the construction of the High Aswan Dam.

It has taken roughly eighty years for our introduction of the suppression of fire to show its effects. Only now, decades after the instigation of livestock grazing and fire suppression into northern Arizona and eastern Oregon, has the significance of the changes in the structure and composition of forests in many areas become evident. The ecological degradation of the ponderosa pine forests in recent times was, ironically, caused by the growth of *too many* trees. This increase in the density of trees was in turn caused by the introduction of livestock grazing and the suppression of fire, which have shifted the open, parklike, pre-settlement forests of huge, stately old trees to dense, closed-canopy stands of less-vigorous young trees—an entirely different forest ecologically.

During the last eighty to a hundred years, the forest floor has shown a general increase in the number of trees and a corresponding increase in the amount of woody fuels. These new forests also show a decrease in the extent of quaking aspen, which often resprouts from roots following fire, and an increase in those species of trees that are more tolerant of the shaded conditions in closed-canopy forests.

Those who study historical fires intensively have failed to document any cases where stand-replacing "crown fires" (those fires that kill the forest by burning through the tops of the trees) occurred in the forests of ponderosa pine of the southwestern United States before 1900. In contrast, however, forests have since 1950 experienced many fires that covered more than five thousand acres and that have totally razed the forests down to mineral soil. Researchers attribute the intensity of these fires to the large amount of woody fuels on the floor of the forests and to the dense stands of young trees within the forests, both of which have become established since 1900.

Some of the trees in these dense thickets, which may include trees of differing ages, have grown into the canopy and form a ladder up which a fire can burn from near the ground into the crowns of the larger trees. Although it is possible that climatic change could account for the increased numbers of large fires, the changes in the forests brought about by more than seventy years of fire suppression is, ironically, the most likely cause of an increasing incidence of large "wildfires."

The development of the High Aswan Dam is the second example of unforeseen effects of many of our introductions. When I was working with a scientific expedition in Egypt in 1963 and 1964, a representative of the Egyptian Ministry of Agriculture spent time with us as we worked just north of the Sudanese border along the Nile. One day three of us from the expedition tried to help this man understand that building—that is, introducing—the High Aswan Dam into the Nile River was an ecological mistake. He could not, however, see beyond the storage of water for irrigation and the generation of electricity—the official government position at that time.

We explained to the Egyptian government representative that building the dam would increase the geographical distribution of the snails that carry the debilitating disease schistosomiasis, a tiny blood fluke, from below the Aswan Dam built by the British in the early 1930s north to at least Khartoum in the Sudan, several hundreds of miles above the new, yet-to-be-completed dam. At that time it was still safe to swim above the British-built Aswan Dam, where the water was too swift and too cold for the snails to live, but it was not safe to swim, or even to catch frogs, in the water below the dam, where the snails already lived.

We told him that the Nile above the high dam would fill

with silt, which would starve the Nile Delta of its annual supply of nutrient-rich sediment and affect farming in a deleterious way. And we told him that the dam could easily become a military target for the Israelis, even as German dams were targets for the British during World War II.

The engineers building the new High Aswan Dam had intended only to store more water and to produce electricity—which they did. But, deprived of the nutrient-rich silt of the Nile's annual flood waters, the population of sardines off the coast of the Nile Delta in the southwestern Mediterranean diminished by ninety-seven percent. In addition, the rich delta, which had been growing in size for thousands of years, is now being rapidly eroded by the Mediterranean, because the Nile is no longer depositing silt at its mouth.

Until the High Aswan Dam was built, the annual sediment-laden waters of the Nile added a millimeter (a little less than a sixteenth of an inch) of nutrient-rich silt to the farms along the river each year. Now that the floods have been stopped by the new dam, the silt not only is collecting upriver from the dam, thus diminishing its water-holding capacity, but also is no longer being deposited on the riverside farms, thus decreasing their fertility. Soon the farmers will have to buy commercial fertilizer—something most of them probably can't afford. In addition, irrigation without flooding causes the soil to become saline, so the Nile Valley, which has been farmed continuously for five thousand years, will within a few centuries have to be abandoned. And finally, schistosomiasis has indeed spread southward to the Sudan.

As we come to recognize the undesirable effects of such introductions as the suppression of fire and the construction of the High Aswan Dam, we must be innovative and daring, and we must focus on controlling the type and amount of processes, substances, and technologies that we *introduce* into an ecosystem to effect a particular outcome. With prudence in our decisions about what to introduce into an ecosystem and how to do it, we can have an environment of desirable quality to support a chosen lifestyle, an environment that can still produce a good mix of products and amenities, but on an ecologically-sustainable basis.

Looking ahead to all effects of introduction is the answer. If we ensure that any material introductions we make into the environment would be biodegradable as food for organisms like bacteria, fungi, and insects, then our "waste" would be their nutriment. In addition, if we use solar- and wind-based energy instead of fossil fuels, and if we recycle all nonrenewable resources in perpetuity, we will shift our pattern of thought from one that is ecologically exploitive to one that is ecologically friendly and sustainable.

We can in fact recycle much, much more than we do, not only the quantity of materials we presently recycle but also the types of materials that we recycle. When I was in Taos, New Mexico, in 1989, for example, someone was constructing a motel and had its entire frame erected when a terrific windstorm suddenly blew the whole frame over. The insurance company insisted that all the *new* lumber, which had been used only to erect the motel's frame, had to be burned. The company would not allow anyone to reuse the lumber out of the fear of being sued if someone somehow got hurt. That fear caused an unmitigated and inexcusable waste of perfectly good lumber.

With a little forethought, the company could have protected itself simply by having the user of the lumber sign a waiver declaring the company not liable for any potential accidents from use of the lumber in building. As it is, we do not, so far as I know, recycle usable lumber; instead, we liquidate old-growth forests and burn "unsafe," "usable," often new lumber.

The construction industry engages in many wasteful practices. Having lived for two years in Las Vegas, Nevada, where housing developments run rampant, I am appalled at just how wasteful the construction industry really is. This is especially true when companies are oriented strictly toward quantity and are in a hurry.

Waste that threatens the environment and human life rather than sustaining it must be relegated to the strictly-linear materialistic economics of the twentieth century. The twenty-first century must begin the era of balances, of cyclic-linear ecologically-sound economics in which the health and welfare of our home planet takes precedence over our puny, selfish, materialistic wants. We must understand and accept that it is the collective thoughts, practices, substances, and technologies that we introduce into the environment that determine the way the landscape will respond to our presence and our social necessities over time. This new way of introducing things into the environment will, of course, require new policies.

Policy

Laws and legal mandates contain inherently conflicting language about what may and may not be allowed in the name of management, although the intent of the law is usually abundantly clear. But agencies, either because of tradition or because of the instruction of a political administration, all too often use the interpretation of a specific policy to get around a given law and its mandates, even one with clear intent. Policy is thus used to meet corporate/political desires rather than to meet the ecological necessities of the environment for which the law was originally intended; witness the extended struggle over the Endangered Species Act.

Policy is therefore a seriously weak link within agencies, because values cannot be legislated or mandated by law. So, despite the best intentions of public law, policy is used by those with vested economic/political interests to "legally" circumvent the law.

Then, to fix the problems resulting from such immoral uses of policy, policy is used to justify rewarding or subsidizing agency personnel, industrialists, and politicians to cause them to fulfill not only their legal duties but also their moral obligations to the public, present and future. Such incentives are moral bribes.

If we are to remain within our cultural capacity, we must manage for a desired condition of the landscape—which means that policy must reflect, both in letter and in spirit, the law and its mandates. If we are to have an environmental policy that is commensurate with ecological sustainability and cultural capacity, therefore, it must be achieved by a consensus of the people, not the self-serving agendas of the agencies, which are at the mercy of the self-serving agendas of Congress, the presidential administration, and private industry. For an environmental policy to be authentic and workable, we also must achieve consensus on a policy that protects the ecological integrity of the environment and its cultural capacity from the irreversible negative aspects of development.

To create and accept sound policies on environment and development, we must first agree that the long-term health of the environment takes precedence over the short-term profits to be made through careless or continual development. Then we must agree that ecological sustainability is primarily an issue of managing *ourselves* in terms of cultural capacity and only secondarily an issue of managing our environment. We thus come to a different kind of distinction about sustainability: nothing can or will be sustained without our first deciding what we choose to sustain and develop, and why, and what we choose not to sustain or develop, and why.

Converting Nature's landscape into a culturally-oriented landscape requires a balance between the paths of development that are sustained and those that are not. In some situations, development is consistent with creating an enjoyable, productive, and sustainable culturally-oriented landscape—cultural capacity. But everything that is sustained or developed in a finite world is chosen selectively. Only in a constantly-expanding world could we avoid the choices of items to sustain and develop, and in what way, and why—or those items not to sustain and develop.

The type of development that we choose is based on and controlled by policies, stated and unstated. Each policy is either a true or a false reflection of public law; in that sense, the path of development may be more or less cooperative and environmentally benign or more or less competitive and environmentally malignant. But whichever path we choose, that choice is ours. We cannot escape it.

This brings us back to the question of sustainability. We cannot manage sustainability for its ownsake, because sustainability is most often regarded in terms of some one thing: corn, salmon, water, cattle, trees, and so on. Beyond that, every ecosystem evolves inevitably toward a critical state in which a minor event sooner or later leads to a catastrophic event, one that alters the ecosystem in some way.

As a young Douglas fir forest grows old, for example, it converts energy from the sun to living tissue, which ultimately dies and accumulates as organic debris on the floor of the forest. There, through decomposition, the organic debris releases the energy stored in its dead tissue. A forest is, therefore, a dissipative system in that energy acquired from the sun is dissipated gradually through decomposition or rapidly through fire.

Of course, rates of decomposition vary: A leaf rots quickly and releases its stored energy rapidly. Woody material, on the other hand, rots much more slowly, often over centuries. As the woody material accumulates, so does the energy stored in its fibers. Before their suppression, fires burned frequently enough to generally control the amount of energy stored in the accumulating woody debris by burning it up, thus protecting the forest for decades, even centuries, from a catastrophic fire that would kill the forest.

Over time, however, a forest eventually builds up enough woody debris to fuel a catastrophic fire. Once available, the fuel needs only one or two very dry, hot years with lightning storms to ignite such a fire, which kills the forest and sets it back in succession to the earliest stage of grasses and herbs. From this early stage a new forest again evolves toward the

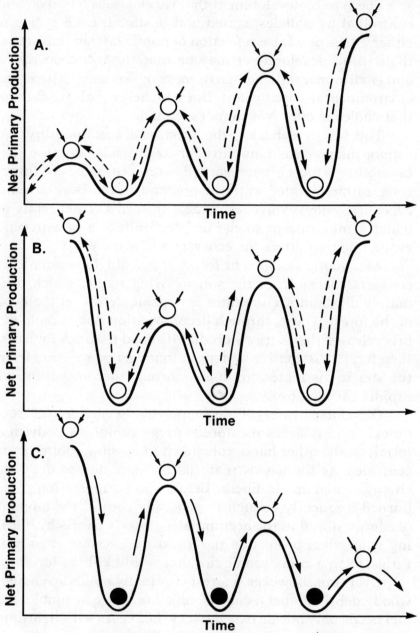

old-growth stage, again accumulating stored energy in dead wood, again organizing itself toward the next critical state, a catastrophic fire, which starts the cycle over.

After a fire, earthquake, volcanic eruption, flood, or landslide, a biological system may eventually be able to approximate what it was through resilience—the ability of the system to retain the integrity of its basic relationships (Fig. 16). A 700-year-old forest that burned could, therefore, be replaced by another, albeit different, 700-year-old forest on the same acreage. In this way, despite a series of catastrophic fires, a forest ecosystem could remain a forest ecosystem. In

Figure 16. *Balancing the Ball:* The existence of a particular ecosystem is a tenuous balancing act. An ecosystem (the ball balanced on the peak) is in a constant state of disequilibrium from the pressure of forces outside itself (solid arrows above the ball). Such a system responds to external pressures by internal, self-reinforcing feedback loops. In addition, the system tends continually to organize itself from one critical state to another over time (dashed, two-way arrows). *Net primary production* is simply the maximum amount of living plant tissue that the system can produce at any one time in a particular stage of its development; thus the higher the peak on which the ball rests, the greater the net primary production. In the top row, A, you see an ecosystem representing its early development on the left and maximum development on the right. This system is constantly moving from one state to another over time. B shows an ecosystem in which a catastrophic disturbance, such as a fire, has temporarily set back one of its developmental stages (solid, one-way arrows in the trough between peaks and balls) and thereby temporarily reduced its net primary production. This is somewhat analogous to a student being held over for another year in the third grade rather than advancing to the fourth grade with his or her classmates. In C is an ecosystem in which a severe, prolonged disturbance, such as the cumulative effects of air pollution, has set the system back in several of its developmental stages and greatly reduced its net primary production over a protracted period of time. Although such a system may or may not recover, depending on the type and severity of the disturbance, it could evolve in unknown ways to a new set of selective pressures.

this sense, the old-growth forests of western North America have been evolving from one catastrophic fire to the next, from one critical state to the next.

Because of the dynamic nature of the evolving ecosystems and because each system is constantly organizing itself from one critical state to another, we can only "manage" an ecosystem for its possible evolution, not for a sustained yield of products. The only sustainability for which we can manage, therefore, is whatever ensures an ecosystem's ability to adapt to evolutionary change (such as warming of the global climate) in a way that may be favorable for us. In other

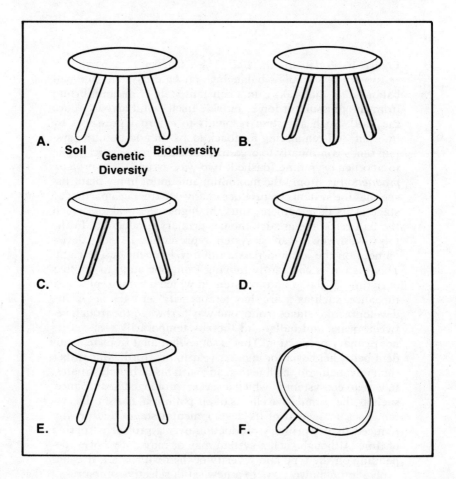

words, we need to manage for choice, which is synonymous with biodiversity, which is in turn an ecological insurance policy for the flexibility of future choice. One way to insure future flexibility is through planning for redundancy.

Biodiversity

With or without the human hand, every ecosystem adapts in some way. Our heavy-handedness precludes our ability to guess, much less to know, what kind of adaptations will emerge. We must therefore pay particular attention to ecological redundancy, of which biodiversity is the "nuts and bolts."

Each ecosystem contains built-in redundancies, which means it contains more than one species that can perform similar functions. Such redundancies give an ecosystem the

Figure 17. *The Three-Legged Stool:* Redundancy in the biological functions of various species is an environmental insurance policy built into every ecosystem. An ecosystem needs diversity of at least three important kinds: diversity of soil, genetic diversity, and biodiversity (A). If one thinks of each of these kinds of diversity as an individual leg of an old-fashioned, three-legged milking stool, it becomes clear that if we lose one leg (one kind of diversity), the stool will fall over, as in F. In reality, however, a considerable amount of functional redundancy is built into an ecosystem, which means that more than one species can perform the same or a very similar function. This results in a stabilizing effect similar to having a six-legged milking stool, but with two legs in each of three locations, as in B. Thus, if one leg is removed (C), it makes no difference which one it is; the stool will remain standing. If a second leg is removed (D), the location of the removed leg is crucial because if it is removed from the same place as the first leg in (C), the stool will fall. If a third leg is removed (E), the location of the removed leg is even more crucial, because removal has now pushed the system to the limits of its stability, and it is courting ecological collapse. The removal of one more piece, no matter how well intentioned, will cause the system to collapse (F).

resilience either to resist change or to bounce back after disturbance. But we have little knowledge about which species do what and the way in which they do it (Fig. 17). So when we tinker willy-nilly with an ecosystem's structure to suit our short-term economic desires, we lose species to extinction and thus reduce the ecosystem's biodiversity. With decreased biodiversity, we lose choices for management, which directly affects the Earth's cultural capacity and therefore our lifestyles. The loss of biodiversity may so alter the ecosystem that it can no longer produce what we valued it for in the first place: a desired lifestyle.

If we want to choose the quality of our lifestyle by determining the cultural capacity of the land over time, we must abandon the cherished mechanical notion of sustained yield. We must instead shift our attention to managing for a sustainable array of choices—which means we must afford the maximum protection to the existing biodiversity, regardless of the apparent short-term economic and political costs.

To those who insist that we can't convert capitalism to an ecologically-friendly form quickly enough to protect existing biodiversity, I point out that at the beginning of World War II we transformed our entire economy to a wartime basis in a matter of a year or so. And in a similarly short time we changed it back again to a peacetime economy at the end of the war. The mechanism that allowed us to shift to the wartime economy and back again was simply a choice of priorities. Similarly, a shift to an ecologically-friendly economy today, which will also serve for tomorrow, is a choice of industrial/political priorities.

We must make the only viable choice we can: to convert our society consciously into an ecologically-friendly version of capitalism as quickly as possible through the purposeful protection of biodiversity as our major source of renewable energy and the novelty of environmental adaptation. After all, the selection of items to sustain and not to sustain in our capitalistic system is a choice of priorities in economic allocation—of wants, desires, needs, and demands as opposed to necessities.

Long-term ecological wholeness and biological richness of the landscape must become the measure of economic health. If we want the land to be able to provide for us, we must do our best to care first and foremost for land. This matter of caring for the land brings us to the patterns we create across the landscape.

Patterns Across the Landscape

Spatial patterns we see on landscapes result from complex interactions among physical, biological, and social forces. Most landscapes have also been influenced by the cultural patterns of human use, so the resulting landscape is an ever-changing mosaic of unmanaged and managed patches of habitat, which vary in size, shape, and arrangement.

The pattern of changes in the North American forest before the Europeans settled here was closely related to topography and to the pattern of Nature's disturbances, especially fire. When the Europeans began to disturb the landscape through such introductions as livestock grazing and the suppression of fire, changes they made altered the patterns of our forests and ranges only selectively, because they accompanied human settlement and the consequent exploitation of the land. Nevertheless, those human-created disturbances began to cause unforeseen changes in the landscape, changes we are now having difficulty dealing with.

A disturbance is any relatively discrete event that disrupts the structure of a population and/or community of plants and animals, or disrupts the ecosystem as a whole and thereby changes the availability of resources and/or restructures the physical environment. We can characterize cycles of ecological disturbances ranging from small grass fires to major hurricanes by their distribution in space and the size of disturbance they make, as well as their frequency, duration, intensity, severity, synergism, and predictability.

In the Pacific Northwest, for example, vast areas of un-broken forest that were at one time in our National Forest System have been fragmented by clearcutting and have been rendered homogeneous by cutting small patches of old-growth timber, by converting these patches into plantations of genetically-selected nursery stock, and by leaving small, uncut patches between the clearcuts. This "staggered-setting system," as it is called, required an extensive network of roads. So before half the land area was cut, almost every water catchment was penetrated by logging roads. And the whole of the National Forest System became an all-of-a-piece patchwork quilt with few, if any, forested areas large enough to support those species of birds and mammals that required the interior of the forest as their habitat.

Changing a formerly diverse landscape into a cookie-cutter sameness has profound implications. The spread of such ecological disturbances of Nature as fires, floods, wind-storms, and outbreaks of insects, coupled with such distur-bances of human society as urbanization and pollution, are important processes in shaping the landscape. The function of those processes is influenced by the diversity of the existing landscape pattern.

Disturbances vary in character and are often controlled by physical features and patterns of vegetation. The varia-bility of each disturbance, along with the area's previous history and its particular soil, leads to the existing vegeta-tional mosaic.

The greatest single disturbance to the ecosystem is human disruption—introductions of practices, substances, and technologies. These disruptions result most often from our attempts to control the size—minimize the scale—of the various cycles of Nature's disturbance with which the eco-system has evolved and to which it has become adapted. Among the most obvious (and well intentioned) is the suppression of fire.

As we struggle to minimize the scale of Nature's disturbances in the ecosystem, we alter the system's ability to resist
or to cope with the multitude of invisible stresses to which
the system adapts through the existence and dynamics of the
very cycles of disturbance that we "control." Today's forest
fires, for example, are more intense and more extensive than
in the past because of the build-up of fuels since the onset
of fire suppression. Many forested areas are primed for catastrophic fire. Outbreaks of plant-damaging insects and diseases spread more rapidly over areas of forest and rangeland
that have been stressed through the removal of Nature's own
disturbances, to which they are adapted and which control
an area's insects and diseases.

The precise mechanisms by which ecosystems cope with
stress vary, but one mechanism is tied closely to the genetic
selectivity of its species. Thus, as an ecosystem changes and
is influenced by increasing magnitudes of stresses, the replacement of a stress-sensitive species with a functionally
similar but more stress-resistant species preserves the ecosystem's overall productivity. Such replacements of species—redundancy—can result only from within the existing
pool of biodiversity. Nature's redundancy must be protected
and encouraged.

Human-introduced disturbances, especially fragmentation of habitat, impose stresses with which the ecosystem is
ill adapted to cope. Biogeographical studies show that "connectivity" of habitats with the landscape is of prime importance to the persistence of plants and animals in viable
numbers in their respective habitats—again, a matter of biodiversity. In this sense the landscape must be considered a
mosaic of interconnected patches of habitats, like vegetated
fencerows, which act as corridors or routes of travel between
patches of farm forest, livestock allotments, or other suitable
habitats.

Whether populations of plants and animals survive in a
particular landscape depends on the rate of local extinctions

from a patch of habitat and on the rate with which an organism can move among patches of habitat. Those species living in habitats isolated as a result of fragmentation are therefore less likely to persist. Fragmentation of habitat, the most serious threat to biological diversity, is the primary cause of the present global crisis in the rate of biological extinctions. On public lands much, if not most, of the fragmentation of the habitat is a "side effect" of management policies that stress the short-term production of commodities at the long-term expense of the environment. Actually, there are, however, no "side effects"—only unintentional effects!

Modifying the connectivity among patches of habitat strongly influences the abundance of species and their patterns of movement. The size, shape, and diversity of patches also influence the patterns of species abundance, and the shape of a patch may determine the species that can use it as habitat. The interaction between the processes of a species' dispersal and the pattern of a landscape determines the temporal dynamics of its populations. Local populations of organisms that can disperse great distances may not be as strongly affected by the spatial arrangement of patches of habitat as are more sedentary species.

Our responsibility now is to make decisions about patterns across the landscape while considering the consequences of our decisions on the potential cultural capacity of the generations of the future. The decisions are up to us, but one thing is clear: although the current trend toward homogenizing the landscape may help maximize short-term money profits, it devastates the long-term biological sustainability and adaptability of the land and thus devastates the long-term cultural capacity. Our greed thus disrupts the stability of the future.

It's not the relationship of numbers that confers stability on ecosystems, it's the relationship of patterns. Stability flows from the patterns of relationship that have evolved among the various species. A stable, culturally-oriented system, even a very diverse one, that fails to support these co-evolved relationships has little chance of being sustainable.

To create viable culturally-oriented landscapes we must stop managing for fragmentation by focusing on such commodity-producing artifacts as forest clearcuts, agricultural fields, and livestock-grazing allotments. Because ecological sustainability and adaptability depend on the connectivity of the landscape, we must ground our culturally-designed landscapes within Nature's evolved patterns and take advantage of them if we are to have a chance of creating a quality environment that is both pleasing to our cultural senses and ecologically adaptable.

We must move toward connectivity of the landscape. If we are to have adaptable landscapes with desirable cultural capacities to pass to our heirs, we must focus on two primary things: (1) caring for and "managing" for a sustainable connectivity and biological richness between such areas as forest clearcuts, agricultural fields, and livestock-grazing allotments within the context of the landscape as a whole, and (2) protecting existing biodiversity—including habitats—at any price for the long-term sustainability of the ecological wholeness and the biological richness of the patterns we create across its landscapes.

The Window of Our Cultural Soul

The shift from attempting to "manage" Nature through economics, science, and technology (which all too often assumes the attitude of pillaging) to the sacred act of gardening with Nature through spirituality and art is a shift from the intellectual pursuit of arrogance through coercion and control to the spiritual pursuit of humility through cooperation and coordination. To understand this shift, however, we must first have some concept of the meaning embodied in the words "spirituality" and "art."

Spirituality

" 'Spiritual' refers to the experience of being related to or in touch with an 'other' that transcends one's individual sense of self and gives meaning to one's life at a deeper than intellectual level."[39] In a spiritual experience, therefore, one encounters something larger or greater than oneself. We need not conceptualize the "other" that we encounter in any traditionally religious terms.

The transcendent other may be seen as a supernatural deity, such as God, or as a natural entity, such as the Earth. It may be something existing objectively "out there," like the process of evolution, or it may be a subjective inner phenomenon like creative inspiration. It may originate independently of the human sphere, like wilderness, or it may be a product of human culture, like a community. For some people, the "other" may not even be a specific, definable entity but might instead be an undefinable sense of being "grounded" or "centered," a feeling that gives meaning to existence.

Regardless of the way this sense of the transcendent "other" is encountered and experienced, it is more than just a passing, casual occurrence. It gives meaning to one's life in some important way and helps define one's life in the greater context of the Universe. The experience is felt at some undefinable level of "knowing" that is far deeper than that of intellectual knowledge. It is usually difficult if not impossible for us to put such an experience into words, but we feel it in our hearts, and it may stir powerful emotions in us. Although we encounter experiences of this kind in many contexts and settings, we may find their primary setting to be Nature.

Nature is often more than a setting for a spiritual experience. She can conjure other images in our personal and social psyches. According to psychologist Carl Jung, our human psyche has different levels or layers, much as an onion has a number of different layers. Immediately below the level of our conscious awareness lies the personal unconscious, including our personal feelings, attitudes, and memories, which we have repressed and "cut off" from our conscious awareness. At a deeper level lies what Jung called the "collective unconscious," which contains the basic, intuitive patterns of behavior, emotions, and imagery common to all humans through time. These intuitive patterns, or "archetypes," not only guide but also give meaning to our interactions with other human beings and with the Universe as a whole.

Archetypes function like templates in the unconscious mind, where they give rise to the symbolic images that enter conscious expression through dreams, myths, religious experiences, and spontaneous fantasies. One of the most important ways in which archetypes express themselves is through both positive and negative "projection," a psychological phenomenon through which we experience the contents of the unconscious mind outside of ourselves as if they belonged to someone or something else. This is analogous to an image on film being projected or cast outward through the lens of the projector and viewed at some distance on a screen: A person sitting in the audience is unaware of the projector and perceives only the "independent" image on the screen.

A classic example of a negative projection with which I think we can all identify is that of an "enemy." If I can identify an enemy, I can project (through my lens) the unconscious, repressed traits that I detest about myself and with which I refuse to deal (the film) onto someone or something else (the neutral, unaware screen). I can thus hate what I think my enemy stands for without having to acknowledge and deal with the fact that what I "see" in my enemy is my own repressed self-loathing. I think I can avoid dealing with my repressed self-loathing by projecting it onto the screen of an innocent person. In so doing, I think the unwanted reflection I see belongs to the other person rather than to my own inner self.

What, you might ask, has this got to do with spirituality and Nature? Consider that Nature is viewed by some as an enemy to be conquered, by others as a commodity to be converted into money, and by still others as a representation of spirituality. All of these perceptions can be thought of as projections of unconscious archetypes onto various elements of the environment or onto Nature as a whole. Here, one might ask what is being projected onto Nature, why it is being projected, and what implications these projections may have both for the individual and for the collective psyche.

Today people turn to the literature of mythology in order to understand the symbolic portrayals of the archetypes that are active in the collective psyche of human culture. From this vantage point, one approach to understanding the spiritual significance of Nature is to study the gods and goddesses who have been associated throughout human history with the various aspects of Nature. In Greek mythology, for example, there is Demeter, the goddess of vegetation, fertility, and agriculture; Pan, the unrefined deity of woods and fields; and many others, some of which are not necessarily gods and goddesses but lesser spirits.

Mythological characters still inspire the imagination of contemporary people and are sometimes used to capture feelings and spiritual portents that defy definition. Artemis, the Moon Goddess of the forest and the hunt, for example, has been chosen as the "Goddess of Conservation," and Gaia, the Earth Goddess, has been adopted as the personification of the deep-ecologist's view of the Earth as a whole, living organism.

The most compelling example is the archetype of the Great Mother, a powerful psychological complex that can have either a positive, nurturing effect or a negative, destructive effect on the psychological development of an individual. The concept of "Mother Nature" or "Mother Earth" in her benevolent and malevolent moods is a personification of this archetype, which is a recurrent and increasing projection onto Nature.

Unconscious archetypes have powerful effects on the way people experience, relate to, and behave in the world. It is therefore important for the conscious mind to be able to relate in a constructive way to the material of the unconscious archetypes. This conscious relation to the archetypes has traditionally been the function of mythological symbols, rites, and rituals of a religious nature.

Myths provide balance between self-expression and self-restraint, between self-protection and self-restriction. Myths limit human cultures so that nonhuman beings can also find homes in the body of the Earth. Because wisdom cannot depend on perfect knowledge, which is nonexistent, myths are the bridge between imperfect knowledge and the perfect knowing that reaches beyond knowledge, for which there is no expression.

But in our modern Western culture we have lost the spiritual meaning of and the cultural guidance from most of our ancient symbols and rituals. So in this era of spiritual bankruptcy and symbolic illiteracy, people are beginning to turn back to Nature to give expression to the archetypal experiences that are no longer evoked by traditional religious images and rituals.

When archetypes are projected onto Nature's unaltered environments, these environments evoke powerful emotions of profound significance to the individual. Experiences of this kind are critical to spiritual/psychological health because they draw people, individually and collectively, toward both a connection with Nature in the greater context of the Universe and a relationship with the transcendent archetypes that underlie their individual and their collective cultural personalities.

So long as the archetypal projections remain unconscious, there will be severe problems in our society, because we do not realize that our experiences come from within our psyches, and we will instead believe that they are due entirely to something "out there." Thus a person who is projecting an archetype tends to perceive the world in terms of subjective opposites, ideals, and absolutes, a projection that blinds the person to the objective nature of the "other" onto which the archetype is being projected. This blindness causes people to disregard objective information, to hold unrealistic expectations, and to behave in rigid, even fanatical ways.

Healthy relationships with both people and things require one to become conscious of the archetypal projections in one's own perceptions and behavior and to see the difference between the inner archetype and the outer object or person onto which it is being projected. Withdrawing unwanted projections through conscious awareness is a frightening and painful process, one that involves feelings of loss and disillusionment. Ultimately, however, it leads to a balanced, free, and realistic appreciation of both the inner subjective and the outer objective aspects of the Universe, and to what may be termed Cosmic Consciousness.

As we become aware of the way we project archetypes onto Nature, we acquire a sort of "double vision," and experiencing Nature becomes like peering out of a house through a pane of window glass. Through the window we see objects that lie outside the house, and simultaneously we see reflections of things that lie inside the house. Similarly, we can observe the workings of the outer world of Nature through physics and biology while at the same time Nature reflects back to us the inner workings and images of our own psychological world. This phenomenon is perhaps most clearly illustrated in the night sky, where stars and constellations bear names and images of our mythological heritage while concurrently serving as an entry into the scientific understanding of the physical universe. And it is through art that this "double vision" of the inner and the outer are expressed simultaneously.

Art

Art is not only the expression of this "double vision" but also a window to our souls. In this sense, art and mythology are one. They embody an inner experience expressed in an outer, symbolic manner through the conscious production or arrangement of sounds, colors, forms, movements, or other elements in a way that affects the sense of beauty, the sense of Self. Although most people probably think of art specifically as the production of beauty in a graphic or plastic medium, art also encompasses the sheer enjoyment of beauty for its own sake.

The historic foundations of much of our contemporary American sense of aesthetics in landscapes are found in European and American art and literature. The works of seventeenth, eighteenth, and nineteenth century painters and critics concerned with the beauty of the fine arts both depicted and evoked images of neat, tidy landscapes. Although they bore a resemblance to Nature's landscapes, they had been cleansed of Nature's seemingly untidy aspects.

These stylized, English landscapes became the nineteenth-century models of American parks, private gardens, and valued landscape scenes, much as they are today. To me, this British notion of tidiness equates with a compulsive sense of having to control the environment. It is a translocation of European myth from the Old World in which it evolved to the New World, where it was out of place, where it was forcibly superimposed on an environment totally different from that of Europe.

During the eighteenth century, however, writers and painters began to see beauty in the apparently chaotic, clearly wild images of a continent with greater physical and biological diversity than that of Europe. Baron Fredrich von Humboldt of Germany was one of these people. As a founding father of modern geography, he was acutely aware of the effect beautiful landscapes had on the human imagination and of the relationship landscapes forged between our inner world of ideas and feelings and our outer world of physical things. Humboldt recognized the different quality of enjoyment and feelings evoked by viewing a forest or a meadow as opposed to those conjured by dissecting a plant.

John Ruskin, the English art critic, although not a geographer by title, advanced many of Humboldt's ideas. For him, the individual elements of the late-eighteenth-century landscape were to be dissected for description and observation and then synthesized for an understanding of the whole. Ruskin found such understanding to hinge on a knowledge of the relationships among geological processes, climate, and other physical processes. Within these relationships, said Ruskin, were the essential components necessary to give expression to a landscape's innate beauty, unity, and harmony, should one wish to express them. In other words, Ruskin saw that a landscape was a matter of characterizing the whole in terms of its pieces and its pieces in terms of the whole.

Despite advances in viewing landscapes with an eye toward their artistic beauty, Americans needed to evolve a landscape myth of place in time, a myth that would be unique to North America. Americans became increasingly convinced that transferring a sense of European landscape myth to the North American continent was no longer tenable. But it wasn't until the 1930s and 1940s that Aldo Leopold, the father of American ecology, gave voice to the need for a conscious "land aesthetic." Such an aesthetic, wrote Leopold, must deal not only with Nature's landscapes but also with humanity's cultural landscapes. It must be a land aesthetic grounded in ecological awareness and sensitivity as well as in sound landscape husbandry.

Leopold valued the historical aspects of a landscape in that its history gave him an intimate knowledge of the way it came to be as it was. He valued its nonvisual characteristics in the sense of its ability to act as a "soundscape" of Nature's music—such characteristics as the songs of birds, insects, trees, and of the wind; as a "touchscape" of such textures as the physical feel of a tree's bark, the prick of a rose's thorn, and the coolness of flowing water; as a "smell-scape" of such odors as the perfume of flowers and the tang of ozone after a thunderstorm. He valued the possibilities the land offered for myriad intimate interactions between himself and Nature in a particular area for which he could evolve a particular sense of place and of well-being.

Today there are two approaches to landscape, the objective and the subjective. The objective approach focuses on the visual aspects, which are composed of form and elements, and views human beings as separate from the landscape. The landscape can affect people and people can affect it through manipulation, but there is no "communication" between them—something that makes irrelevant a search for meaning in a landscape. This view allows for the concentration on specific elements of a landscape as commodities at the expense of the long-term health of the whole.

The subjective approach, on the other hand, offers insight into values and meanings. It attends to the structural and functional characteristics of a particular place as well as human responses to them. It can be thought of as the result of people projecting their archetypal emotions, feelings, and ideas onto their surroundings in such a way that a knowledge of the landscape is gained through personal interaction with it.

People "communicate" with the landscape. In so doing they change the landscape and are changed by it, because conversation is not limited to a discourse between humans or even to the present. And to converse with any part of Nature is to be in unity with it, whatever it is—even with the stars. So our communication with our respective landscapes is not only relevant but also critical both to the well-being of human society and to the long-term health of the landscapes themselves. That sort of communication brings us to the notion of gardening.

And a Sense of Gardening

Gardening is the act in which spirituality and art merge into the context of Nature's landscape. It is where we use the form and function of Universal Laws to transpose in graphic form the cultural beauty and spiritual harmony of our inner landscape to the fluid medium of Nature's outer landscape. Gardening is the conscious marriage of cultural myth and Universal Laws of Being. To garden is to bring Nature, art, and our souls into harmony with one another in such a way that one cannot tell where Nature ends and art begins, and vice versa.

To garden the Earth, be it a tiny garden in a backyard, a city park, a prairie, or a forest, we must begin by gardening our minds and our souls. James Allen, British philosopher, states this beautifully:

A man's mind may be likened to a garden, which may be intelligently cultivated or allowed to run wild; but whether cultivated or neglected, it must, and will, *bring forth*. If no useful seeds are *put* into it, then an abundance of useless weed seed will *fall* therein, and will continue to produce their kind.

Just as a gardener cultivates his plot, keeping it free from weeds, and growing the flowers and fruits which he requires, so may a man tend the garden of his mind, weeding out all the wrong, useless, and impure thoughts, and cultivating toward perfection the flowers and fruits of right, useful, and pure thoughts. By pursuing this process, a man sooner or later discovers that he is the master gardener of his soul, the director of his life. He also reveals, within himself, the laws of thought, and understanding, with ever-increasing accuracy, how the thought forces and mind elements operate in the shaping of his character, circumstances, and destiny.[40]

Only when we have the discipline to garden the inner landscape of our minds and our souls, weeding out all inharmonious thoughts, will our inner harmony be consummated in the outer landscape. Whether we wish to admit it or not, says ecological restorationist William Jordan, the world really is a garden that invites, even requires, our constant participation and habitation. In this sense, gardening the Earth means to negotiate a new reality with Nature, one that is based on Universal Laws and on our spiritual evolution, because the patterns created on the landscape by a society are a true "pictorial" reflection of its collective spiritual attainment and ecological understanding as well as the economics of its "management." Note that the root word for both *ecology* and *economics* is based on the Greek word for *house*. Ecology is the study of the house, and economics is its management.

I say "spiritual attainment," because gardening is an act born out of our love for the Earth. Love creates an openness to experience, an unfolding without judgment. It expands awareness of and compassion for oneself and others in relationship, and its intimacy permits connectivity of distance—even unto the generations of the future. Love personalizes the Universe while keeping it intrinsically free unto itself.

It was from this sense of a personalized, loving relationship with the Earth that Aldo Leopold wrote: "The average dolled-up estate merely proves what we will some day learn to acknowledge: that bread and beauty grow best together. Their harmonious integration can make farming not only a business but an art; the land not only a food-factory but an instrument for self-expression, on which each can play music of his own choosing." It is hard for us, said Leopold, to visualize that creating an artistically-beautiful landscape is not the prerogative of "esthetic priests" but of "dirt farmers." A farmer designs fields with plowshare and seed; a farmer not only wields spade and pruning shears but also determines the presence or absence of plants and animals in a particular place and time. In this sweep of human thought are the seeds of change, "including, perhaps, a rebirth of that social dignity which ought to inhere in land-ownership."[41]

I would today change the notion of "land-*ownership*" to land-*trusteeship*, because we "own" nothing but our thoughts and our behavior. Everything else we merely borrow both from Nature and from our children, and their children, and theirs into the blue haze of the future's horizon. In addition, ownership connotes the present in the present for the present, but trusteeship connotes the maintenance and protection of the principle, held in trust by adults in the present for the benefit of the future—the children, the trustees.

I feel a sense of trusteeship when nature writer Wendell Berry writes about farming, which, he says, "cannot take place except in nature; therefore, if nature does not thrive, farming cannot thrive." We know, too, says Berry, that we are an inseparable part of Nature, that we do not stand safely outside of Her. We are in Nature and of Nature simply because we exist, and beyond that, we *are* Nature while we use Her. If Nature cannot thrive as and while we use Her, human society cannot thrive. Therefore, "the appropriate measure of farming [gardening] . . . is the world's health and our health, and these are inescapably *one* measure."

If, says Berry, all farmers on all farms would accept the responsibility of knowing where they are—in whose garden—and of consulting the "genius of the place," they would ask Nature what She would be doing with that place if no one were farming it. They would ask what Nature would permit them to do there and how they best could do it with the least harm to the place and its nonhuman and human neighbors. And they would ask what Nature would help them to do. Then, after each question, knowing that Nature will respond, they would attend carefully to Her response.[42]

Farming is therefore "gardening" when it is done by Nature's measure, which is predicated on the answers Nature has given to a farmer's questions about his or her particular place. This means that "farmers must tend farms that they know and love, farms small enough to know and love, using tools and methods that they know and love, in the company of neighbors that they know and love."[43]

Gardening is giving to the Earth and all its inhabitants, including ourselves, the only things of value that we each have to give: our love, our trust, and our respect. The very process of gardening is thus the process through which we become attuned with Nature and, through Nature, with ourselves. To engage in the act of gardening is to commune with and to know the God in ourselves, in one another, and in all of Nature. To treat the Earth in the sacred manner of gardening as a vehicle to know God is our global imperative if we want to coexist as truly equitable and peaceful human societies. To garden the earth is to love Nature.

13

A QUESTION OF MORAL CHOICE

As human beings, we participate in the creation of the world in which we live, because our very existence and that of every other living thing is involved in this on-going act of Creation. As conscious co-creators, each generation of human beings is the moral ecological guide for the generations to come. In this sense, our impressions of our ancestors are reflections of the care they took of the land we inherited. As ancestors of the generations of the future, we will have their impressions of us mirrored in the care we take of the land they inherit.

Thus, if we would leave a more favorable impression than we received, we must begin now, consciously, to create a new paradigm for our trusteeship of the land, one based on a sense of place and permanence, a sense of ecological health and sustainability, a sense of creation and landscape artistry, and a sense of humility and humanity. Although such a harmonious union between people and the Earth is not new in the world, it is new to our modern Western psyche. It is the act of sacred participation with the Earth through which we give expression to the artistry and the beauty that for so long has lain dormant in our souls.

The images we see on the landscape are but reflections in our social mirror of the way we treat ourselves and one another. As we compete and fight and live in fear, so we destroy the land; as we cooperate and coordinate and live in love, so we heal the land. It cannot be otherwise, because reflected on the collective outer landscape of the Earth we see the individual inner landscape of our being. We see ourselves reflected in the Universal mirror of the way we care for the land, which sustains and nurtures us, because we and the land are one.

So the question is: how do we participate in creating our world, and to what extent? To answer this question, we must decide if: (1) we are going to create our society in such a way that its effects on the land are environmentally compatible with our society, or (2) we are going to create our society in such a way that its effects on the land are environmentally hostile to our social existence. On the one hand, we accept our responsibility as trustees of Nature's bounty and act accordingly; on the other, we alienate ourselves from our own planet. The choice is ours, and *we must choose!*

Two things are clear: First, nothing will change the effect of our choices on the collective outer landscape until we first change the cause in our individual inner landscapes; nothing will change until we move toward conscious simplicity in both our inner and our outer lifestyles. Second, the only way to save the existence of human society on Planet Earth—and perhaps someday even humanity itself—is through unequivocal cooperation and coordination not only between and among human beings and societies but also between humanity and the Earth. This, then, becomes the moral issue of balance between our inner and our outer landscapes.

Do We Owe Anything to the Future?

Do we owe anything to the future? If so, we must understand and accept that there are no external fixes for internal moral imperatives; there are only internal shifts of consciousness and morally-correct intentions and behavior. We must also understand and accept that all we can bequeath to the generations of the future is options—the right to choose as we have done.

To protect that right of choice, we must ask new, morally-right, future-oriented questions, questions that determine the quality of life we wish to have and that we wish our children to be able to have. We need to determine first and foremost how much of a given resource is necessary to leave intact in the environment as a biological reinvestment in the health and continued productivity of the ecosystem. We must, at any cost, be it economical or political, protect the quality of the soil, water, and air of our home planet if humanity and its society is to survive. We also must view the environment from the standpoint of biological and cultural necessities as opposed to limitless cultural wants, desires, needs, and demands, and, if necessary, alter our lifestyles to reflect what the ecosystem can in fact sustainably support.

We must account for the intrinsic ecological value of all natural resources as well as for their conversion potential into money, and we must accept that the long-term health of the environment takes precedence over the short-term profits to be made through exploitation and continual development. Concurrently, we must convert our society—immediately, rapidly, consciously, and unconditionally—to a version of capitalism that views long-term ecological wholeness and biological richness of the environment as the measure of long-term economic health.

To this end, it is imperative that we pass clearly-stated, precisely-worded, unambiguous laws in which the intent is so simply stated that it cannot be distorted and hidden by bureaucratic policy. We must create environmental policy commensurate with ecological sustainability and cultural capacity, and we must simultaneously create policy that protects the ecological integrity of the environment and cultural capacity from the irreversible negative aspects of continual development. Such policies must be achieved by popular consensus to protect them from the self-serving agendas of the agencies, which are at the mercy of self-serving agendas of Congress, the presidential administration, and private industry.

We must also accept that the only sustainability for which we can manage is one that ensures the ability of an ecosystem to adapt to evolutionary change—which means we must manage for choice (for maximum biodiversity) regardless of the economic and political costs. In turn, biodiversity can be protected only if we manage for a desired condition of the landscape and only if we abandon our cherished but unworkable notion that industrial resources are capable of a "sustained" ever-increasing yield. To achieve such a desired condition, we must stop today's practice of managing for fragmentation of the landscape by focusing only on commodity-producing resources. We must instead focus on and manage for the connectivity of habitats to help ensure the ecological wholeness and the biological richness of the patterns we create across the landscape.

Finally, if we are to be successful guardians of the future's right of choice, we must unfailingly manage the only thing we can really manage—ourselves—in such a way that we conscientiously live within the ecologically-moral confines of our cultural capacity. The importance of living within our cultural capacity cannot be over-emphasized, because when all is said and done, the great and only gift we can give our children is the right of choice and something of value from which to choose.

We the people are the trustees of the future's options; we must therefore find and test our moral and political courage. The body politic must act in an other-centered, future-oriented manner, regardless of perceived short-term economic hardships and political uncertainties.

We already have most of the laws and mandates necessary to give us license to manage our environment in an ecologically-sound manner. Now we must find the moral courage and the political will to follow both the intent and the spirit of those laws for the long-term good of the people, present and future. If current laws are not morally sound, better ones can be passed as necessary. The choice is ours—a choice of morality.

What Legacy Shall We Leave the Children?

As our individual pilgrimages on Earth draw to a close, what are we leaving, individually and collectively, to those who follow—fear, myopia, competition, and their attendant deprivation or love, cooperation, coordination, and their attendant abundance? Eleanor Roosevelt, the activist wife of President Franklin D. Roosevelt, addressed this question when she said, "We have reached a place where it is not a question of 'can we live in the same world and cooperate' but 'we must live in the same world and learn to cooperate.'" In view of the critical economic and cultural instability and moral decay—or more correctly *because* of the critical economic and cultural instability and moral decay—faced by society today, we have a choice to make, a choice of legacy to leave to the generations of the future.

The choice is between the continuation of the old, worn-out, immorally-arrogant, commodity-oriented, materialistic legacy of "I want and demand mine now" and a new, vibrant, morally-balanced, spiritual-oriented legacy of necessities and options for the present balanced with the necessities and options required by the future. The heart of our choice lies in the grand opportunity of the future, an opportunity hidden in the impending surge of cultural evolution, which is not without its element of freedom—the freedom of an evolving system in the moment of its transformation. A moment in this sense may be from five to ten years for a human social system as opposed to from 50,000 to 100,000 years for a biological species.

When the critical instability occurs—which it does more frequently in highly specialized systems, such as human societies, than it does in generalists, such as the human species itself—there is freedom of choice. This is the fork in the road where a new species or social system diverges from the old. Choice is always available, because complex systems, such as biological species and human societies, inevitably contain new possibilities of replacing themselves. Such replacements are better-adapted successors that are more fit to live under the new conditions than are the carry-over members of the old, dominant system itself.

A species like a mouse cannot, so far as we know, exercise conscious foresight and take purposeful action during its moment of evolutionary transformation from one species to another. But human societies, should they choose to, can be purposeful, foresighted systems during their moments of transformation, because their individual human members have the ability to act consciously and collectively.

And it is precisely because human social systems can choose their own evolutionary path that they have a moral responsibility to the generations of the future to exercise the morality of that choice. As I've said before, conscious cultural evolution is guided by those individuals with the wisdom to ask farsighted, socially-penetrating, balanced, present- and future-oriented questions like these: How can we participate with our environment so that we can build our cultural expression into the landscape within the governance of Nature's Laws? How can we participate with our environment in such a way as to protect the patterns across the landscape, a way that makes possible its ability to adapt to changing conditions? How can we use the Earth while at the same time protecting biodiversity and, through biodiversity, the

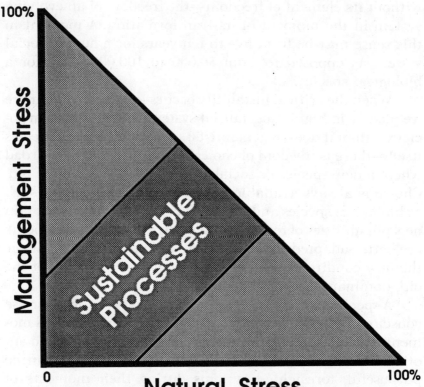

Figure 18. *Stress Limits:* "Managing" ecosystems means engaging in a balancing act between Nature's stresses and humanity's cultural stresses. We can "manage" an ecosystem for products on a sustainable basis if we are careful to remain within the stress threshold in which the ecosystem is self-repairing and self-sustaining in the sense of being able to once again approximate its condition at the time humans disturbed it. The higher the natural stress, the lower the management stress must be; the lower the natural stress, the higher the management stress can be—but always within the limits of the ecosystem's ability to sustain its processes.

sustainability of the ecological processes that make adaptation possible? How can we participate with a particular place, be it a city lot, a farm, or a forest, to balance Nature's evolutionary stresses with society's cultural stresses in such a way as to protect not only the sustainability of the eco-system and its processes but also our cultural capacity over time? (Fig. 18).

It is, after all, the questions we ask that will in the end determine which baton we pass as our legacy to the next generation. And that baton will reflect some of the many faces of creation and some of the many faces of extinction in all their multitudinous dimensions, faces that are but a re-flection of the Eternal Mystery.

NOTES

1. *The Holy Bible, Authorized King James Version* (Iowa Falls, IA: World Bible Publishers), Genesis Chapter 1, Verse 2.

2. "Rare fish faces extinction," *The Corvallis Gazette-Times*, Corvallis, Oregon, October 4, 1989.

3. Louise H. Emmons, "Tropical rain forests: why they have so many species, and how we may lose this biodiversity without cutting a single tree," *Orion* 8 (1989): 8–14.

4. Sue Cross, "Pair rescue legends as Tlingit tongue dies," *The Corvallis Gazette-Times*, November 15, 1987.

5. Eloise Salholz, David L. Gonzalez, Harry Hurt III, and Pat Wingert, "Say it in English," *Newsweek* (February 20, 1989), pp. 22–23.

6. Michael Kiefer, "Fall of the Garden of Eden," *International Wildlife*, (July-August 1989): 38–43.

7. Allan Chen, "Unraveling another Mayan mystery," *Discover* (June 1987), pp. 40, 44, 46, 48–49.

8. John G. Neihardt, *Black Elk Speaks* (Lincoln, Nebraska: University of Nebraska, 1961).

9. Wendell Berry, "The road and the wheel," *Earth Ethics*, 1 (1990): 8–9.

10. Marion Clawson, "Forests in the long sweep of American history,"

Science 204 (1979): 1168–1174.

11. Susana Hayward, "Land's wealth may doom remote tribe," *The Corvallis Gazette-Times*, December 27, 1978.

12. Gerald Gold and Richard Attenborough, "The unfinished revolution," *Heart*, Autumn (1983):17–19, 108–112.

13. Luna B. Leopold, "Ethos, equity, and the water resource" *Environment* 2 (1990): 16–42.

14. D.J. Chasan, *Up for grabs, inquiries into who wants what* (Seattle, WA: Madrona Publications, 1977).

15. *The Holy Bible, op. cit.,* Numbers, Chapter 35 Verse 34.

16. Verne Gross Carter and Timothy Dale, *Topsoil and civilization*, Rev. Ed. (Norman, OK: University of Oklahoma Press, 1974).

17. W.C. Lowdermilk, *Conquest of the land through seven thousand years.* Agricultural Information Bulletin No. 99, United States Department of Agriculture, Soil Conservation Service. (Washington D.C.: United States Government Printing Office, 1975).

18. Joseph Campbell, *The Power of Myth* (New York, NY: Doubleday, 1988).

19. Robert V. Bartlett, "Adapt or get out: The Garrison Diversion project and controversy," *Environmental Review* 12 (1988): 57–74.

20. Donald Worster, *Rivers of Empire: Water, aridity, and the growth of the American West.* (New York, NY: Pantheon Books, 1985), p. 329.

21. Wallace Stegner, "The function of aridity," *Wilderness* (Fall 1987):17–18.

22. James Allen, *As a man thinketh.* (New York, NY: Grosset & Dunlap, 1981).

23. "Last dusky seaside sparrow dies," *The Corvallis Gazette-Times*, June 18, 1987.

24. Victor Frankl, *Man's search for meaning* (New York, NY: Pocket Books, 1963).

25. William K. Stevens, "New eye on nature: The real constant is eternal turmoil," *The New York Times*, July 31, 1990.

26. Ervin Laszlo, "The crucial epoch," *Futures* (February 1985): 2–23.

27. Roberta Ulrich, "Growth fuels coastal-protection laws," *The Oregonian*, Portland, Oregon, June 16, 1991.

28. Daniel B. Wood, "Report details decline of Hawaiian paradise," *The Oregonian*, November 7, 1991.

29. Roberta Ulrich, "Forest Service seeks court-review shield," *The Oregonian*, June 15,1991.

30. World Commission on Environment and Development, *Our common future* (New York, NY: Oxford University Press, 1987).

31. Ivan Illich, "The shadow our future throws," *Earth Ethics* 1(1990): 3–5.

32. Elizabeth Ann R. Bird, "The social construction of nature: Theoretical approaches to the history of environmental problems," *Environmental Review* 11 (1987): 255–264.

33. John R. Platt, "Strong inference," *Science* 146 (1964): 347–353.

34. Harold T. Shapiro, "The willingness to risk failure," *Science* 250 (1990): 609.

35. David W. Orr, "The question of management," *Conservation Biology* 4 (1990): 8–9.

36. Norman Jacob, "Towards a theory of sustainability," *Trumpeter* 6 (1989): 93–97.

37. M. Campbell, "7 B.C. fisheries ordered closed after poisons found in shellfish," *The Globe and Mail*, Toronto, Ontario, Canada, November 24, 1989.

38. Garrett Hardin, "Cultural carrying capacity: a biological approach to human problems," *BioScience* 36 (1986): 599–606.

39. Herbert W. Schroeder, "The spiritual aspect of nature: a perspective from depth psychology," *Proceedings of Northeastern Recreation Research Conference*, Saratoga Springs, New York, April 8 1991 (in press).

40. James Allen, *op. cit.*

41. Aldo Leopold, "The conservation ethic," *Journal of Forestry* 31 (1933): 634–643.

42. Wendell Berry, "Taking nature's measure," *Harper's Magazine* (March 1990): 20–22.

43. *Ibid.*

GLOSSARY

Aggregation: a group gathered together in a mass or sum so as to constitute a whole.

Bering-Chukchi platform: a connection of land (presently under water) between what is now northeastern Siberia and Alaska. As the Cascade Mountain Ranges grew and changed, the Bering-Chukchi platform (also called the trans-Bering land bridge) between North America and Eurasia was intermittently inundated and exposed. When fully exposed, it formed a flat isthmus about 994 miles wide between what is now northeastern Siberia and Alaska.

Biotic: composed of plants and animals.

Boreal: northern.

Calcium carbonate: a colorless or white crystalline compound that occurs naturally in chalk, limestone, marble, and other forms.

Cambium: in woody vegetation, the layer of living cells (the innermost living bark) that lies just under the outer bark.

Carbohydrate: any of a group of chemical compounds, including sugars, starches, and cellulose, containing carbon, hydrogen, and oxygen only.

Carbon: a naturally abundant nonmetallic element that occurs in many inorganic and in all organic compounds.

Carbonate: to charge with carbon dioxide gas.

Carrying capacity: the number of individuals of a species that can live in an area without degrading the habitat that supports them.

Cell: the smallest structural unit of an organism that is capable of independent functioning.

Clay: a very fine-grained sediment that becomes plastic and acts like a lubricant when wet. Clay consists primarily of hydrated silicates of aluminum and is used widely in making bricks, tiles, and pottery.

Climatic cycle: the cyclic changes in weather patterns in a geographical area over time.

Climax: the culminating stage in plant succession for a given site where the vegetation is self-reproducing and has thus reached a stable condition through time; see also "subclimax."

Climax forest: a forest plant community that represents the culminating stage of forest succession for a particular site; see also "climax."

Community: a group of one or more populations of plants and/or animals using a common area; an ecological term used in a broad sense to include groups of plants and animals of various sizes and degrees of integration.

Compound: a substance composed of two or more chemical elements or things.

Conifer: the most important order of the Gymnospermae, comprising a wide range of trees, mostly evergreens that bear cones and have needle-shaped or scalelike leaves; timber commercially identified as softwood.

Coniferous: of or pertaining to conifers.

Coniferous forest: a forest dominated by cone-bearing trees; see also "conifer."

Constellation: any of 88 groups of stars, which are considered to resemble and are named after various mythological characters, inanimate objects, and animals.

Continuum: a continuous extent, succession, or whole, no part of which can be distinguished from neighboring parts except by arbitrary division.

Cycling: to occur in or pass through a cycle; to move in, or as if in, a circle.

Decay: in wood, the decomposition by fungi or other microorganisms resulting in softening, progressive loss of strength and weight, and changes in texture and color.

Deciduous: pertaining to any plant organ, such as a leaf, that is shed naturally; perennial plants that shed their leaves and are therefore leafless for some time during the year.

Decompose: to separate into component parts or elements; to break down; to decay or putrefy.

Diversity: the relative degree of abundance of species of plants and animals, functions, communities, habitats, or habitat features per unit of area.

Dynamic: characterized by or tending to produce continuous change.

Ecological: an adjective that identifies a relationship between living organisms and their non-living physical environment.

Ecosystem: all the living organisms interacting with their non-living physical environment, considered as a unit.

Electron: a subatomic particle that has a negative electric charge.

Erosion: the group of processes, including weathering, dissolution, abrasion, corrosion, and transportation, by which earthy or rock material is removed from any part of the earth's surface.

Eutrophic: a word used to describe a body of water in which the increase of mineral and organic nutrients has reduced the dissolved oxygen, producing an environment that favors plant life over animal life.

Fauna: animals collectively, especially the animals of a particular region or time.

Floodplain: a plain bordering a stream or river that is subject to flooding.

Flora: plants collectively, especially the plants of a particular region or time.

Forest: generally, that portion of the ecosystem characterized by tree cover; more particularly, a plant community predominantly of trees and other woody vegetation that grows close together.

Forest floor: the surface layer of a soil that supports forest vegetation.

Formation: the primary geological unit of stratigraphy in rock. It refers to a succession of strata useful for the description and mapping of an area.

Fruiting body: the reproductive organ of a fungus.

Function: the natural or proper action for which an organism or habitat or behavior has evolved.

Gene pool: narrowly, the genic material of a localized interbreeding population; broadly, the genetic resources or materials of a species throughout its entire geographical distribution.

Genus: the first word in a binomial (two-part) or scientific name.

Glacier: a huge mass of laterally-limited moving ice that originated from compacted snow.

Glacial: of or pertaining to a glacier.

Gradient: a rate of inclination, a slope; an ascending or descending part; an incline.

Graminae: the taxonomic family to which grasses belong.

Grass: any species of plant that is a member of the family Graminae, characteristically having narrow leaves, hollow, jointed stems, and spikes or clusters of membranous flowers borne in smaller spikelets; such plants collectively.

Grassland: an area, such as a prairie or meadow, of grass or grasslike vegetation.

Gravel: any unconsolidated mixture of rock fragments and pebbles.

Gymnospermae: a group of woody plants having a naked seed; for example, a seed not enclosed in an ovary.

Habitat: the sum total of environmental conditions of a specific place occupied by a plant or animal, or a population of such species.

Heartwood: the inner layers of wood that, in a growing tree, have ceased to contain living cells and in which the reserve materials, such as starch, have been removed or converted into more durable substances.

Herb: pertaining to or characteristic of a non-woody plant as distinguished from a woody plant.

Herbaceous: pertaining to or characteristic of an herb or non-woody plant as distinguished from a woody plant.

Hydrological cycle: the cycle of the way water falls as rain and/or snow, sinks into the soil and is either stored or flows below ground, runs over the surface of the soil in streams and rivers on their way to the sea, and evaporates into the atmosphere to be cycled again as rain and/or snow.

Inorganic: involving neither organic life nor the products of organic life; not composed of organic matter, especially minerals; see "organic."

Inorganic compound: a chemical compound that does not involve organic products; see "inorganic" and "organic."

Inorganic materials: anything that does not involve organic products; see "inorganic" and "organic."

Integrity: the state of being unimpaired; soundness; completeness; unity.

Interglacial: between glacial epochs.

Intermittent: starting and stopping at intervals, such as a stream whose flow is interrupted periodically.

Jam: fallen trees and other woody debris blocking, congesting, or clogging a stream or river.

Landslide: the dislodging and fall of a mass of earth and rock.

Lichen: a plant that is actually two plants in one; the outer plant is a fungus that houses the inner plant, an alga.

Macroclimate: the overall, prevailing climate of the times as it affects the continent.

Macrohabitat: the larger habitat within which an organism dwells, such as a forest.

Mammal: an animal that has hair on its body during some stage of its life and whose babies are nurtured initially by their mother's milk.

Marine: of the ocean.

Meander: to follow a winding and turning course, such as streams that flow through level land; also said of a bend in a stream that has been cut off from the main channel by the stream's having shifted its course.

Microbe: microscopic organism.

Microclimate: as I am using it here, the climate of an immediate area as determined by the topography and the vegetation of the area, which exerts a local influence over the prevailing, overall climate of the times, the macroclimate.

Microhabitat: the small, specialized habitat in which an organism dwells, such as a log (microhabitat) within a forest (macrohabitat).

Mineral: any naturally occurring, homogeneous, inorganic substance that has a definite chemical composition and characteristic crystalline structure, color, and hardness.

Mineral soil: soil composed mainly of inorganic materials and with a relatively low amount of organic material.

Montane: of or pertaining to the mountains.

Morphology: the biological study of the form and structure of living organisms.

Morphological: of or pertaining to morphology.

Neutron: an electrically-neutral subatomic particle with a mass 1,839 times that of an electron. A neutron and a proton combine to form nearly the entire mass of an atomic nucleus.

Non-nucleated: to lack a nucleus; see "nucleus."

Nucleated: to possess a nucleus; see "nucleus."

Nucleic acid: any member of either of two groups of complex compounds found in all living cells, which are composed of purines, pyrimidines, carbohydrates, and phosphoric acid.

Nucleus: a central thing or part around which other things are grouped. In biology, a nucleus is a complex, usually spherical, protoplasmic body within a living cell that contains the cell's hereditary material and that controls the cell's metabolism, growth, and reproduction.

Organic: of, pertaining to, or derived from living organisms; of or designating compounds containing the element carbon; see "inorganic."

Organic combinations: mixtures of organic substances.

Organic compound: a chemical compound that involves carbon and is derived from living organisms; see "inorganic" and "organic."

Organic matter in soil: materials derived from plants and animals, much of it in an advanced state of decay.

Organism: any living individual of any species of plant or animal.

Parent material: the original rock from which a particular soil is derived in a particular location.

Pebble: a small stone eroded smooth.

Permafrost: permanently frozen subsoil that is continuous in underlying polar regions and occurring locally in perennially frigid areas.

Physiology: the biological science of essential and characteristic life processes, activities, and function.

Physiological: of or pertaining to physiology.

Pit-and-mound topography: the roughened surface of the floor of a forest caused by the residual pits, or holes, in the ground that are left as the roots of a tree are torn out of the soil when a tree is blown or falls over and the accompanying root wad with its intact roots of the tree, soil, and rocks that forms a mound next to the pit.

Process: a system of operations in the production of something; a series of actions, changes, or functions that brings about an end or result.

Protein: any of a group of complex nitrogenous, organic compounds of high molecular weight that contain amino acids as their basic structural units and that occur in all living matter and are essential for the growth and repair of animal tissue.

Proton: a stable, positively charged subatomic particle with a mass 1,836 times that of an electron.

Quark: a hypothetical subatomic particle having an electric charge that is one-third to two-thirds that of an electron. Quarks are proposed as the fundamental units of matter.

Rootwad: the mass of roots, soil, and rocks that remains intact when a tree, shrub, or stump is uprooted.

Sand: loose, granular, gritty particles of worn or disintegrated rock, finer than gravel and coarser than dust.

Sediment: material suspended in water; the deposition of such material onto a surface, such as a stream bottom, underlying the water.

Scientific name: the binomial or two-word latinized name of an organism; the first word describes the genus, the second the species.

Silt: a sedimentary material consisting of fine mineral particles intermediate in size between sand and clay.

Snag: a standing dead tree from which the leaves and most of the branches have fallen; such a tree is broken off but still more than twenty feet tall.

Soil: earth material so modified by physical, chemical, and biological agents that it will support rooted plants.

Species: a unit of classification of plants and animals consisting of the largest and most inclusive array of sexually reproducing and cross-fertilizing individuals that share a common gene pool.

Species richness: the variety of species that inhabit a particular area.

Stump: the woody base of a tree left in the ground after the stem breaks off and falls.

Subclimax: a stage in the ecological succession of a plant or animal community immediately preceding the climax and often persisting because of the effects of fire, flood, or other major disturbance.

Subspecies: a subdivision (a division of lower rank) of a taxonomic species, usually based on characteristics that indicate variation as a result of geographical distribution.

Symbiosis: the relationship of two or more different organisms living in a close association that may be but is not necessarily of benefit to each; sometimes the relationship is obligatory to one or more of the organisms in the relationship.

Symbiotic: two different organisms living together in relationship.

Topography: the physical features of a place or region.

Tundra: a treeless area between the ice cap and the tree line of arctic regions, having a permanently frozen subsoil and supporting low-growing vegetation, such as lichens, mosses, and stunted shrubs. Tundra also occurs above the tree line on high mountains; this is termed "alpine tundra" as opposed to "arctic tundra."

Volcanic: of or resembling an erupting volcano; produced by or discharged from a volcano.

Volcano: a vent or opening in the earth's crust through which molten lava and gases are ejected.

Water-holding capacity: a measure of the ability of soil, wood, or some other substance to soak up and hold water.

REFERENCES

A course in miracles; Manual for teachers. Tiburon, California: Foundation for Inner Peace, 1975.

Allen, James. *As a man thinketh*. New York: Grosset & Dunlap, 1981.

Allison, Ira S. "Fossil Lake, Oregon, its geology and fossil faunas." *Studies in Geology*, No. 9. Corvallis, Oregon: Oregon State University (1966):1–48.

Amaranthus, M.P., and D.A. Perry. "The effect of soil transfers on ecto-mycorrhizal formation and the survival and growth of conifer seedlings on old, nonforested clearcuts." *Canadian Journal of Forest Research* 17 (1987): 944–950.

Anderson, W.T. *To govern evolution, further adventures of the political animal*. Orlando Florida: Harcourt Brace Jovanovich, 1987.

Bak, Per, and Kan Chen. "Self-organizing criticality." *Scientific American* (1991): 46–53.

Barrett, Thomas S. "The sky's the limit." *Earth Ethics* 1 (1990): 1.

Baumhoff, M.A. and R.F. Heize. "Postglacial climate and archaeology in the desert west." pp. 697–707. In: *The Quaternary of the United States*. J.E. Wright, Jr., and D.G. Frey, (Eds.). Princeton, New Jersey: Princeton University Press, 1967.

Berry, Wendell. "The road and the wheel." *Earth Ethics* 1 (1990): 8–9.

Bird, Elizabeth Ann R. "The social construction of nature: Theoretical approaches to the history of environmental problems." *Environmental Review* 11 (1987): 255–264.

Bochemühl, Jochen. *Dying forests, a crisis in consciousness.* Gloucestershire, United Kingdom: Hawthorn Press, 1986.

Botkin, Daniel B. "A grandfather clock down the staircase: stability and disturbance in natural ecosystems." pp. 1–10. In *Forests: Fresh Perspectives from Ecosystem Analysis.* R.H. Waring, Ed. *Proc. 40th Ann. Biol. Colloquium.* Corvallis, Oregon: Oregon State University Press, 1979.

Buber, Martin. *I and Thou.* New York: Charles Scribner's Sons, 1970.

Bucke, R.M. *Cosmic Consciousness, a study in the evolution of the human mind.* New York: E.P Dutton & Company. 1923.

Cooke, Robert. "Lake Erie has improved, but complete recovery is unlikely." *LA Times-Washington Post Service.* In *The Oregonian*, Portland, Oregon, June 16, 1991.

Cooper, J.C. *An illustrated encyclopedia of traditional symbols.* New York: Thames and Hudson. 1978.

Corn, Paul Stephen and James C. Fogleman. "Extinction of montane populations of the northern leopard frog (*Rana pipiens*) in Colorado." *Journal Herpetology* 18 (1984): 147–152.

Covington, W. Wallace, and Margaret M. Moore. "Changes in forest conditions and multiresource yields from ponderosa pine forests since European settlement." Unpublished report, submitted to J. Keane, Water Resources Operations, Salt River Project, Phoenix, AZ., 1991.

Crawley, R. *Translation of the complete writings of Thucydides.* New York: Random House. 1951.

Creasy, Rosalind. "Ecosystem gardens." *Orion* 5 (1986): 26–39.

Davis, Margaret B. "Lags in vegetation response to greenhouse warming." *Climatic Change* 15 (1989): 75–82.

Davis, Margaret B., and C. Zabinski. "Changes in geographical range resulting from greenhouse warming effects on biodiversity in forests." In R.L. Peters and T.E. Lovejoy (eds.), *Consequences of global warming for biodiversity: Proceedings of the World Wildlife Fund Conference,* 1991. New Haven, Connecticut: Yale University Press. In press.

DeAngelis, D.L., W.M. Post, and C.C. Travis. *Positive feedback in natural systems.* Berlin, Germany: Springer-Verlag, 1986.

Delcourt, Hazel R., and Paul A. Delcourt. "Quaternary landscape ecology: Relevant scales in space and time." *Landscape Ecology.* 2 (1988): 23–44.

Delcourt, Paul A., and Hazel R. Delcourt. 1985. "Dynamic landscapes of East Tennessee: an integration of paleoecology, geomorphology, and archaeology." University of Tennesse, Knoxville. Department of Geological Science, *Studies in Geology 9* (1985): 191–220.

De Monnin, Joyce. "Seabird may join owl as threatened." *The Corvallis Gazette-Times*, Corvallis, Oregon, June 18, 1991.

de Santillana, G., and H. von Dechend. *Hamlet's mill: an essay on myth and the frame of time.* London: Macmillan, 1969.

Devall, Bill, and George Sessions. *Deep ecology: living as if nature mattered.* Layton, Utah: Peregrine Smith, 1985.

Dillon, L.S. "Wisconsin climate and life zones in North America." *Science* 123 (1956): 167–176.

Dix, R.L. "A history of biotic and climatic changes within the North American grassland." pp. 71–89. In *Grazing in terrestrial and marine environments.* D.J. Crisp (Ed.). England: Blackwells Science Publishing, 1964.

Dobson, Andy, Alison Jolly, and Dan Rubenstein. "The greenhouse effect and biological diversity." *Tree* 4 (1989): 64–68.

Dobzhansky, T. "What is a species?" *Scientia* 61 (1937): 280–286.

Dobzhansky, T. *Genetics of the evolutionary process.* New York: Columbia University Press, 1970.

Dorf, E. "Climatic changes of the past and present." *American Scientist* 48 (1960): 341–346.

Durbin, Kathie. "Marbled murrelet may join threatened species." *The Oregonian*, Portland, Oregon, June 18, 1991.

Egerton, Frank N. "Pollution and aquatic life in Lake Erie: early scientific studies." *Environmental Review* 11 (1987):189–205.

Ehrlich, Paul. "Changing our minds." *Earth Ethics* 1 (1990): 6–7.

Fetcher, N. and G.R. Shaver. "Environmental sensitivity of ecotypes as a potential influence on primary productivity." *American Naturalist* 136 (1990): 126–131.

Flynn, John. "Forest without trees." *Amicus Journal*, Winter (1991): 28–33.

Franklin, Jerry F. and Miles A. Hemstrom. "Aspects of succession in coniferous forests of the Pacific Northwest." pp. 212–229. In *Forest Succession.* D.E. Reichle (Ed.). New York: Springer-Verlag, 1981.

Franklin, Jerry F., and Richard T.T. Forman. "Creating landscape patterns by forest cutting: ecological consequences and principles." *Landscape Ecology* 1 (1987): 5–18.

Fryer, J.H., and F.T. Ledig. "Microevolution of the photosynthetic temperature optimum in relation to the elevational complex gradient." *Canadian Journal of Botany* 50 (1972): 1231–1235.

George, C.J. *The role of the Aswan Dam in changing fisheries of the southwestern Mediterranean. In*: The careless technology. M.T. Farvar and J.P. Milton (eds.). New York: Natural History Press, 1972.

Ghiselin, M.R. "A radical solution to the species problem." *Systematic Zoology* 23 (1974): 536–544.

Graham, A. and C. Heimsch. "Pollen studies of some Texas peat deposits." *Ecology* 41 (1960): 751–763.

Grayson, Donald K. "On the Holocene history of some northern Great Basin lagomorphs." *Journal of Mammal* 58 (1977): 507–513.

Grayson, Donald K. "Mount Mazama, climatic change, and Fort Rock Basin archaeofaunas." pp. 427–457. In *Volcanic activity and human ecology*. New York: Academic Press, 1979.

Grayson, Donald K. 1987. "The biogeographic history of small mammals in the Great Basin: Observations on the last 20,000 years." *Journal of Mammal* 68 (1987): 359–375.

Greber, Brian J., and K. Norman Johnson. "What's all this debate about overcutting?" *Journal of Forestry* 89 (1991.): 25–30.

Griffin, J.B. "Late Quaternary prehistory in the northeastern woodlands." pp. 655–667. In *The Quaternary of the United States*.

Grossinger, R. *The night sky*. Los Angeles, California: J.P. Tarcher. 1988.

Guilday, J.E., P.W. Parmalee, and H.W. Hamilton. "The Clark's Cave bone deposits and the late Pleistocene paleoecology of the Central Appalachian Mountains of Virginia." *Carnegie Museum of Natural History Bulletin* 2 (1977): 1–87.

Hardin, Garrett. "An ecolate view of the human predicament." *The Environmental Fund*, Monograph Series (1984): 1–14.

Harmon, Mark E., William K. Ferrel, and Jerry F. Franklin. "Effects on carbon storage of conversion for old-growth forests to young forests." *Science* 247 (1990): 699–702.

Harris, Larry D. 1984. *The fragmented forest*. Chicago, Illinois: University of Chicago Press, 1984.

Harris, Larry D., and Chris Maser. "Animal community characteristics." In *ibid*, pp. 44–68.

Highsmith, R.M., Jr., and A.J. Kimerling (Eds). *Atlas of the Pacific Northwest (6th Ed.)*. Corvallis, Oregon: Oregon State University Press, 1979.

Hoekstra, Thomas W., Timothy F.H. Allen, and Curtis H. Flather. "Implicit scaling in ecological research, on when to make studies of mice and men." *BioScience* 41 (1991): 148–154.

Holling, C.S. "Resilience and stability of ecological systems." *Annual Review of Ecological Systems* 4 (1973): 1–24.

Hoopes, Roy. "Turning out the light." *Modern Maturity*, June-July (1988): 29–33, 88.

Hopkins, D.M. "Cenozoic history of the Bering Land Bridge." *Science* 129 (1959): 1519–1528.

Hughes, J.D. 1990. "Goddess of conservation." *Forest and Conservation History* October (1990): 191–197.

Hurley, Andrew. "The social biases of environmental change in Gary, Indiana, 1945–1980." *Environmental Review* 12 (1988): 1–19.

Indonesia Forestry Community. "Indonesia: Tropical forests forever." *Journal of Forestry* 88 (1990): 26–31.

Jacobson, Jodi L. "Holding back the sea." *Futurist* 24 (1990): 20–27.

Jaffe, L.W. *Liberating the heart: spirituality and Jungian psychology*. Toronto, Ontario, Canada: Inner City Books, 1990.

James, William. *The varieties of religious experience*. New York: Penguin Books, 1982.

Jordan, William R., III. "Restoration and the reentry of nature." *Orion* 5 (1986): 14–25.

Jung, Carl G. "On the nature of the psyche." pp 159–234. In *The collected works of C.G. Jung* (vol. 8). Read, H. and others (eds.). New York: Pantheon, 1960.

Jung, Carl G. *Man and his symbols*. New York: Dell Publishers, 1964.

Jung, Carl G. *Memories, dreams, reflections*. New York: Random House, 1965.

Kellogg, C.E. "We seek, we learn." pp. 1–11. In *Soil: The yearbook of agriculture*. United States Department of Agricualture. Washington, D.C.: United States Government Printing Office, 1957.

Kennedy, Christina B., James L. Sell, and Ervin H. Zube. "Landscape aesthetics and geography." *Environmental Review* 12 (1988): 31–55.

Knize, Perri. "The mismanagement of the National Forests." *The Atlantic Monthly*. October (1991): 98–112.

Koopes, Clayton R. "Efficiency/equity/esthetics: towards a reinterpretation of American conservation." *Environmental Review* 11 (1987): 127–146.

Kraenzel, C.F. *The Great Plains in transition.* Oklahoma: University of Oklahoma Press, 1955.

Kriebel, H.B. *Patterns of genetic variation in sugar maple.* Ohio Agricultural Experiment Station Research Bulletin 791, Wooster, Ohio: 1957.

Kunisawa, B.N. "A nation in crisis: The dropout dilemma." *National Education Association,* January (1988): 61–65.

Lancaster, John. "As Utah's salt flats disappear an unusual alliance emerges." *LA Times-Washington Post Service.* In *The Oregonian,* Portland, Oregon, June 16, 1991.

Lancaster, John. "Public land, private profit." *Journal of Forestry* 89 (1991): 20–22.

Laszlo, Ervin "The crucial epoch." *Futures,* February (1985): 2–23.

Ledig, F. Thomas. "Human impacts on genetic diversity in forest ecosystems." *Oikos.* In press.

Ledig, F.T., and D.R. Korbobo. "Adaptation of sugar maple along altitudinal gradients: photosynthesis, respiration, and specific leaf weight." *American Journal of Botany* 70 (1983): 256–265.

Leopold, Luna B. *Water: A primer.* California: W.H. Freeman, 1974.

Leopold, Luna B. "Ethos, equity, and the water resource." *Environment* 2 (1990): 16–42.

Leviton, Richard. "Environmental illness." *Yoga Journal* November/December (1990): 43–53, 95–100.

Lovelock, J.E. *Gaia: a new look at life on Earth.* New York: Oxford University Press, 1979.

Lowdermilk, W.C. *Conquest of the land through seven thousand years.* Agricultural Information Bulletin No. 99, United States Department of Agriculture, Soil Conservation Service. Washington, D.C.: United States Government Printing Office. 1975.

Magnuson, John J. "Long-term ecological research and the invisible present." *BioScience* 40 (1990): 495–501.

Magnuson, J.J., C.J. Bowser, and A.L. Beckel. "The invisible present: long term ecological research on lakes." *L & S Magazine.* University Wisconsin, Madison. Fall (1983): 3–6.

Manley, S.A.M. "Genecology of hybridization in red spruce (*Picea rubens* Sarg.) and black spruce (*Picea mariana* [Mill.] BSP)." Ph.D. Dissertation, Yale University. New Haven, Connecticut: 1975.

Manley, S.A.M., and F.T. Ledig. "Photosynthesis in black and red spruce and their hybrid derivatives: ecological isolation and hybrid inviability." *Canadian Journal of Botany* 57 (1979): 305–314.

Martin, Clyde S. "Forest resources, cutting practices, and utilization problems in the pine region of the Pacific Northwest." *Journal of Forestry* 38 (1940): 681–685.

Marvin, Rob. "The earth churns, moans, breathes, and the 'living rocks' keep rollin' on." *The Oregonian*, Portland, Oregon, (1991): April 18.

Maser, Chris. *Forest Primeval: The Natural History of an Ancient Forest.* San Francisco, California: Sierra Club Books, 1989.

Maser, Chris. "On the "naturalness" of natural areas: a perspective for the future." *Natural Areas Journal* 10 (1990): 129–133.

Maser, Chris. "Authenticity in the forestry profession." *Journal of Forestry* 89 (1991): 22–24

Maser, Chris. *The Redesigned Forest.* San Pedro, California: R. & E. Miles, 1988.

Maslow, Abram H. 1968. *Toward a psychology of being (2nd. ed.).* New Jersey: D. Van Nostrand, 1968.

Maslow, Abram H. 1970. *Religions, values, and peak experiences.* New York: Viking Press, 1970.

Mayr, E. "The species concept: semantics vs. semantics." *Evolution* 3 (1949): 371–372.

Mayr, E. "Concepts of classification and nomenclature in higher organisms and microorganisms." *Annals, New York Academy of Science* 56 (1953): 391–397.

Mayr, E. 1963. *Animal species and evolution.* Cambridge, Massachusetts: Belknap Press of Harvard University Press, 1963.

Mayr, E. *Systematics and the origin of species from the viewpoint of a zoologist.* New York: Dover Publications, 1964.

Mayr, E., E.G. Linsley, and R.L. Usinger. *Methods and principles of systematic zoology.* New York: McGraw-Hill, 1953.

Meighan, C.W. "Pacific Coast archaeology." pp. 709–720. In *The Quaternary of the United States.*

Melosi, Martin V. "Energy and environment in the United States: the era of fossil fuels." *Environmental Review* 11 (1987): 167–188.

Merchant, Carolyn. "The theoretical structure of ecological revolutions." *Environmental Review* 11 (1987): 265–274.

Miller, Julie Ann. "Biosciences and ecological intergrity." *BioScience* 41 (1991): 206–210.

Moir, Will H. *Forests of Mount Rainier.* Washington: Pacific Northwest National Parks and Forest Association, 1989.

Monastersky Richard. "Time for action, the world embarks on the torturous road toward a climate treaty." *Science News* 139 (1991): 200–202.

Morrison, Peter H., and Frederick J. Swanson. *Fire history and pattern in a Cascade Range landscape.* United States Department of Agriculture Forest Service General Technical Report PNW-GTR-254. Portland, Oregon: Pacific Northwest Research Station, 1990.

Naess, Arne. "Sustainable development and the deep long-range ecology movement." *Trumpeter* 5 (1988): 138–142.

Olson, Sherry. "Environments as shock absorbers, examples from Madagascar." *Environmental Review* 12 (1988): 61–80.

Payne, John F. "A viewpoint on endangered species." *Environmental Science and Technology* 25 (1991): 364–365.

Perlin, John. *A Forest Journey: the role of wood in the development of civilization.* New York: W.W. Norton, 1989.

Perry, David A. "An overview of sustainable forestry." *Journal of Pesticide Reform* 8 (1988): 8–12.

Perry, David A. "Landscape pattern and forest pests." *Northwest Environmental Journal* 4 (1988): 213–228.

Perry, D.A., M.P. Amaranthus, J.G. Borchers, S.L. Borchers, and R.E. Brainerd. "Bootstrapping in ecosystems." *BioScience* 39 (1989): 230–237.

Perry, David A. and Jeffrey G. Borchers. "Climate change and ecosystem responses." *Northwest Environmental Journal* 6 (1990): 293–313.

Perry, D.A., J.G. Borchers, S.L. Borchers, and M.P. Amaranthus. "Species migrations and ecosystem stability during climate change: The belowground connection." *Conservation Biology* 4 (1990): 266–274.

Perry, David A. and Jumanne Maghembe. "Ecosystem concepts and current trends in forest management: Time for reappraisal." *Forest Ecology and Management* 26 (1989): 123–140.

Petts, G.E. *Impounded rivers, perspectives for ecological management.* New York: John Wiley & Sons, Inc., 1984.

Péwé, T.L., D.M. Hopkins, and J.L. Giddings. 1967. "The Quaternary geology and archaeology of Alaska." pp. 355–374. In *The Quaternary of the United States.*

Powers, R.F., et al. "Sustaining site productivity in North American forests: Problems and prospects." pp. 49–79. In Gessel, S.P., D.S. Lacate, G.R. Weetman, and R.F. Powers (Eds.) *Sustained productivity of forest soils*, Proceedings 7th North American Forest Soils Conference, Forestry Publication. Vancouver, B.C., Canada: University of British Columbia, 1990.

Rapport, D.J, H.A. Regier, and T.C. Hutchinson. "Ecosystem behavior under stress." *The American Naturalist* 125 (1985): 617–640.

Read, Richard. "Turtle-shell artisans say craft endangered." *The Oregonian*, Portland, Oregon, June 16, 1991.

Reid, Walter V., and Kenton R. Miller. *Keeping options alive, the scientific basis for conserving biodiversity*. Washington, D.C.: World Resources Institute, 1989.

Reisner, Marc. *Overtapped oasis: Reform or resolution for western water*. New York: Viking Press, 1989.

Roberts, A., and K. Tregonning. "The robustness of natural systems." *Nature* 288 (1980): 265–266.

Robinson, Michael C. "The relationship between the U.S. Army Corps of Engineers and the Environmental Community." *Environmental Review* 13 (1989): 1–41.

Rothenberg, David. "A platform for deep ecology." *The Environmentalist* 7 (1987): 185–190.

Routledge, R.D. "The impact of soil degradation on the expected present net worth of future timber harvests." *Forest Science* 33 (1987): 823–834.

Savonen, Carol. "Ashes in the Amazon." *Journal of Forestry* 88 (1990): 20–25.

Schowalter, Timothy D. "Adaptations of insects to disturbance." pp. 235–386. In Pickett, S.T.A., and P.S. White (eds.). *The ecology of natural disturbance and patch dynamics*. New York: Academic Press, 1985.

Sessions, George. "The deep ecology movement: a review." *Environmental Review* 11 (1987): 105–125.

Shaffer, Mark L. "Minimum population sizes for species conservation." *BioScience* 31 (1981): 131–134.

Shannon, Margaret A. "Sociology and public land management." *Western Wildlands* 7 (1981): 3–8.

Shearman, Richard. "The meaning and ethics of sustainability." *Environmental Management* 14 (1990): 108.

Simmons, I.G. "The earliest cultural landscapes of England." *Environmental Review* 12 (1988): 105–116.

Simon, H.A. "The architecture of complexity." *Proceedings of the American Philosophical Society* 106 (1962): 467–482.

Simpson, G.G. "The species concept." *Evolution* 5 (1952):285–298.

Slobodkin, Lawrence B. "On the susceptibility of different species to extinction: Elementary instruction for owners of a world." pp. 226–242. In *The preservation of species*. Norton, B.G. (ed.). Princeton, New Jersey: Princeton University Press, 1988.

Slocombe, D.Scott. "History and environmental messes: A nonequilbrium systems view." *Environmental Review* 13 (1989):1–13.

Sokal, R.R. "The species problem reconsidered." *Systematic Zoology* 22 (1973): 360–374.

Soroos, Marvin S. "The international commons: a historical perspective." *Environmental Review* 12 (1988): 1–22.

Stephenson, R.L. 1967. "Quaternary human occupation of the plains." pp. 685–696. In *The Quaternary of the United States*.

Susuki, David and P. Knudtson. *Genethics, the ethics of engineering life.* Don Mills, Ontario, Canada: Stoddart Publishing, 1988.

Swetnam, T.W. 1990. "Fire history and climate in the southwestern United States." pp. 6–17. In *Effects of Fire in Management of Southwestern Natural Resources*. J. S. Krammers (Tech. Coord.). United States Department of Agriculture, Forest Service General Technical Report RM-191. Fort Collins, Colorado: Rocky Mountain Research Station, 1990.

Thomas, Jack Ward (ed.). "Wildlife habitats in managed forests: The Blue Mountains of Oregon and Washington." United States Department of Agriculture, *Forest Service Agriculture Handbook. No. 533*. Washington, D.C.: United States Government Printing Office, 1979.

Thomas, Jack Ward, Eric D. Forsman, Joseph B. Lint, E. Charles Meslow, Berry R. Noon, Jared Verner. *A conservation strategy for the northern spotted owl. Report of the Interagency Scientific Committee to Address the Conservation of the Northern Spotted Owl*. Washington, D.C.: United States Government Printing Office, 1990.

Tomioka, Ariel. *On the breath of the Gods*. Carmichael, California: Helios House, 1990.

Train, Russell E. "Religion and the environment." *Journal of Forestry* 89 (1991): 12–15.

Trapnell, C.G. "Ecological results of woodland burning experiments in northern Rhodesia." *Journal of Ecology* 47 (1959): 129–168.

Turner, Monica Goigel. "Landscape ecology: The effect of pattern on process." *Annual Review or Ecological Systems* 20 (1989): 171–197.

Turner, Monica G., Eugene P. Odum, Robert Costanza, and Thomas M.

Springer. "Market and nonmarket values of the Georgia landscape." *Environmental Management* 12 (1988): 209–217.

Wells, P.V. "Postglacial vegetational history of the Great Plains." *Science* 167 (1970): 1574–1582.

Whitaker, John O., Jr. "The biological subspecies: an adjunct of the biological species." *Biologist* 52 (1970): 12–15.

Williams, B. "Reflections on the spirit of nature." *Transformation* (1990): 21:5.

Wilson, E.O., and W.L. Brown, Jr. "The subspecies concept and its taxonomic application." *Systematic Zoology* 2 (1953): 97–111.

Worster, Donald. "The vulnerable Earth: toward a planetary history." *Environmental Review* 11 (1987): 87–103.

Yoon, Carol K. "OSU biologist leads research of rare bird." *The Oregonian*, Portland, Oregon, July 11, 1991.

Zarin, Daniel J. "Searching for pennies in piles of trash: municipal refuse utilization in the United States, 1870–1930." *Environmental Review* 11 (1987): 207–222.

Zedler, P.H., C.R. Gautier, and G.S. McMaster. "Vegetation change in response to extreme events: the effect of a short interval between fires in California chapparal and coastal scrub." *Ecology* 64 (1983): 809–818.

Chris Maser is the author of: *Forest Primeval: The Natural History of an Ancient Forest* (San Francisco, CA: Sierra Club Books, 1989), and *The Redesigned Forest* (San Pedro, CA: R & E Miles, 1988, rev. 1992).

If you would like information on Chris Maser's lectures on workshops, you may reach him at:

3303 Tyler Street, Corvallis, OR 97330

PUBLISHER'S NOTE

This logo represents Stillpoint's commitment to publishing books and other products that promote an enlightened value system. We seek to change human values to encourage people to live and act in accordance with a greater and more meaningful spiritual purpose and a true intent for the sanctity of all life.